NEW **MASTERS** OF **POSTER** DESIGN

POSTER DESIGN FOR THE NEXT CENTURY • **JOHN FOSTER, FUSZION COLLABORATIVE**

GLOUCESTER MASSACHUSETTS

ROCKPORT PUBLISHERS

First published in the United States of America by
Rockport Publishers, a member of
Quayside Publishing Group
33 Commercial Street
Gloucester, Massachusetts 01930-5089
Telephone: (978) 282-9590
Fax: (978) 283-2742
www.rockpub.com

Library of Congress Cataloging-in-Publication Data
Foster, John, 1971–
    New masters of poster design : poster design for the next century /
John Foster.
        p.   cm.
    ISBN 1-59253-222-5 (hardback)
    1. Posters—21st century—Catalogs. I. Title.
NC1806.9.F67 2006
741.6'74090511—dc22   2005030663
                                                             CIP

ISBN 1-59253-222-5

10 9 8 7 6 5 4 3 2 1

Design: FUSZION Collaborative

Printed in Singapore

CONTENTS

★ THE NEW MASTERS ★

A Poster Is a Poster and Not a Pipe
A poster has a message. Sometimes. A poster is a sheet of paper without a backside. A poster is a stamp. You can put it on the wall or on the window, on the ceiling or on the ground, upside down or wrong side up. There are young posters that look very old and old posters that never die. A good poster attacks you. A bad poster loves you. And there are "l'art-pour-l'art" posters that love themselves and want to be beautiful. These type of posters confuse the viewer, muddle up his eyes, and force him to look for something in the poster that is not inside. If you like, you can smoke it in your pipe.
—Uwe Loesch

I love the big scale and immediate impact of posters. They're my favorite things to design.
—Paula Scher

★ INTRODUCTION ★

SOMETHING SPECIAL IS HAPPENING

What you are about to see in this book must be considered unexpected at best. As clients found success with other forms of marketing, and communities in general became hostile to the papering of their neighborhoods, the poster waned as a messaging vehicle throughout the 1980s and 1990s. In much the way that the album was replaced by the CD, the poster became a postcard or an email blast—sad days indeed.

Some designers could not just stand by and let this happen. The loss of a storied and majestic medium that had served as a perfect canvas for so long could not be tolerated. Some of the world's best designers turned to the poster as a means of personal expression and as an outlet from more restrictive media. They also set out to prove that the poster could still serve as a powerful tool in communicating a client's message. Breathtaking work from Pentagram, Niklaus Troxler, Michael Schwab, Alain Le Quernec, and many others who plied their trade commercially began to appear. Art Chantry, Alejandro Magallanes, Frank Kozik, Yee-Haw Industries, Ames Bros., Charles S. Anderson, and others taking a more subversive role converged with aboveground and ongoing efforts in music and theater as well as an American Institute of Graphic Arts (AIGA) literacy effort to bring the poster back to prominence.

One project encapsulates this effort: Paula Scher's work for the Public Theater in New York City. Her *Bring in Da Funk* series is probably the best known, but the entire collection of posters is awe-inspiring from one production to the next. A number of people I have spoken to in connection with this book felt the same way I did when they saw these posters in the design annuals (almost a full year after Scher designed them.) The poster is alive. It is powerful, vibrant, and—most important—artful.

The perfect melding of design and marketing power, the theater needed the scale and the scale needed the designers. As Scher stated, posters are her favorite projects to design, and that affection is obvious in every placement of type and selection of art. The audience quickly noted that this was not a one-off labor of love, as Scher was doing it again and again. This was big-time work for a big-time client.

As clients saw this amazing revival, they came to reconsider the poster as a forum. Currently employed by giants such as Target and Starbucks as their main in-store promotion, the poster has reemerged, and I would argue that it is better employed than ever before. It is true that Europe and the United States have very different ideas as to its vitality, and I admit that the days of poster-lined city streets in international capitals are gone. However, the poster has emerged, phoenixlike, in new places and in new ways. We no longer paint the sides of barns—we hang twenty-story banners in downtown New York City. It makes me miss the quaint past, but even more so, it makes me excited for the future.

The future of the poster is now. I give you a few familiar faces and many you should know more about; from the silkscreen guerrillas in the United States to the technology-entranced Europeans to artists from every other continent. This collection showcases the work of the world's finest poster designers at the moment of this medium's rebirth.

On the other hand, this book is just a snapshot of what is going on in the design world. I have never encountered a more difficult task than narrowing my initial list of "new masters" from more than one thousand to just thirty. To say this could have been a collection of volumes rather than profiles is an understatement. The interesting part is that few of these designers were aware of what the others were doing. They may know a few creatives in their genre of work, but they have little knowledge of the state of the poster globally. So pure is their drive that they only know that they are personally fighting to keep this medium alive. They can now enjoy seeing their brothers and sisters in arms.

–John Foster

★ AESTHETIC APPARATUS ★

MINNEAPOLIS, MINNESOTA, USA

THE TIME IS RIGHT

Working side by side at Planet Propaganda, a top U.S. design firm, Dan Ibarra and Michael Byzewski decided to form a haven for their interest in screen-printing. Originally conceived as an outlet for fun and one-off side projects, they quickly became so successful that making the choice to turn Aesthetic Apparatus into their full-time gig was a no-brainer. Building their business around limited-edition screen-printed concert posters, they were one of the first firms to benefit fully from the explosion of this market.

With the path cleared by Frank Kozik and Art Chantry, Aesthetic Apparatus left Wisconsin and headed west to the design hotbed of Minneapolis, fully formed and ready to "break your heart and drink your blood," as they threaten on their website.

Mixed in with their tight design chops is a self-deprecating wit that can be seen in a large portion of their work. Ibarra and Byzewski boast that their work has "secretly snuck into the hearts and minds of a small rather silent group of socially awkward music and design nerds." They have benefited immensely from that great connector of music and design nerds—the Internet—and note that "our business functions as it does because of the Internet. When we're not printing posters or designing, we're packing up online poster orders, keeping up with clients via email, or presenting work to them, also via email. If there were no Internet we never would've existed like we do today, which is pretty funny because we really don't understand how the Internet works."

DESIGN FOCUSED

Not quite ready to assume the mantle of leadership of the new poster movement, Ibarra and Byzewski do, however, see themselves as part of that movement. They add, in analyzing the current crop, that "some people have said that we have inspired folks in regard to the recent wave of design-focused rock posters. Neither of us believes that we did anything new or inventive in regard to our art or our studio or whatever, but it's always flattering to think that someone actually enjoys what we're doing." You won't have to look far in this book or at a local rock club to see that influence.

As for their own inspiration, they find joy in recounting the amazing hand-printed runs of thousands of posters by Anthony Velonis and the other artists of the Works Progress Administration (WPA). They are one of the few firms to admit that they wear their influences on their sleeves—or at least leave them exposed on their posters. "Artist-wise, our influences are pretty easy to guess: Saul Bass, Jeff Kleinsmith [profiled on page 140], Art Chantry, Andy Warhol, Robert Rauschenberg, Raymond Loewy, Paul Rand, Reid Miles, Charles S. Anderson, Tibor Kalman, Yee-Haw Industries, The Bird Machine [Next Wave on page 242], Seripop [profiled on page 154], and Ames Brothers."

INK UNDER YOUR NAILS

Ibarra and Byzewski have an unusual angle on the process, as they print all of their posters by hand. This can lead to interesting results. "Probably the most annoying part of poster making is when the printing goes horribly, horribly wrong. Or when all is said and done and you've printed the poster and you step back to take a look at the finished product and you just hate it. It's heartbreaking. That just happened to us the other day."

Getting their hands dirty and engaging in the entire process has led Ibarra and Byzewski to challenge themselves to produce the most creative solution not only in terms of design but also on press. The inevitable hits and misses have turned into success after raging success, although their remarks belie their learning process. The blurring of lines between print and production extends to those between designer and client. After working for local clubs and building up a solid base of trust, Aesthetic Apparatus makes all creative decisions themselves and sends the final art to the club before going to press. They elaborate, "Honestly, they have never asked for any changes or revisions or anything. We don't even know if they proofread these anymore. I don't even know if they look at them."

Certainly *someone* can't keep their eyes off the posters, as they have a pretty difficult time keeping them on the walls of the clubs and their print runs sell out notoriously fast. If you see something you like, you had better figure out that Internet thing real quick!

"If there were no Internet we never would've existed like we do today, which is pretty funny because we really don't understand how the Internet works."

The
BLACK
KEYS
AKRON, OH

WITH SPECIAL GUESTS
THE CUTS

FIRST AVENUE SEPTEMBER 21, 2004 8PM 21+ID

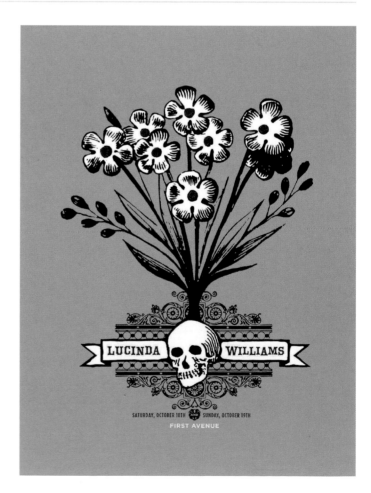

CHRISTIAN
+ ANDREW BRODER + GEORGE CARTWRIGHT
MARCLAY

WITH SPECIAL GUESTS••••••
• CEPIA AND DOSH=
Saturday, August 21< 2004 9PMS8
• TRIPLE ROCK SOCIAL CLUB 21+
Copresented by the Walker Art Center))

Mogwai
WITH PAPA M

THE RAPTURE

+ THE BOGGS
+ REVOLVER

TUESDAY, MAY 6TH, 2003 | 8PM | FIRST AVENUE | 21+ ID

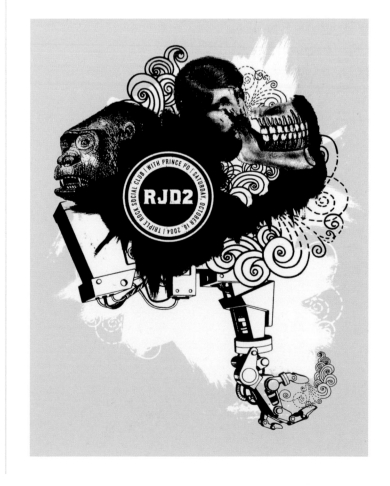

RJD2

INTERPOL

FIRST AVENUE - OCTOBER 19, 2004   WITH SECRET MACHINES AND HAIL SOCIAL   8PM - 21+ID

TITLE: Black Keys Poster
CLIENT: First Avenue
SIZE: 18" x 25" (45.72 x 63.50 cm)
PRINTING PROCESS: Hand screen-printed
INKS: Speedball acrylic screen-printing ink
Are posters what you primarily do for this client? Yes

PROCESS
COMPS PRESENTED: 1
REVISIONS: 0
APPROVAL: Venue management
INVOLVEMENT WITH FINAL PRINTING:
Printed by Aesthetic Apparatus

In designing this poster for an appearance by The Black Keys, Aesthetic Apparatus dove headfirst into the band's inspiration—for the title of their album, that is. Ibarra and Byzewski recount, "The title of their last album, *The Rubber Factory,* is named in honor of the old tire factory in Akron the band practices in." They wanted the typography to be as authentic as possible. "We wanted to give the type a bit of an early or mid-century treatment, to make it feel like it might have been an old tire company logo of some sort."

TITLE: Firewater Poster
CLIENT: 7th St. Entry
SIZE: 17" x 23.5" (43.18 x 59.69 cm)
PRINTING PROCESS: Hand screen-printed
INKS: Speedball acrylic screen-printing ink
Are posters what you primarily do for this client? Yes

PROCESS
COMPS PRESENTED: 1
REVISIONS: 0
APPROVAL: Venue management
INVOLVEMENT WITH FINAL PRINTING:
Printed by Aesthetic Apparatus

It is rare for a design to fall rapidly into place for Aesthetic Apparatus. Not so for this poster for the band Firewater. "Sometimes we'll toil away on a design for days and days until the last second. Here the design, from start to finish, probably took only six to eight hours."

TITLE: Guided by Voices Poster
CLIENT: First Avenue
SIZE: 19" x 25" (48.26 x 63.50 cm)
PRINTING PROCESS: Hand screen-printed
INKS: Speedball acrylic screen-printing ink
Are posters what you primarily do for this client? Yes

PROCESS
COMPS PRESENTED: 1
REVISIONS: 0
APPROVAL: Venue management
INVOLVEMENT WITH FINAL PRINTING:
Printed by Aesthetic Apparatus

Most posters draw on one spark of inspiration from the band being featured. For this one, Ibarra and Byzewski tried to cram every little bit of inspiration they could think of into it! "We're pretty happy with all the ideas and references to the band we squeezed into this poster. The band has always had a fascination with military aircraft, which figure in the design as a reference to a song off the album they were touring on entitled *My Kind of Soldier*. The target is a reference to The Who [a huge influence on the band] and also another military aircraft reference, and the fact that it's over the figure's mouth is a reference to the band name." You can only imagine what they would have done with a larger sheet of paper.

TITLE: Stereolab Poster
CLIENT: First Avenue
SIZE: 18" x 24" (45.72 x 60.96 cm)
PRINTING PROCESS: Hand screen-printed
INKS: Speedball acrylic screen-printing ink
Are posters what you primarily do for this client? Yes

PROCESS
COMPS PRESENTED: 1
REVISIONS: 0
APPROVAL: Venue management
INVOLVEMENT WITH FINAL PRINTING:
Printed by Aesthetic Apparatus

Clearly inspired by the space-age grooviness in the band's music, the type and illustration here are a bit of a departure from the firm's usual work. The poster managed to please almost everyone in this niche industry. *Almost* everyone. Ibarra tells us that "the poster-making community at gigposters.com believes this poster to be 'just right,' 'beautifully done,' 'very nice,' 'makes all other Stereolab posters cry,' 'awesome!' 'coolest new one since Guided by Voices,' 'brilliant,' 'AA+,' 'groovy'—and 'a little more restrained than I'd usually like.'"

TITLE: Lucinda Williams Poster
CLIENT: First Avenue
SIZE: 18" x 25" (45.72 x 63.50 cm)
PRINTING PROCESS: Hand screen-printed
INKS: Speedball acrylic screen-printing ink
Are posters what you primarily do for this client? Yes

PROCESS
COMPS PRESENTED: 1
REVISIONS: 0
APPROVAL: Venue management
INVOLVEMENT WITH FINAL PRINTING:
Printed by Aesthetic Apparatus

The firm just couldn't keep away from the bristled edges of Lucinda Williams's music and history, yet they wanted the glory of her tunes to shine through as well. They soon found themselves working in images that crop up throughout their work: skulls and flowers. They recount, "We wanted to get something that felt rough and dirty but was still beautiful and sweet. Something that related directly to Lucinda, her life, and the lives she describes in her music."

TITLE: Christian Marclay Poster
CLIENT: Walker Art Center
SIZE: 19" x 25" (48.26 x 63.50 cm)
PRINTING PROCESS: Hand screen-printed
INKS: Speedball acrylic screen-printing ink
Are posters what you primarily do for this client? Yes

PROCESS
COMPS PRESENTED: 1
REVISIONS: 0
APPROVAL: Venue management
INVOLVEMENT WITH FINAL PRINTING:
Printed by Aesthetic Apparatus

On occasion, the joys of printing can overtake whatever other projects Ibarra and Byzewski are working on. No matter what they came up with for imagery, they knew the manner in which they would be printing this poster. "We're so, so, so obsessed with printing with process colors right now. It's a phase. Not sure what it is—the brightness of straight CMYK, the noise of overlapping colors, or what. But it makes our eyes very happy."

TITLE: Mogwai Poster
CLIENT: Atomic Records
SIZE: 18″ x 24″ (45.72 x 60.96 cm)
PRINTING PROCESS: Hand screen-printed
INKS: Speedball acrylic screen-printing ink
Are posters what you primarily do for this client? Yes

PROCESS
COMPS PRESENTED: 1
REVISIONS: 2
APPROVAL: Venue management
INVOLVEMENT WITH FINAL PRINTING:
Printed by Aesthetic Apparatus

The tiny finishing touches really make a piece like this rise above its competition on the club wall. Ibarra notes, "This poster was pretty much finished with the colors and layout that you see here, but there was something that wasn't working. It just didn't feel dynamic enough. It was very flat. Michael came up with the idea of having the moose break out of the green box and bleed off the page, and that changed everything. Just that little touch added the layer and depth to the poster that it was missing previously."

TITLE: The Rapture Poster
CLIENT: First Avenue
SIZE: 19″ x 25″ (48.26 x 63.50 cm)
PRINTING PROCESS: Hand screen-printed
INKS: Speedball acrylic screen-printing ink
Are posters what you primarily do for this client? Yes

PROCESS
COMPS PRESENTED: 1
REVISIONS: 0
APPROVAL: Venue management
INVOLVEMENT WITH FINAL PRINTING:
Printed by Aesthetic Apparatus

Aesthetic Apparatus has become well known (and vilified in some quarters) for their use of found or appropriated images in their work. This one breaks from tradition as they allow that "although many of our posters are created via found image and collage, the four horsemen [a Rapture reference they consider pure genius] on this poster are our original drawings. Original drawings traced over images of horses and guys in suits—but still original."

TITLE: RJD2 Poster
CLIENT: The Triple Rock Social Club
SIZE: 19″ x 25″ (48.26 x 63.50 cm)
PRINTING PROCESS: Hand screen-printed
INKS: Speedball acrylic screen-printing ink
Are posters what you primarily do for this client? Yes

PROCESS
COMPS PRESENTED: 1
REVISIONS: 0
APPROVAL: Venue management
INVOLVEMENT WITH FINAL PRINTING:
Printed by Aesthetic Apparatus

Sometimes the struggle to do something new leads to taking a step back and finding the solution you were looking for in what you had already been doing. For this piece, "We wanted to do something that felt a bit more organic than a lot of our previous posters. So drawings were made. They were horrible. So we scrapped all the drawings but held onto the mess we made with a brush and ink and shoved a bunch of found imagery into it." This approach was perfectly appropriate, as "the idea was to have a sort of mishmash of evolution represented, as the music of RJD2 is an audio collage of many sources both old and new."

TITLE: The Thermals Poster
CLIENT: The Triple Rock Social Club
SIZE: 19″ x 25″ (48.26 x 63.50 cm)
PRINTING PROCESS: Hand screen-printed
INKS: Speedball acrylic screen-printing ink
Are posters what you primarily do for this client? Yes

PROCESS
COMPS PRESENTED: 1
REVISIONS: 0
APPROVAL: Venue management
INVOLVEMENT WITH FINAL PRINTING:
Printed by Aesthetic Apparatus

This is the poster in which the influence of hand-printing the work really comes full circle. The firm lets us in on the process. "Whenever we're starting a print run, we always have to pull a couple test prints to see that the image is printing correctly and that the color is right. We tend to print on previous mis-prints of older posters, so after a while these sheets get to be pretty cool and chaotic. When people ask us which poster is our favorite, we always end up telling them about our test prints because we like them so much more than any poster we've made. This Thermals poster was actually an attempt to emulate the look and feel of one of our test prints with the disjointed elements, overlapping colors, and noise."

TITLE: Yeah Yeah Yeahs Poster
CLIENT: First Avenue
SIZE: 17.5″ x 23.75″ (44.45 x 60.33 cm)
PRINTING PROCESS: Hand screen-printed
INKS: Speedball acrylic screen-printing ink
Are posters what you primarily do for this client? Yes

PROCESS
COMPS PRESENTED: 1
REVISIONS: 0
APPROVAL: Venue management
INVOLVEMENT WITH FINAL PRINTING:
Printed by Aesthetic Apparatus

For the Yeah Yeah Yeahs' blend of passion and buzzing angles, "we were going for something both sexy and violent on this—hence the sort of death blob this lovely couple is sharing orally. Oh, and the blood splatters as well." Bumps in the road to final delivery can greatly affect the final product, as Ibarra and Byzewski relate. "The folks who trim our posters decided to make a design decision of their own on this and trimmed them quite a bit smaller than they were supposed to. They did the right thing."

TITLE: Interpol Poster
CLIENT: First Avenue
SIZE: 19″ x 25″ (48.26 x 63.50 cm)
PRINTING PROCESS: Hand screen-printed
INKS: Speedball acrylic screen-printing ink
Are posters what you primarily do for this client? Yes

PROCESS
COMPS PRESENTED: 1
REVISIONS: 0
APPROVAL: Venue management
INVOLVEMENT WITH FINAL PRINTING:
Printed by Aesthetic Apparatus

When approached to do a poster for the hot new band of the minute, the firm could not resist playing up the almost orgasmic response the media and indie rock kids had to Interpol's arrival on the scene. As Georgia O'Keeffe couldn't be licensed to fit their budget, they had to figure out their own forms of subtlety for the desired final impression. Ibarra says, "Yeah, the image is supposed to be kind of vaginal."

FRANÇOIS CASPAR

PARIS, FRANCE

BEAUTIFUL FOR A MOMENT

"The nicest compliment I've had is when a simple passerby said that seeing my poster in his street has made his everyday life more beautiful for a moment," says designer François Caspar. The impressive list of galleries and museums that show his work and the awards he has won probably feel pretty good as well. Caspar's bold sense of design, use of large central imagery, and inherent playfulness generate a classic appeal with a French twist.

Caspar's work for theater productions has garnered most of the attention. When asked why he designs posters for theater, he recalls, "I couldn't answer that question two years ago, but now I remember that I went to the Ariane Mnouschkine Theatre when I was eight years and that I have been fascinated with theater ever since." In addition, "Working on a theater poster is working on the imagination itself. It is telling a story in as short a manner as possible," and this is what invigorates him: the journey and the challenge.

Caspar no longer ponders his design as he did when he was young. "We are what we do, and there are so many solutions when I design a poster," he says, reflecting on the styles and design movements that have influenced his work. When asked about his place in design, he responds, "I asked myself this question when I was a student. Now I don't care. I do what I believe in and try to find my own way. The secret is to let your life come into your poster, to let its story become yours and vice versa. What else can you do? I could tell you every event of my life by describing my posters," he smiles.

THE REAL SEARCHERS
Caspar's influences from the masters are "Cassandre for construction, Hartfield for political positioning, Cieslewicz for generosity, and Savignac for humor. But I'm more influenced by art painting in general," he admits. "Like surrealism or constructivism, and primitives. What would design be without the artists? To me, they are the real searchers." Striving for the artistic application of his concepts drives his poster work above those around him. Unafraid of technology, he embraces it in a way that furthers his goal but does not overtake it.

Caspar appreciates every step of producing a poster and is hooked on silkscreening and the subsequent ink smell, "which makes me drunk and happy." He relishes photographing Paris at night and snaps pictures of his favorite shoes. He picks up a pair of scissors, or a brush, or a pen, and then looks forward to manipulating the results on his trusted computer. Once he completes a design he really gets to work, explaining that when posters are in press "is when I really take control of the process." His bold colors certainly attest to that.

JUST ENOUGH
Now Caspar does more with less. "I wanted to design ten posters a month before. Now I know I would lose my soul if I worked at that rate. I prefer to take more time so as not to mess up. I'll never get rich with this anyway. I now choose my clients for poster projects. We have to fit. If not, there is no way I can make a good poster. This might sound strange, but I need carte blanche, even if I have less work." For him, "the poster is a synthesis of graphic design competencies: conceptualization, typography, layout, and personal expression. This expression must enrich the information, without damaging it, to amplify its impact. To paraphrase Milton Glaser, I would say that I look not for the less but for the just enough."

"I could tell you every event of my life by describing my posters."

THEATRE DE LA TETE NOIRE
Bouli Miro
Avec
Jacques Courtès
Sébastien Crinon
Sylvie Gauduchon
Stéphane Jaubertie
Marène N'Diaye
Elsa Royer
Texte Fabrice Melquiot
mise en scène Patrice Douchet
Scénographie et costumes
Danièle Rozier
Musique
Jacques Trupin
Lumières
Damien Grossin
Assistante à la mise en scène
Erika Von Rosen
Formes animées
Pascale Blaison
Régie son
Raphaël Guédec
Création Théâtre de la Tête Noire
Coproduction
Théâtre des Jeunes Années
CDN, Lyon

La Jeune fille suppliciée sur une étagère

Mise en scène de Marc-Ange Sanz
d'après le récit d'Akira Yoshimura
Avec Laurence Mongeaud et Nobuko Matsumya

Scénographie Jean-Claude Leparc
Son/Vidéo Stéphane Gombert
Lumières Gilles Bouscarle

Traduction Rose-Marie Makimo-Fayolle – Actes Sud Papiers
Spectacle réalisé par L'Empreinte et Cie en coproduction avec le CCAM Scène Nationale de Vandœuvre–Lès–Nancy
avec le soutien financier du Conseil Régional de Lorraine et de la DRAC Lorraine

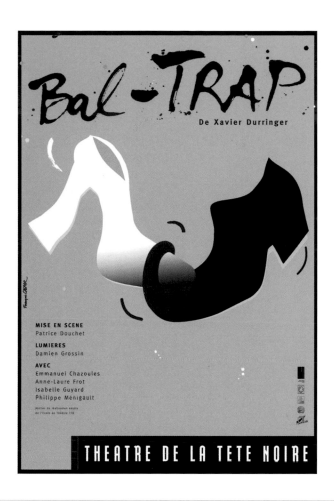

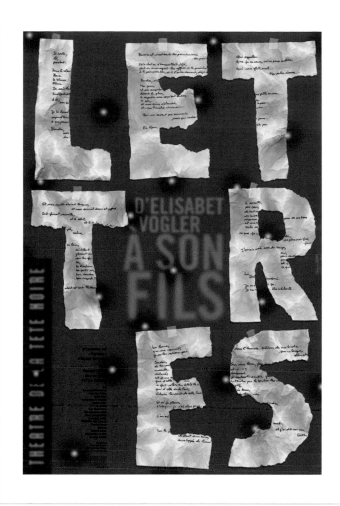

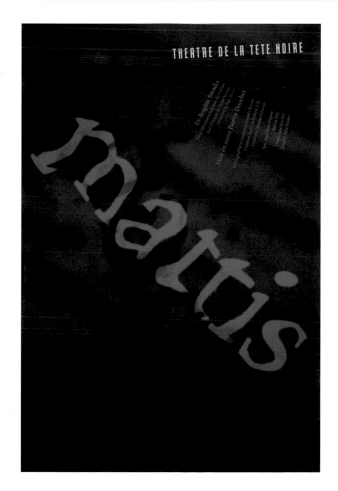

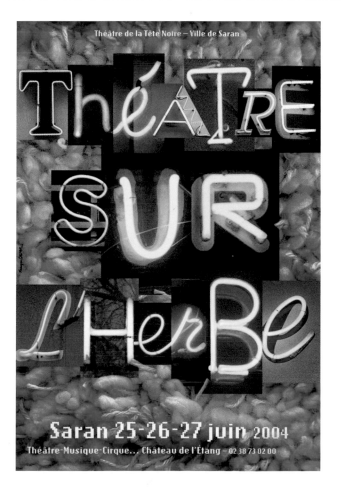

DEHORS

THEATRE DE LA TETE NOIRE

DEVANT LA PORTE

Mise en scène
PATRICE DOUCHET

Scénographie
DANIÈLE ROZIER

Musique
JACQUES TRUPIN

Régie générale
DAMIEN GROSSIN
assisté de
RAPHAËL QUÉDEC
ULYSSIA MARCHAIS
assistant à la mise en scène : Ulyssia Marchais

Avec
CÉLINE CAUSSIMON
ÉRIC CÉNAT
JEAN-CHRISTOPHE COCHARD
SÉBASTIEN CRINON
PHILIPPE FAUCONNIER
SYLVIE GAUDUCHON
HUBERT GODON
MARTINE HÉQUET
MARIE LANDAIS
DOMINIQUE MAILLOCHON
ISABELLE MELMOUX
DANIEL PINAULT

De WOLFGANG BORCHERT
Traduit de l'allemand par J.-B. O.

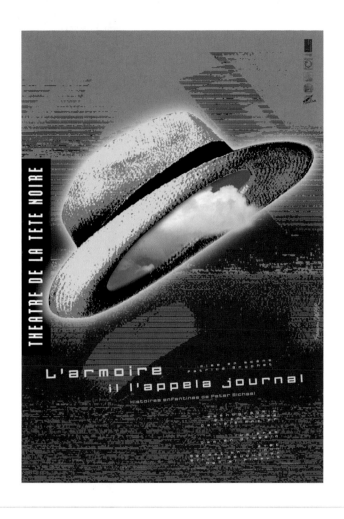

TITLE: *Bouli Miro*
CLIENT: Black Head Theatre
SIZE: 47.24" x 68.90" (120 x 175 cm)
PRINTING PROCESS: Silkscreen
INKS: 3 color
Are posters what you primarily do for this client? No

PROCESS
COMPS PRESENTED: 3
REVISIONS: 1
APPROVAL: Director
INVOLVEMENT WITH FINAL PRINTING:
Prepared for production and press inspected

"Bouli Miro is the name of the teenage hero in the play, " explains Caspar. "This kind of title is difficult to design for, as it gives no clues to the audience what the play is about. " Caspar knew he wanted "to give a feeling of the end of the story—something funny." Using his "laughable fashion shoes" for props, he also took photos of real bananas and tennis shoes to work from for his final image.

TITLE: *The Girl Tortured on a Rack*
CLIENT: l'Empreinte et Cie (The Fingerprint
and Company)
SIZE: 47.24" x 68.90" (120 x 175 cm)
PRINTING PROCESS: Silkscreen
INKS: 2 color
Are posters what you primarily do for this client? Yes

PROCESS
COMPS PRESENTED: 2
REVISIONS: 3
APPROVAL: Director
INVOLVEMENT WITH FINAL PRINTING:
Prepared for production and press inspected

Caspar confesses, "I really thought I was collapsing while reading this script, " which was adapted from the work of Japan's Akira Yoshimura and "describes how the dead body of a girl is methodically cut up for scientific needs and then burned to ashes. " He knew the themes of "eroticism, voyeurism, and identity" he wanted to convey, as well as "keeping a little mystery in this image."

TITLE: *Bal Trap*
CLIENT: Black Head Theatre
SIZE: 47.24" x 68.90" (120 x 175 cm)
PRINTING PROCESS: Silkscreen
INKS: 3 color
Are posters what you primarily do for this client? No

PROCESS
COMPS PRESENTED: 3
REVISIONS: 1
APPROVAL: Director
INVOLVEMENT WITH FINAL PRINTING:
Prepared for production and press inspected

Caspar employs a methodical process for his design work for the Black Head Theatre, with which he has a long and continuing relationship. "First I read the play," he says. "Then I discuss it with the director of the theater, who is also the director of the play. We have a discussion about his vision of the text. We can't put all of the topics in one poster, so we choose a single message. Then I present black and white sketches and we choose one concept that I can continue to work on. This method makes us focus first on the idea; then, in the second stage, the artistic work will start," he says. "The idea comes out very fast," but it is a process, so time is important. For *Bal Trap*, "I wanted to play with erotic shapes without showing any real details. Once, a journalist from the TV channel ARTE told me, 'I see the female sex, I see the tongue, but I see male sex with the female shoe.' I replied, 'Well, everybody can have his own phantasms.'" To piece together the actual art, Caspar "used cut paper to make the shoes. Put my fingers into the ink—I love it! And last but not least, I used the computer to put all of this together."

TITLE: *Letters of E. Vogler to Her Son*
CLIENT: Black Head Theatre
SIZE: 47.24" x 68.90" (120 x 175 cm)
PRINTING PROCESS: Silkscreen
INKS: 4-color process
Are posters what you primarily do for this client? No

PROCESS
COMPS PRESENTED: 2
REVISIONS: 3
APPROVAL: Director
INVOLVEMENT WITH FINAL PRINTING:
Prepared for production and press inspected

"This may be the most interesting concept I have developed for a poster, " says Caspar of this exploration of a play about perception. He enjoys the poster's "ability to be read at different distances. What is sharp? What is blurred? What is readable, and what is suggested? " He wonders, "Is it the reality or the reflection? What is the front, and what is behind?" The challenge to the viewer is exactly the desired effect.

TITLE: *Mattis*
CLIENT: Black Head Theatre
SIZE: 47.24" x 68.90" (120 x 175 cm)
PRINTING PROCESS: Silkscreen
INKS: 3 color
Are posters what you primarily do for this client? No

PROCESS
COMPS PRESENTED: 3
REVISIONS: 5
APPROVAL: Director
INVOLVEMENT WITH FINAL PRINTING:
Prepared for production and press inspected

Moving past his first concept, which involved fire and its polar opposite, water, Caspar took his lead from the end of the play, where the main character drowns in murky dark. "I could show the end of the story because the audience feels his impending drowning right from the beginning," he explains. He laughs that for once he was able to contain the "visual pollution" of the required logos in a tiny corner.

TITLE: *Festival Theater on the Grass*
CLIENT: Black Head Theatre
SIZE: 47.24" x 68.90" (120 x 175 cm)
PRINTING PROCESS: Silkscreen
INKS: 4-color process
Are posters what you primarily do for this client? No

PROCESS
COMPS PRESENTED: 3
REVISIONS: 5
APPROVAL: Director
INVOLVEMENT WITH FINAL PRINTING:
Prepared for production and press inspected

Using his working time to bounce around Paris for inspiration, "taking pictures of signs for shops, bars, and restaurants for the lighted letters," Caspar found himself "using a carpet shop for the background." Conveying a sense of excitement to tie into the nighttime staging, he went for "a Charlie Chaplin limelight feeling."

TITLE: *Outside in Front of the Door*
CLIENT: BLACK HEAD THEATRE
SIZE: 47.24" x 68.90" (120 x 175 cm)
PRINTING PROCESS: Silkscreen
INKS: 3 color
Are posters what you primarily do for this client? No

PROCESS

COMPS PRESENTED: 3
REVISIONS: 5
APPROVAL: Director
INVOLVEMENT WITH FINAL PRINTING:
Prepared for production and press inspected

Caspar feels this poster is a good example of his current way of working. "I continue to enjoy working with cut paper, ink, paint, paintbrushes, etc., but these days I am using the scanner much in the way I used the photocopier before," he says. He used this high-tech tool much in the way he used handwork of the past to form the maniacal, clownish, zipper mouth that taunts the viewer.

TITLE: *He Named the Wardrobe Newspaper*
CLIENT: Black Head Theatre
SIZE: 47.24" x 68.90" (120 x 175 cm)
PRINTING PROCESS: Silkscreen
INKS: 4-color process
Are posters what you primarily do for this client? No

PROCESS

COMPS PRESENTED: 3
REVISIONS: 5
APPROVAL: Director
INVOLVEMENT WITH FINAL PRINTING:
Prepared for production and press inspected

Caspar designed two posters for this play. "First, the theater wanted to appeal to kids. But after the play ran, they realized it was really made for adult spectators, as it was too complex." Caspar jumped at the opportunity to represent the "madness, dreams, and poetry" he saw in the production and created a new and improved version.

TITLE: *Spring Awakening*
CLIENT: Black Head Theatre
SIZE: 47.24" x 68.90" (120 x 175 cm)
PRINTING PROCESS: Silkscreen
INKS: 4 color
Are posters what you primarily do for this client? No

PROCESS

COMPS PRESENTED: 3
REVISIONS: 1
APPROVAL: Director
INVOLVEMENT WITH FINAL PRINTING:
Prepared for production and press inspected

"This play was marketed to teenagers," says Caspar. "They put the posters up in schools, but they kept getting stolen!" Speaking of stealing, for his design for the production, which "talks about the awakening of love in a very religious society," Caspar stole the hands of Albrecht Dürer's *Melancholia* to create his edgy and modern illustration technique. Caspar struggled with "combining dogma and lust— a nineteenth-century text with a modern ethos," in making the final image.

TITLE: The Great Unisson
CLIENT: City of St. Jean de la Ruelle
SIZE: 47.24" x 68.90" (120 x 175 cm)
PRINTING PROCESS: Silkscreen
INKS: 4-color process
Are posters what you primarily do for this client? No

PROCESS

COMPS PRESENTED: 3
REVISIONS: 1
APPROVAL: Director of culture for the city
INVOLVEMENT WITH FINAL PRINTING:
Prepared for production and press inspected

This piece was designed for a summer music festival where "everybody can play any kind of music in the same place at the same moment. What a noise!" exclaims Caspar. When a musician hits a bad note, "we call it *a duck*," he notes. So he chose the funny little duck to complete his image, being careful to select a bass that works in as many genres of music as possible. He thinks it was funny that "the teachers at the festival were a little afraid of this idea, but their students loved it."

RESPONSIBILITY

Fang Chen is a thinking man's poster designer. He constantly works to elevate the level of creative thinking in the world, and one of the ways in which he pursues that goal is through designing posters. "From the beginning of my career, I have worked as an art educator, and I have taught graphic design at the university level for more than ten years," says Chen.

"As a teacher of design, I feel a responsibility to practice design—I choose poster design—because good teaching is based on professional knowledge, and practice is essential to effective learning. Designing posters, for me, is not only a commercial pursuit but also a philosophical endeavor."

Chen was lucky to succeed in poster design, given the diminished state of the medium in China at the beginning of his career. Writing pointed him in that unexpected direction. Chen wrote and edited a series of books, entitled *The World Masters*, that showcased five graphic designers from England, Germany, Japan, and the United States. "Because it was the first art book series to introduce internationally recognized and influential contemporary designers and their masterpieces to China, the publisher decided to promote the series as *The World Masters*," he explains. Chen "proposed designing some promotional posters for the series, and the publisher agreed."

"The posters promoting the series were attached to the packaging distributed to bookstores or posted on the wall at book fairs. A lot of readers not only bought the book but also asked to purchase the posters. The publisher told me that the sales of the books had flourished *and* that the promotional posters had been stolen by fans during the book fair!" The pieces not only disappeared from bookstores but also earned international acclaim. "Since that time, I have loved the poster, and I believe it is one of the best ways to show my ideas and creativity," says Chen.

YIN AND YANG

Chen's homeland is integral to his solutions. "I was born and raised in China, and the country's cultural history has influenced my art and design profoundly. In my work, I try to explore and present a personal understanding of hybrid visual statements that combine traditional Chinese culture and contemporary world context. It's interesting that some people have mentioned that my black and white posters appear to be rooted in a Western design tradition rather than the Chinese soil." Chen often portrays all of humankind through his simple, ambiguous figures, yet he has

also chosen "the strongest possible way to convey the images—using only black and white, which is based on the traditional Chinese philosophical idea of yin and yang." For Chen, this duality is relevant because "yin and yang can also be used to represent dialectic concepts such as brightness and darkness, hopefulness and hopelessness, victor and victim. Black and white are my favorite colors in my posters; they serve to reveal, to question, and potentially to clarify the dynamic relationships between subjective and objective worlds. Black and white offers perhaps the richest potential for my work because it is so pure and significant in our perception."

Chen is researching the strength and power of image as a "universal language" in poster design. He believes this approach to design represents a new direction for contemporary poster expression, especially during this time of increasing globalization. The clean, sharp, and strong image possesses a unique value as a transcendent communication medium.

A SENSE OF PRIDE

In the past few years, Chen has been teaching in the United States. He now takes even more pride in the performance of his students than that of his own work. His students placed their work in the Seventh Mexico International Poster Biennial, and won first place at the Fortieth Annual *Print* Magazine Student Competition. Chen is eagerly awaiting the future of design, as his students will help shape it. Chen believes that the "idea is the soul of poster, and a good concept is the fruit of an educational, analytical, and intuitive process. A creative poster designer has to have wide cultural scope, intellectual depth, and solid general knowledge." This is the premise of his teaching.

"There are so many things to do during our brief lifetimes," Chen says, "but very little we can actually achieve. So I try to do the best I can. As an artist and educator, I am proud of having chosen poster design as my career because it represents one of the most difficult challenges and requirements for creativity."

"Designing posters, for me, is not only a commercial pursuit but also a philosophical endeavor."

Hello. I'm Poster

Workshop Poster

EPCC
Northwest
Library
Room 109

Tuesday
Jan. 28
11:30 a.m.

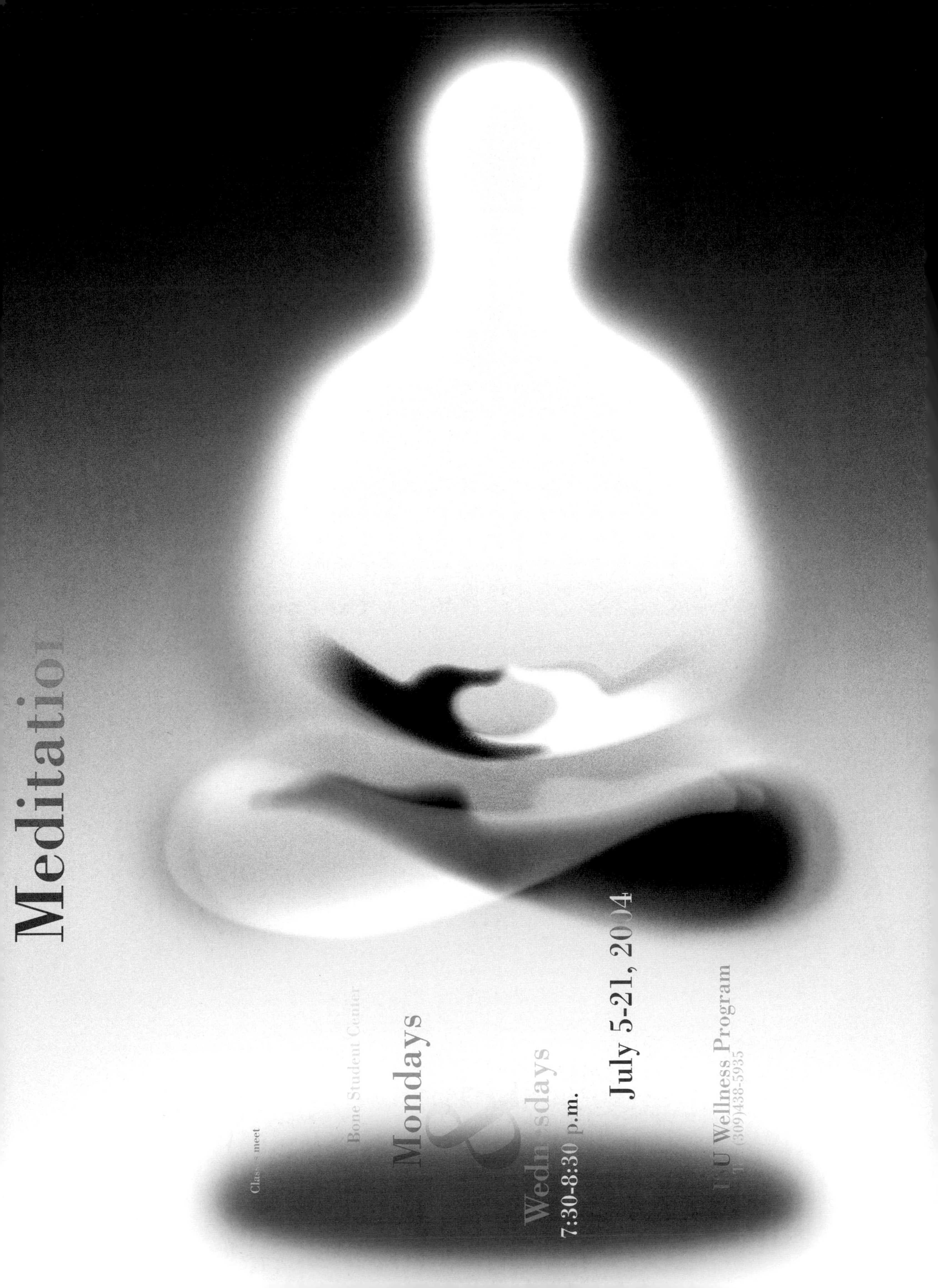

Meditation

Classes meet

Bone Student Center

Mondays & Wednesdays
7:30-8:30 p.m.

July 5-21, 2004

ISU Wellness Program
(309)438-5935

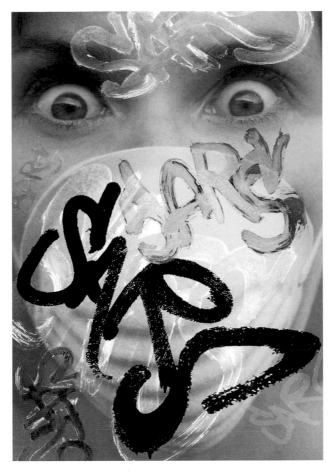

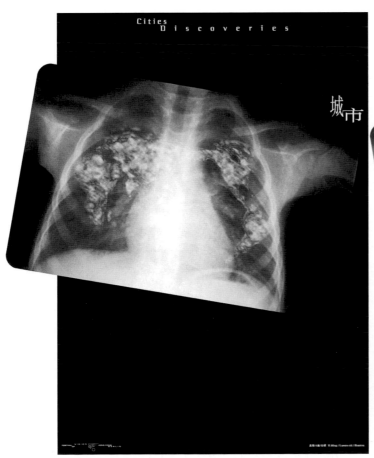

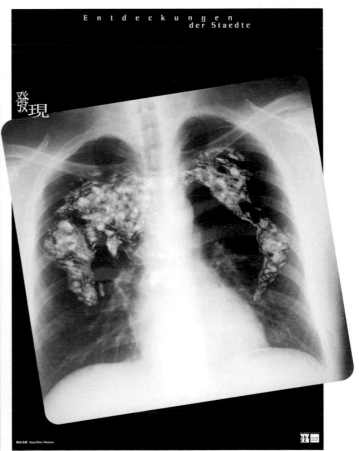

TITLE: Hello, I'm Poster!
CLIENT: El Paso Community College
SIZE: 27.56" x 39.37" (70 x 100 cm)
PRINTING PROCESS: Offset
INKS: Black
Are posters what you primarily do for this client? Yes

PROCESS

COMPS PRESENTED: 1
REVISIONS: 0
APPROVAL: Fang Chen
INVOLVEMENT WITH FINAL PRINTING:
Prepared for production and press inspected

"A good designer maximizes both communication and aesthetics in a limited circumstance when he or she designs a poster," says Chen. To promote a lecture and workshop, Chen was given a canvas on which to "showcase my personal understanding of what a poster should be." His presentation is simple yet "so dynamic and strong that it could pierce the wall and paper sheet and shake hands with the reader and the audience."

TITLE: Meditation
CLIENT: UTEPISU
SIZE: 27.56" x 39.37" (70 x 100 cm)
PRINTING PROCESS: Offset
INKS: Black
Are posters what you primarily do for this client? Yes

PROCESS

COMPS PRESENTED: 1
REVISIONS: 0
APPROVAL: Fang Chen
INVOLVEMENT WITH FINAL PRINTING:
Prepared for production and press inspected

"For years I was thinking of creating a poster to demonstrate a lofty oriental aesthetic realm of solemn and quiet," says Chen. Inspired by meditation and aided by the computer, he created a figure "without detail in order to leave room for the audience to see themselves in a typical pose of meditation." Working in his familiar black and white, Chen "elevated the figure with the aid of an emphasized shadow beneath the body. Typography was not only applied to give the necessary verbal information but also to support the elevation compositionally as well."

TITLE: Fear-SARS; Fear-MAN
CLIENT: UTEPISU
SIZE: 27.56" x 39.37" (70 x 100 cm) for each
PRINTING PROCESS: Offset
INKS: Black
Are posters what you primarily do for this client? Yes

PROCESS

COMPS PRESENTED: 1
REVISIONS: 0
APPROVAL: Fang Chen
INVOLVEMENT WITH FINAL PRINTING:
Prepared for production and press inspected

Fang Chen created a two-piece poster series in response to the Severe Acute Respiratory Syndrome (SARS) crisis that occurred in East Asia and North America. Chen's design serves to "warn people of the violent relationship between human beings and animals. Studies show that this mysterious and fatal disease came originally from a civet cat that people killed, cooked, and ate. On the flip side, animals certainly feel that humans are a fatal disease. So people fear SARS just as animals fear mankind!" Chen notes, "During the time of SARS, nearly everybody wore a mask out in public and in the street, so the animal in my poster also wears a mask because it fears mankind as a deadly force."

TITLE: City Discovery
CLIENT: Festival of Vision Hong Kong/Berlin
SIZE: 27.56" x 39.37" (70 x 100 cm)
PRINTING PROCESS: Offset
INKS: 4-color process
Are posters what you primarily do for this client? Yes

PROCESS

COMPS PRESENTED: 1
REVISIONS: 0
APPROVAL: Festival organizer
INVOLVEMENT WITH FINAL PRINTING:
Prepared for production and press inspected

The organizer of an invitational poster exhibition invited fifty Southeast Asian professional designers and fifty children under the age of ten to participate in the event themed "City Discovery." The hope was that "the posters would result from an interaction between a professional designer and a child less than ten years old, and the final work would include the points of view of a child and an adult." Chen points out that one can discover many things in a city but everyone, regardless of age or location, faces the same serious problem of pollution. For this design, Chen obtained two X-rays, one of a five-year-old child and one of an adult, both showing infected lungs. On these he superimposed the shape of a world map, creating a two-piece poster reflecting urban environmental issues. Both were exhibited in Hong Kong and Berlin.

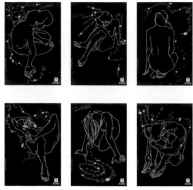

TITLE: Qichyuan Record Poster/Calendar
CLIENT: China Educational Book Import
and Export Corporation
SIZE: 22.8" x 34.6" (57.91 x 87.88 cm) for each
PRINTING PROCESS: Offset
INKS: Black
Are posters what you primarily do for this client? Yes

PROCESS
COMPS PRESENTED: 1
REVISIONS: 0
APPROVAL: Record company manager
INVOLVEMENT WITH FINAL PRINTING:
Prepared for production and press inspected

Sometimes poster concepts come together quickly. Chen explains, "The manager of a record company in Guangzhou, China, registered a new brand, Qichyuan, for his music record products and invited me to create a poster to promote his new brand and record products. When I accepted this commission, I immediately generated an idea for the poster campaign. The idea came from my experience and impression ten years ago, when I was a graduate student an Academy of Fine Arts. Whenever we drew a model in our studio, we always turned on a record player so the model could keep a relaxed pose in front of us. I found the models, both male and female, accompanied with the light music, would contort their bodies to show a kind of natural rhythm like that of the music. Quickly I captured the impression with a fountain pen and lines, spending around five to ten minutes on each drawing." Chen chose six line drawings from his early studio work and modified them to become a series of six posters, hoping audiences would associate them with music immediately. He notes that the posters were designed as a calendar in the hope that the series could exert a subtle influence on audiences for an entire year.

TITLE: AIDS!
CLIENT: UTEPISU
SIZE: 27.56" x 39.37" (70 x 100 cm)
PRINTING PROCESS: Offset
INKS: Black
Are posters what you primarily do for this client? Yes

PROCESS
COMPS PRESENTED: 1
REVISIONS: 0
APPROVAL: Fang Chen
INVOLVEMENT WITH FINAL PRINTING:
Prepared for production and press inspected

"I tried to avoid using cliché when designing this poster about AIDS," Chen explains. "People have seen too many condoms in this type of poster." Chen wanted a bold visual statement and quickly arrived at one. "The helmet is a vital metaphor in this poster; meanwhile, it has a moral function and partially hides the penis, as genitalia appearing in public might be too offensive."

★ CYAN ★

BERLIN, GERMANY

SHARED CONVICTIONS

cyan—always lowercase—has brought a sense of intensity to the German design scene. Daniela Haufe and Detlef Fielder worked together elsewhere before deciding to concentrate on their cultural work and form their own studio, where they were joined by Julia Fuchs and Katja Schwalenberg. They quickly found themselves feted in international magazines and collections. The firm was even identified by Neville Brody as one of the few worth watching in Germany.

Due to their extraordinary ability to unify content, form, and image on a single sheet of paper, the poster is a natural vehicle for their talents.

Haufe and Fielder share their design convictions with the emerging generation of new German and European designers through their teachings and lectures at the Academy of Visual Arts in Leipzig, where they are both professors. "The poster is integral to the learning process. In our teachings, we always try to make the poster the subject of discussion—and we make the students get involved with this medium." They also are involved with the internationally recognized association, 100 Beste Plakate (100 Best Posters), working with people and communities interested in keeping up poster design. They support the medium through international festivals, associations, and publications, helping to keep the poster vibrant.

A CERTAIN RADICALISM

Given that cyan will surely go down in history as one of the most innovative German firms of their time, and given their scholarly pursuits, it is particularly interesting to hear their thoughts on past masters of poster design, among whom they count Toulouse-Lautrec, John Hartfield, Raymond Savignac, Rodchenko, Piet Zwart, and Wolfgang Weingart. "We are influenced by posters that managed to change the style of an era through a certain radicalism." Somehow, that Haufe and Fielder are drawn to radical solutions does not come as a surprise to me. The challenging thought behind the work they consider great seems to shape their selections, as their own work shows little of its influence.

Speaking of influence, cyan reveals a more obvious basis for their work. "Besides the fine art, music, and photography—think Bauhaus, Cartier-Bresson—of various epochs, it is mostly everyday life that influences us." For example, "we once bought a colored striped sweater, out of which came the colors for our following layouts. The sweater as a piece of clothing also became one of our favorites!"

AHEAD OF THEIR TIME

"Designing a poster is an elementary design exercise," say Haufe and Fielder. "First of all, there is the size of a poster. The other dimension you have to work, unlike in designing a book or a brochure, is that a poster also always has to win out over its environment." In addition, they point out, the designer must take into account the poster's effect when viewed from various distances. To create a poster that draws attention at first sight, but is still interesting on the second view, means concentrating all of your creative energy into a single panel. There is no room for anything less than a flawless execution. This imperative, plus "dealing with a huge amount of text and twenty or more logos," they laugh, makes the challenge of creating a poster that is both legible and attractive a daunting but rewarding task.

Some studios seem to be five years ahead of their time. cyan, with their inventive color palettes, eye-catching patterns, and blazingly intense presentation, is one of those firms. Given its heavy influence on Germany's young designers, by whom Haufe and Fielder are revered like rock stars, one can only imagine what the future will hold. Luckily, we can view the work presented here and dream.

"Designing a poster is an elementary design exercise."

ANDRES ROTO
BOSS PHONIA
HAR

D

3.
7.–
27.
7.

schweiz

klanginstallation

kirchenschiff

N

2003

vernissage
mi
2.
7.
2003
um
18h

lange
nacht
so
27.
7.
2003
bis
24h

öffnungszeiten
mi
bis
so

von
14h
bis
20h

singuhr —
hœrgalerie
in
parochial
klosterstraße 67
10179 berlin-mitte
u-bahnhof klosterstrasse u2
s-bahnhof alexanderplatz
veranstaltet
von
kunst in parochial
tel+fax 030 —- 24 72 44 65

www.singuhr.de

mit unterstützung der av. kirchengemeinds marien, initiative neue musik berlin, berliner senatsverwaltung für wissenschaft, forschung und
kulturpro'mkreise – schweizer kulturstiftung, a-dim – stiftung für musik,

G

S

u

h

R

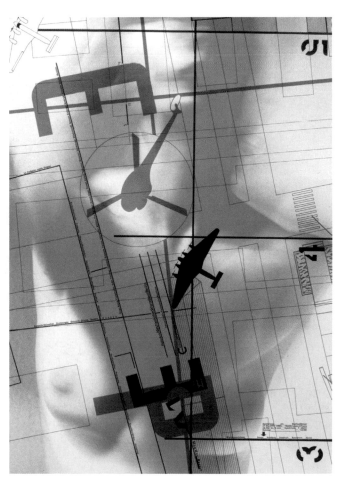

TITLE: "Singuhr"—Sound Art Gallery
at Parochial Church 1997
CLIENT: Kunst in Parochial E.V.
SIZE: 32.8" x 46.4" (84.1 x 118.9 cm)
PRINTING PROCESS: Silkscreen
INKS: 3 color
Are posters what you primarily do for this client? Yes

PROCESS
COMPS PRESENTED: 1
REVISIONS: 0
APPROVAL: Head of association
INVOLVEMENT WITH FINAL PRINTING:
Prepared for production and press inspected

"Singuhr" is an experimental sound/music project, based in Berlin, that uses the Parochial Church as a venue for contemporary music and its carillon's nickname as its title. The first poster cyan completed for "Singuhr" was designed to help establish a new location for the event as well as the annual theme. The new location concept was expressed by "a rooster crowing loudly for attention and a ventilator bringing fresh wind into the old church, but also resembling a clock." Once they felt comfortable with that solution, Haufe and Fielder tackled incorporating the annual theme, which was "resonance." "We proceeded to put three regular waves on top of each other. The resulting impression of irregularity is a conscious visual deception of the viewer: an intellectual reflection on resonances," they explain.

TITLE: "Singuhr"—Sound Art Gallery
at Parochial Church 2003
CLIENT: Kunst in Parochial E.V.
SIZE: 39" x 54.6" (100 x 140 cm)
PRINTING PROCESS: Silkscreen
INKS: 2 color
Are posters what you primarily do for this client? Yes

PROCESS
COMPS PRESENTED: 1
REVISIONS: 0
APPROVAL: Head of association
INVOLVEMENT WITH FINAL PRINTING:
Prepared for production and press inspected

"The curator's concept for this season of 'Singuhr' was very strict," notes cyan. "It explored the possibilities of transferring the basic idea of jazz into the field of sound installations." Haufe and Fielder decided to strip down their approach accordingly to convey clear, distinct sound and the feeling that the notes that are not played in music are just as important as those that are. After a great deal of thought, "we translated this aspect by designing a purely typographical black and white poster," says cyan.

TITLE: Urban + Aboriginal XVI "Recent and Ancient Music from Korea"
CLIENT: Freunde Guter Musik Berlin E.V.
SIZE: 23.2" x 32.8" (59.4 x 84.1 cm)
PRINTING PROCESS: Offset
INKS: 4-color process
Are posters what you primarily do for this client? Yes

PROCESS
COMPS PRESENTED: 1
REVISIONS: 0
APPROVAL: Head of association
INVOLVEMENT WITH FINAL PRINTING:
Prepared for production

In creating imagery for a festival of traditional and contemporary Korean music, which ranges from classical interpretations to electronic sounds played on original instruments, cyan wanted to relate the look to its cultural context. To stay as authentic as possible while still applying their modern touch, cyan took inspiration from traditional patterns and the colors that are most prominent in Korean culture.

TITLE: Better Days
CLIENT: Cie. Toula Limnaios
SIZE: 32.8" x 46.4" (84.1 x 118.9 cm)
PRINTING PROCESS: Offset
INKS: 2 color
Are posters what you primarily do for this client? Yes

PROCESS
COMPS PRESENTED: 3
REVISIONS: 0
APPROVAL: Choreographer and composer
INVOLVEMENT WITH FINAL PRINTING:
Prepared for production and press inspected

In designing a poster for a dance piece by the Compagnie Toula Limnaios, the studio meant to create a contrast to its content. Here the five dancers are somewhat isolated from each other, unlike on stage. Each one is living in a personal parallel world, escaping to the outer world in their dreams. "This outer world was shown on television screens on the stage during the production," explains cyan, which also designed the black and white stage set and the video work. Haufe and Fielder played up that aspect with "the apparently happy family situation shown on the photograph of the poster, creating a feeling that is both contrary and equal to the complex atmosphere of the piece," explains cyan. "Better days?" One has to ask.

TITLE: "Singuhr"—Sound Art Gallery
at Parochial Church 2005
CLIENT: Kunst in Parochial E.V.
SIZE: 39" x 54.6" (100 x 140 cm)
PRINTING PROCESS: Silkscreen
INKS: 4 color
Are posters what you primarily do for this client? Yes

PROCESS
COMPS PRESENTED: 1
REVISIONS: 1
APPROVAL: Head of association
INVOLVEMENT WITH FINAL PRINTING:
Prepared for production and press inspected

The focus of the 2005 edition of "Singuhr" was "the creation of invisible but perceptible soundscapes," Haufe and Fielder explain. "Each visitor experiences the soundscapes individually and differently." The firm tried to capture that feeling visually by overprinting the moiré patterns to create a sort of "sound cluster, similar to the one that arises in and around the head of a visitor to the gallery."

TITLE: Suite in Parochial
CLIENT: Kunst in Parochial E.V.
SIZE: 39" x 54.6" (100 x 140 cm)
PRINTING PROCESS: Silkscreen
INKS: 3 color
Are posters what you primarily do for this client? Yes

PROCESS
COMPS PRESENTED: 1
REVISIONS: 0
APPROVAL: Head of association
INVOLVEMENT WITH FINAL PRINTING:
Prepared for production and press inspected

Designing a poster for a sound and art festival entitled "Suite in Parochial," the studio noted "a sound installation, a daily listening room, and various sound performances by international electronic sound artists" while trying to identify "the underlying theme of all the events, which was the attempt to interpret a suite electronically." The final piece is "the attempt to put the spherical aspect and the punctual impulses into a rigorous, eye-catching form," explains cyan.

TITLE: "Singuhr"—Sound Art Gallery at Parochial Church 2004
CLIENT: Kunst in Parochial E.V.
SIZE: 39" x 54.6" (100 x 140 cm)
PRINTING PROCESS: Silkscreen
INKS: 4 color
Are posters what you primarily do for this client? Yes

PROCESS
COMPS PRESENTED: 1
REVISIONS: 0
APPROVAL: Head of association
INVOLVEMENT WITH FINAL PRINTING:
Prepared for production and press inspected

The 2004 "Singuhr" exhibit required "the artists to design their spaces, not only in an electronic fashion but also by using physical phenomena (Bunsen burner, capacitors, etc.) to create and amplify the sound," says cyan. "Therefore, we worked with images and drawings out of an old physics schoolbook," to capture the feel and to connect to science-based imagery.

TITLE: Twentieth Anniversary of Friends of Good Music
CLIENT: Freunde Guter Musik Berlin E.V.
SIZE: 39" x 54.6" (100 x 140 cm)
PRINTING PROCESS: Silkscreen
INKS: 3 color
Are posters what you primarily do for this client? Yes

PROCESS
COMPS PRESENTED: 1
REVISIONS: 0
APPROVAL: Head of association
INVOLVEMENT WITH FINAL PRINTING:
Prepared for production and test printed

TITLE: Fifteenth Anniversary of Friends of Good Music
CLIENT: Freunde Guter Musik Berlin E.V.
SIZE: 39" x 54.6" (100 x 140 cm)
PRINTING PROCESS: Offset
INKS: 6 color
Are posters what you primarily do for this client? Yes

PROCESS
COMPS PRESENTED. 1
REVISIONS: 0
APPROVAL: Head of association
INVOLVEMENT WITH FINAL PRINTING: Prepared for production and press inspected

The Freunde Guter Musik ("Friends of Good Music") began as a promotional operation over twenty years ago. Haufe and Fielder explain, "The range of concerts they organize runs the gamut from avant-garde to pop to techno and everything in between." The concerts are presented in different venues depending on the demands of the performance, leaving the company with no real home. The search for space led to the studio to develop imagery based on that exploration. "The spaces constructed in the posters relate to the content and also reflect the changing status of the group. The fifteenth-anniversary poster shows a somewhat blurry, undefined space. The living room atmosphere of the one created five years later is, in contrast, almost cozy," says cyan.

TITLE: MagMec Berlin
CLIENT: Bauhaus Dessau Foundation
SIZE: 26.9" x 38.2" (69 x 98 cm)
PRINTING PROCESS: Offset
INKS: 3 color
Are posters what you primarily do for this client? No

PROCESS
COMPS PRESENTED: 1
REVISIONS: 0
APPROVAL: Professor of architecture
INVOLVEMENT WITH FINAL PRINTING:
Prepared for production and press inspected

"MagMec was a student project dealing with the world of shopping," and the firm was to promote the exhibition of this work. The group of design students from the Rosenheim design school in Bavaria had developed fourteen projects represented in designs and drawings to be shown at Bauhaus Dessau. "The challenge was to balance the overall design concept while providing common ground for the various projects and preserving the individuality of each of the presented student works," Haufe and Fielder explain. "Legibility of the text was not a primary issue. The client wanted us to capture the feeling foremost, and it seemed to be more important to represent the architectural character and social commentary of the works in the design."

★ ODED EZER ★

GIVATAYIM, ISRAEL

WHAT IS A TYPOGRAPHER DOING IN HERE?

Oded Ezer is somewhat of an anomaly for this book because he is primarily a typographer. He is at the forward edge of Hebrew type design and now leads a small movement concerned with three-dimensional typography in Israel. This passion for type has found him at an odd destination—the poster. Each year he works on an "ongoing project: the Nonprofit Item Project, or NPI, as I call it," he says. "I use these posters as a platform to disseminate my conclusions and suggestions for typographical design."

If the description sounds dry, then you had better look at the work again. It has garnered awards from as far away as New York and Japan. Drawn to the "high sex appeal of the poster, which I consider somewhere between graphic design and art," Ezer makes viewers question everything they thought they knew about type in an amazingly sophisticated yet direct manner.

For his NPI projects, Ezer structures his work with three rules: He always uses low-budget, everyday materials; he always works by hand; and he uses color only when necessary. His goal is to speak about form, and his need to work by hand is likely a reaction to using the computer for commercial design. "By the time I am working on these pieces I am fed up with the computer from my other work. I feel like there are more possibilities when I work with my hands."

HONESTY

"When designing my posters, I see myself as someone who uses his abilities to change and reshape the visual appearance of our environment in a way that will reflect the reality instead of hiding it. I see this not only as a visual or professional act but also a political one," says Ezer. What he strives for most is honesty. At the end of the day, honesty is all he really wants from design. It is what he believes a poster's success hinges on. Striving for honesty, he draws on a "variety of contemporary fields, such as architecture, music, science, and the philosophies of our time. As an Israeli, I am, of course, influenced by the cultural, national, and political environment of my country." A student of design, he has learned a great deal from the masters, but he is also doing everything he can to be a trailblazer in his own right.

HOW DO LETTERS LOOK?

If some of this comes across as intellectual and serious—well, it is. But it is also a very human exercise. Ezer explains, "As a designer, I feel deeply obligated to make an impact on my community by pushing the borders of Hebrew typography and graphic design in order to create a new pluralistic environment. As a matter of fact, I give it the utmost priority, and this was the main reason I engaged in the profession." His dedication cannot be questioned when you view his tiny handmade sculptures of type forms, sometimes as small as 2 inches (5 cm), manipulated into dancing for the camera.

This sense of exploration keeps Ezer challenged. "Some of the questions I often ask myself while creating are: How does typography behave in different situations? What do letters do when they are happy? How do they look when they are shy? How will a letter act when it is slapped or kissed? How will typographic design look in ten, twenty, fifty, one hundred years? What are the borders of readability, on the one hand, and typographic expressiveness, on the other? How can one use the tension between literal meaning and visual meaning in typographic work?"

When you hear his communication with his typographic children and see the results of the interplay, the passion as well as the innate artistic ability comes shining through. Somehow it seems appropriate that he showcase these tiny sculptures in such a larger than life format.

"I feel like there are more possibilities when I work with my hands."

מהכתב העברי לאורך ההיסטוריה // ומצורות הכתבים הלועזיים

מדוע לא להוסיף מקורות השראה נוספים

פניה לשדות אחרים // העתקת העקרונות שלהם לשדה העיצוב הטיפוגרפי // תביא ליצירת צורות חדשות בתחום הזה.

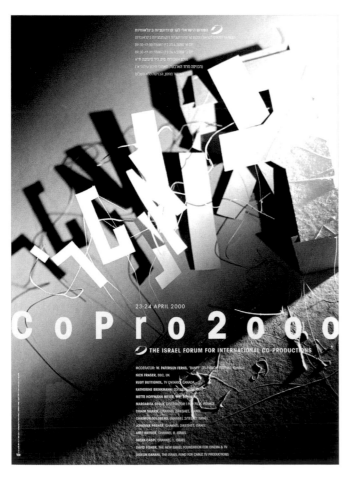

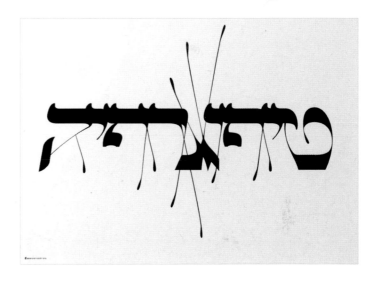

TITLE: Plastica
CLIENT: Oded Ezer
SIZE: 26.77" x 37.01" (68 x 94 cm)
PRINTING PROCESS: Offset
INKS: Black
Are posters what you primarily do for this client? Yes

PROCESS
COMPS PRESENTED: 1
REVISIONS: 0
APPROVAL: Oded Ezer
INVOLVEMENT WITH FINAL PRINTING:
Prepared for production and press inspected

Producing his "manifest for Hebrew type designers," Ezer was drawn to the work of French designer Philippe Starck and motivated by his own interest in insects. He was desperate to "design a three-dimensional typeface that stands on its own feet. If viewed from above, you can actually read the sculpture, but the idea is to give it life." After photographing his typebugs, he overlaid small lines of type that serve as his "manifests," challenging commonly held notions about typography. The main influences on Hebrew typographers until now "have been ancient Hebrew and Latin," says Ezer. "I declared that they should also be influenced by nature, architecture, philosophy, mathematics, and new technology in order to fully enrich the field of typography."

TITLE: Now
CLIENT: Oded Ezer
SIZE: 26.77" x 37.01" (68 x 94 cm)
PRINTING PROCESS: Offset
INKS: Black
Are posters what you primarily do for this client? Yes

PROCESS
COMPS PRESENTED: 1
REVISIONS: 0
APPROVAL: Oded Ezer
INVOLVEMENT WITH FINAL PRINTING:
Prepared for production and press inspected

Paying typographic homage to a close friend, Israeli visual communicator and designer David Tartakover, Ezer began his own take on the Peace Now logo. "*Now* is half of Peace Now," the name of an Israeli peace movement, explains Ezer. "David had designed the logo for the cause, and because he is a good friend I knew he wouldn't mind my making my own interpretation." Ezer signifies progress toward building peace in his country by using nails to assemble his typography.

TITLE: CoPro2000
CLIENT: Israel Forum for Co-Productions
SIZE: 26.77" x 37.01" (68 x 94 cm)
PRINTING PROCESS: Offset
INKS: Black
Are posters what you primarily do for this client? Yes

PROCESS
COMPS PRESENTED: 1
REVISIONS: 0
APPROVAL: Forum manager
INVOLVEMENT WITH FINAL PRINTING:
Prepared for production and press inspected

Working with photographer Amos Rafaeli, Ezer set about promoting a film festival by building "the word *documentary* in Hebrew as if it had just been caught on film in the middle of an action." It was inspired by the mid-1980s posters for the Holland Festival designed by Studio Dumbar, but Ezer's design met with resistance. "The client was not as crazy about this as I was. It seemed too experimental, but they were forced to use it due to time constraints. Once it was up on the streets, it was so different from what was being done, especially printed in black and white, that it had a huge impact."

TITLE: Alef
CLIENT: Oded Ezer
SIZE: 26.77" x 37.01" (68 x 94 cm)
PRINTING PROCESS: Offset
INKS: Black
Are posters what you primarily do for this client? Yes

PROCESS

COMPS PRESENTED: 1
REVISIONS: 0
APPROVAL: Oded Ezer
INVOLVEMENT WITH FINAL PRINTING:
Prepared for production and press inspected

Alef is "the first letter of the Hebrew alphabet, and it is the first letter of the words for 'God' and 'Man,'" says Ezer. "It has a way of linking things, and it suggests we all have a little bit of God in us." Exploring this link, Ezer tried to "bend the two edges of the letterform so they nearly touch—much in the same way God and Adam's fingers nearly touch in Michelangelo's Sistine Chapel painting." Ezer used close photography to capture the delicate nature of the bend; the actual model was only 2 inches (5 cm) wide.

TITLE: *The Chorus of the Opera*
CLIENT: Check the Gate Productions
SIZE: 26.77" x 37.01" (68 x 94 cm)
PRINTING PROCESS: Offset
INKS: Black
Are posters what you primarily do for this client? Yes

PROCESS

COMPS PRESENTED: 1
REVISIONS: 0
APPROVAL: Two directors and the company owner
INVOLVEMENT WITH FINAL PRINTING:
Prepared for production and press inspected

"This incredibly sad film," says Ezer, "tells the tale of singers who have given up their dreams of becoming a soloist to join the chorus in the opera. So the poster was meant to look appropriately somber." The company was concerned no one would attend a film promoted in such a bleak fashion. Ezer retorted, "The film is sad. I cannot lie. I cannot produce a happy solution." He was fired from the project. "I loved the poster and printed it myself and sent it around the world to great acclaim. Six months later, the producers called me and had heard about the success and hoped they could have some posters for themselves." Still smarting, Ezer says, "I saw their point in firing me and hope they saw my point in telling them no. You have to believe in the design. Design should tell the truth."

TITLE: Typography
CLIENT: Oded Ezer
SIZE: 26.77" x 37.01" (68 x 94 cm)
PRINTING PROCESS: Offset
INKS: Black
Are posters what you primarily do for this client? Yes

PROCESS

COMPS PRESENTED: 1
REVISIONS: 0
APPROVAL: Oded Ezer
INVOLVEMENT WITH FINAL PRINTING:
Prepared for production and press inspected

This is the only piece in this series executed on the computer. How odd that Ezer's letterforms are similar whether they are drawn or sculpted or vectorized! This work is like a bridge between "Plastica" (page 39) and the work of another typographer, Raphael Frank. "Frank designed in the twentieth century, and I created this in some way as an homage to his work," says Ezer. "This piece also shows how typography can have an appeal like that of calligraphy."

TITLE: Stami Veklumi ("Unimportant and Nothing")
CLIENT: Oded Ezer
SIZE: 26.77" x 37.01" (68 x 94 cm)
PRINTING PROCESS: Offset
INKS: 4-color process
Are posters what you primarily do for this client? Yes

PROCESS

COMPS PRESENTED: 1
REVISIONS: 0
APPROVAL: Oded Ezer
INVOLVEMENT WITH FINAL PRINTING:
Prepared for production and press inspected

Using the title of a poem by the Israeli poet Yona Volach, "Stami Veklumi"—a conversation between "Unimportant" and "Nothing," Ezer worked to capture the feeling of the words in his poster. The poem "is about nothing and boredom," says Ezer. "When I thought about materials I wanted to work with, chewing gum immediately came to mind. I worked with it very quickly to make my own typographic poetry." As the feel of the gum was essential to the look of the piece, he had photographer Shaxaf Haber work in color. "I did what the material asked me to do," Ezer explains.

HAKOBO (JAKUB STEPIEN)

LODZ, POLAND

NEW KID ON THE BLOCK

America is not the only place young designers have latched on to the silkscreen movement to promote a subculture. Poland's music and skateboard scene has spawned an unlikely hero: a designer whose work hangs side by side in museums with Europe's finest masters. Working under the guise Hakobo on the street and under his own name in the museum circles, Jakub Stepien has served notice that the next wave of Polish poster designers already has a champion.

Trained at the Academy of Fine Arts in Lodz, Stepien is well aware of the designers that have come before him in Poland's long love affair with the poster. He enjoys being part of this national tradition of making posters. For Stepien, the creative process "evolves peacefully" right down to "printing the poster, when it becomes a material thing." Covering a piece of paper with paint brings him simple joy.

Stepien does not view his youth as a barrier. "My age is not important. The most important thing is that I have something to say and if I can express it visually, I should. I have worked at getting to the point I am now since I was a child. I was always drawing, painting, and practicing the graphic language."

STREET GEOMETRY

Although he wishes his posters were contemporary, Stepien has bridged the past with a modern sensibility. His client base alone brings a current value to his work as well as his work situation. "The home computer is a large influence on shaping my graphic style." In this vein, he is reminded of "Eli Lissitzky, Rodczenko, and others who dreamed of a day when the computer would aid this type of design. I like their simplicity, typography—the geometric style."

The clean sensibility and element of stacking or building that pervades Stepien's work is an influence of his industrial surroundings. He also envelops himself in "sport and street style, modern fashion—the kind you see every day, not from the catwalks—the poor, trashy typography used everywhere in Poland." Stepien combines this with "a love of nature and of sincerity, an interest in prehistoric and primitive art, and a fetish for modern decorative tapestry."

The interest in primitive art, along with his uncanny sense of geometry, informs his work and goes a long way toward conveying the immediacy with which it speaks to the audience.

CONNECT

Stepien truly loves the poster. "My interest in it reflects my whole life. It broadens my horizons, it keeps me in touch with the design world, it lets me meet interesting people around the world. It is the most interesting medium. It lets me express myself and connect with what I see, what I want to say, and what I think."

Stepien expresses the wish that his designs "were close to people, literally close to their body." In this he follows in the footsteps of his mother, a fabric designer in a huge factory. He thus has branched out into "walking posters," or street clothing adorned with his designs. He explains, "If somebody likes my graphic, he can show that by wearing it rather than by stealing a poster."

"I was always drawing, painting, and practicing the graphic language."

asp

godz.21
16.11.2001
FUXÓWKA

FORUM FABRICUM:KONCERT-*LOCKO RICHTER & JURA* (ACID JAZZ,TRIP HOP,HOUSE,FUNK-*Mr.WORRY*)
WYSTAWA-*EDYTA I MARCIN FORYS* (FOTOGRAFIA,TKANINA,INSTALACJE,SITODRUK)+DJ J A S M A N
DYSTRYBUCJA ZAPROSZEN OD 08.11.2001 *prokadencja@bluenet.pl*

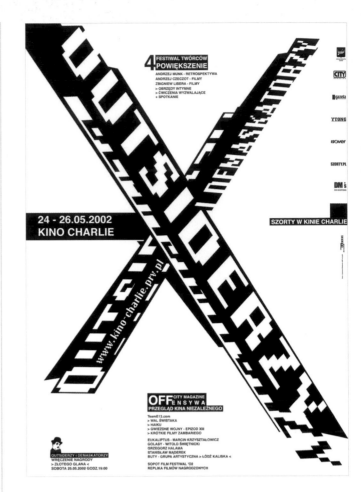

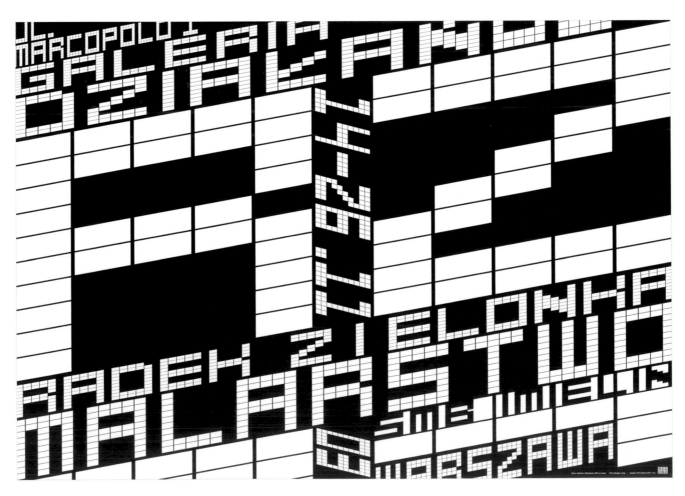

TITLE: Fuxówka ("A Greenhorn's Party")
CLIENT: Forum Fabricum
SIZE: 39.37" x 27.56" (100 x 70 cm)
PRINTING PROCESS: Silkscreen
INKS: 2 color
Are posters what you primarily do for this client? No

PROCESS
COMPS PRESENTED: 1
REVISIONS: 1
APPROVAL: Party contact
INVOLVEMENT WITH FINAL PRINTING:
Printed by Hakobo

The solution for this piece did not come easily to Stepien, who notes, "There was a long road between the first and last version of this poster." But he struck on a connection. "In Poland, young students are called *cats*. That's why there is a crazy cat symbolizing a new students' party." The poster was a raging success. "The final effect surprised me alot. Everybody liked it, especially the students."

TITLE: CKOD
CLIENT: Cool Kids of Death
SIZE: 39.37" x 27.56" (100 x 70 cm)
PRINTING PROCESS: Silkscreen
INKS: 2 color
Are posters what you primarily do for this client? Yes

PROCESS
COMPS PRESENTED: 1
REVISIONS: 0
APPROVAL: Band member
INVOLVEMENT WITH FINAL PRINTING:
Printed by Hakobo

Stepien gets a lot of attention, due in part to his initiative. He designed this poster influenced by the dynamic music from the second album by Cool Kids of Death, a band in which a college friend is a vocalist. The intersecting typographic elements that seem to fly past and cut into one another, and the simple red and black palette came to him quickly. "Nobody asked me to do it—it was just an impulse," he says. He printed the posters by hand and presented them to the group as a gift.

TITLE: Outsiders and (People Denouncing)
CLIENT: Charlie Cinema
SIZE: 39.37" x 27.56" (100 x 70 cm)
PRINTING PROCESS: Silkscreen
INKS: Black
Are posters what you primarily do for this client? Yes

PROCESS
COMPS PRESENTED: 4
REVISIONS: 6
APPROVAL: Cinema committee
INVOLVEMENT WITH FINAL PRINTING:
Printed by Hakobo

Creating a poster for a film festival, Stepien strove for the obvious. "I wanted to create a symbol of going beyond." With intersecting typography and dimensional shapes in a direct black and white fashion, Stepien feels he succeeded in making "a poster that combines a road sign, celluloid, and my typography" to promote the festival. He notes that sometimes less thought is more in his "short way of thinking."

TITLE: Hakobo
CLIENT: Z.o.o. Gallery in Warsaw
SIZE: 39.37" x 27.56" (100 x 70 cm)
PRINTING PROCESS: Silkscreen
INKS: 2 color
Are posters what you primarily do for this client? Yes

PROCESS
COMPS PRESENTED: 1
REVISIONS: 1
APPROVAL: Gallery
INVOLVEMENT WITH FINAL PRINTING:
Printed by Hakobo

Stepien designed this poster for solo exhibitions of his work in Lodz and Warsaw. Now he looks back on it as "a very symbolic piece." He wanted to graphically reflect his progress and used a temple constructed in his honor to do so. "This speaks directly to my art. Each level is a symbol of a new step in my work."

TITLE: Beyond the Red Horizon
CLIENT: Center for Contemporary Art in Warsaw
SIZE: 37.40" x 25.59" (95 x 65 cm)
PRINTING PROCESS: Offset
INKS: 4-color process
Are posters what you primarily do for this client? No

PROCESS
COMPS PRESENTED: 8
REVISIONS: 7
APPROVAL: Art Center committee
INVOLVEMENT WITH FINAL PRINTING:
Prepared for press

Designing the promotional poster for an exhibit of contemporary art from Poland and Russia, Stepien was heavily influenced by "a painting by a vanguard Russian artist of the 1970s, Erik Bulatow, called *The Red Horizon*. The colors are taken from this painting, and they also recall the colors of the new flag of Russia after the fall of communism." Stepien combined these with his modern typography to reference the contemporary collection of work.

TITLE: It Began
CLIENT: Futro Club in Lodz
SIZE: 39.37" x 27.56" (100 x 70 cm)
PRINTING PROCESS: Silkscreen
INKS: Black
Are posters what you primarily do for this client? No

PROCESS
COMPS PRESENTED: 1
REVISIONS: 1
APPROVAL: Club contact
INVOLVEMENT WITH FINAL PRINTING:
Printed by Hakobo

Club music is important to Stepien. In this case, it coincided perfectly with his interest in other cultures. "I was inspired by African music and the culture in general, as the poster was to promote an event with African music." Using an African aesthetic, Stepien wove an almost startlingly graphic, mythical icon into the typography and captured the vibe for the evening of music.

TITLE: Lodz
CLIENT: Manhattan Gallery in Lodz
SIZES: 198.43" x 93.70" (504 x 238 cm)
PRINTING PROCESS: Silkscreen
INKS: 4-color process
Are posters what you primarily do for this client? No

PROCESS

COMPS PRESENTED: 5
REVISIONS: Many
APPROVAL: Gallery committee
INVOLVEMENT WITH FINAL PRINTING:
Printed by Hakobo

"The city of Lodz was promoting a new look with an exhibition. Formerly it was a promised land for four nations. Germans, Russians, Jews, and Poles came here, but now it is a city of football fans and unemployment," says Stepien. The exhibition was "a discussion about the difference between stereotypes and the city's contemporary identity." Dealing with one of the city's important issues—the constant clash between hooligan fans of its two soccer clubs—Stepien wove in two more important links. "The poster has a knitted facture, which is both a symbol of the textile industry, on which the city was built in the nineteenth century, and a scarf for a football fan. The typography relates to the vanguard typography of Stanislaw Strzeminski, an important artist of Polish and Lodz constructivism."

TITLE: RZ
CLIENT: Imielin Gallery
SIZE: 39.37" x 27.56" (100 x 70 cm)
PRINTING PROCESS: Silkscreen
INKS: Black
Are posters what you primarily do for this client? Yes

PROCESS

COMPS PRESENTED: 1
REVISIONS: 0
APPROVAL: Artist
INVOLVEMENT WITH FINAL PRINTING:
Printed by Hakobo

Asked by a friend to design a poster promoting his first solo exhibition in a small gallery in Warsaw, Stepien found himself drawn to both the art and the artist. "The poster depicts his art, influenced by geometrical abstract shapes. Playfully, I exposed his initials—R Z—for Radek Zielonka in the shapes."

TITLE: Dydo Poster Gallery
CLIENT: Dydo Poster Gallery in Kraków
SIZE: 39.37" x 27.56" (100 x 70 cm)
PRINTING PROCESS: Silkscreen
INKS: 2 color
Are posters what you primarily do for this client? Yes

PROCESS

COMPS PRESENTED: 1
REVISIONS: 1
APPROVAL: Hakobo
INVOLVEMENT WITH FINAL PRINTING:
Printed by Hakobo

Stepien slaved over creating this piece for renowned poster collector Krysztof Dydo to promote his gallery, no doubt inspired by a client he wanted to impress. "It was hard work, as I wanted to create new and exciting typography" that would stand out amidst Dydo's amazing collection. Stepien admits he was only partially successful. "Krysztof said that he did not understand it—but he likes it," and he displays it proudly.

TITLE: Transformers
CLIENT: Center for Contemporary Art in Warsaw
SIZE: 70.87" x 47.24" (180 x 120 cm)
PRINTING PROCESS: Inkjet
INKS: 4-color process
Are posters what you primarily do for this client? Yes

PROCESS

COMPS PRESENTED: 1
REVISIONS: 0
APPROVAL: Exhibition curator
INVOLVEMENT WITH FINAL PRINTING:
Printed by Hakobo

Stepien used the title of the exhibition as his jumping-off point, as it had to do with "the political, cultural, and economic transformation in both Poland and Russia. Unfortunately, the curators changed their minds on the title, and I had to start all over again. But despite this, we all liked the posters so much that we decided to print it and include it in the exhibition. The letters are Polish except the F, which is a Russian Cyrillic." The colors reference the new Russian flag much in the way the *Red Horizon* piece does.

TITLE: Beauty as a Paining Effect
CLIENT: Contemporary Art Gallery BWA
SIZE: 37.40" x 25.59" (95 x 65 cm)
PRINTING PROCESS: Offset
INKS: 2 color
Are posters what you primarily do for this client? No

PROCESS

COMPS PRESENTED: 10
REVISIONS: 7
APPROVAL: Gallery committee
INVOLVEMENT WITH FINAL PRINTING:
Prepared for press

Discussing his poster for an exhibition about the conceptual idea of beauty, Stepien notes, "I wanted to create a visual connecting beauty and trash in order to show that for someone trash is beautiful and for another the same item is disgusting. To express this idea, I used weird typography, as it is simultaneously repellent and tempting." The only problem is that Stepien's work remains true to his brilliant simplicity and engaging forms despite his efforts, so no one is likely to find the typography "repellent."

★ HAMMERPRESS ★

KANSAS CITY, MISSOURI, USA

TOUCH ME, FEEL ME

The maker of the most tactile posters featured in this book, Hammerpress of Kansas City, carries on a proud tradition of printing that requires a different approach to design than that of many contemporaries—the beloved letterpress. Designer and printer Brady Vest is one in a long line of devotees to this printing process. With its metal type and custom-engraved plates biting into the paper, this age-old process provides vivid color and the unique characteristics of hand-set type and borders married to custom images.

Letterpress was the manner in which printed materials were produced for hundreds of years, and it instantly gives each piece a nostalgic feel.

Hammerpress may practice an old-school way of printing, but that mindset is not reflected in its creativity, just in its craftsmanship. Hammerpress often incorporates idiosyncratic illustrations and found art with typesetting and block printing. Combined with vibrant inks and overlapping elements, the result is an intoxicating mix of the past and the future on a single sheet of paper. The designers also have a playful streak that comes out when you learn a little of the behind-the-scenes goings-on in the print shop. The firm's unique approach to design is its single parameter for each piece: The last element inserted into the current piece must form the first element of the one to follow. This makes for a string of posters forever linked by the studio but invisible to the viewer, and it keeps the designers challenged at every turn.

Each poster bleeds into the firm's other work as well. Vest says, "We try to keep the boundaries open between the format and function of different kinds of work. The poster work is a direct influence on smaller, more commercial work, and vice versa."

TOUCH ME, TEACH ME

Long in love with Jim Dine's drawings and etchings, Vest had something closer to home to absorb as an influence. "The father of a friend in my high school art class was an art professor at the local university. [The work] blew me away! There was a real physicality and history to the work that I had never seen before. Areas of the paper nearly disintegrated from drawing and erasing so many times." This fascination with the effect of process continued in college, where Vest's printmaking instructor was Hugh Merril. "His work, at the time, was mostly sequential series of etchings, and he would pull a whole body of work off of one zinc etching plate until it was just a thin sheet of metal with holes eaten through it. The medium was not just a production method but an integral part of the work as well."

Assorted ephemera pop into Vest's consciousness as well. He confesses to regular study of "Asian pharmacy boxes, matchbook art, old tickets, old billboards with nothing on them, and old grade-school textbook covers." Almost anything printed is fair game. Vest admits that, to him, a successful poster "is primarily a beautiful print." He knows "this may go against some opinions of what a well-designed poster should be but we at Hammerpress are not as concerned with illustrating an idea as we are concerned with working the print to make something that is really unusual and new and exciting while advertising an event."

ABSOLUTE CREATIVE CONTROL

Hammerpress has served to bring some peace to Vest and his crew as well. When he started out as a college student doing posters and packaging for friends' bands, "it was a total labor of love and completely trial and error." As designing became a full-time job, he found himself embroiled in the day-to-day drudgery of printing for other firms and agencies. Vest admits, "Mentally, I couldn't justify the posters for quite a while because there is not a lot of money in them." Finally giving in, he got back to "doing stuff I enjoyed with absolute creative control. It became a way to balance myself."

It doesn't take much effort to visualize Vest lovingly nestling metal type together to form the beginning of another balanced day.

"The medium was not just a production method but an integral part of the work as well."

MYSTERIOSO

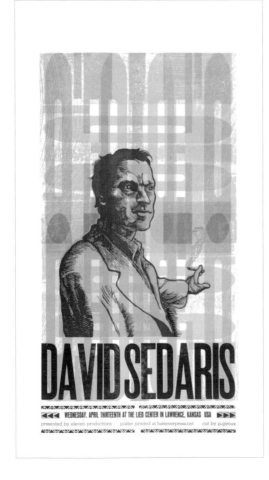

TITLE: Mysterioso
CLIENT: Hammerpress
SIZE: 6" x 9" (15.24 x 22.86 cm)
PRINTING PROCESS: Letterpress
INKS: Various
Are posters what you primarily do for this client? No

PROCESS

COMPS PRESENTED: 1
REVISIONS: 0
APPROVAL: Hammerpress
INVOLVEMENT WITH FINAL PRINTING:
Printed by Hammerpress

Again altering the elements of one of Vest's "miniature posters," the Mysterioso print accentuates the detail available when working smaller, which is something computer-designed posters don't need to address. Vest points out that "the smaller format allows for some things you cannot accomplish in our larger posters due to the scale of some of the lead type and ornaments." These projects are a bridge between what the Hammerpress designers can accomplish on their invitation and small-format jobs and their beloved poster work.

TITLE: Belle & Sebastian and the Polyphonic Spree
CLIENT: Eleven Productions
SIZE: 14" x 22" (35.56 x 55.88 cm)
PRINTING PROCESS: Letterpress
INKS: Various
Are posters what you primarily do for this client? Yes

PROCESS

COMPS PRESENTED: 1
REVISIONS: 0
APPROVAL: Promoter
INVOLVEMENT WITH FINAL PRINTING:
Printed by Hammerpress

Two posters for different performers with shows a few weeks apart allow the viewer to see the quirky way Vest can work. "These were worked on in a sequential manner, and many of the compositional elements are basically the same," says Vest. "I started with two stacks of paper, then ran the first two or three layers through on both stacks and started to address them separately and make them into two different posters. Imagine 500 sheets of blank paper walking hand in hand down a pathway and somewhere along the way they get mad at each other and take opposite paths at a fork in the road. Then a couple of days later, the two paths meet up again, and they both arrive at the intersection and realize that they really aren't that different after all. They're friends again!"

TITLE: David Sedaris
CLIENT: Eleven Productions
SIZE: 14" x 26" (35.56 x 66.04 cm)
PRINTING PROCESS: Letterpress
INKS: Various
Are posters what you primarily do for this client? Yes

PROCESS

COMPS PRESENTED: 1
REVISIONS: 0
APPROVAL: Promoter
INVOLVEMENT WITH FINAL PRINTING:
Printed by Hammerpress

Writer David Sedaris's performance led the Hammerpress designers to rein in their "obsessive tendencies a bit and not go crazy with the intricate and tiny stuff. I worked with a friend, illustrator Patrick Giroux, who created a hand-carved linoleum cut that was so fantastic and beautiful I didn't want to embellish or distract from it," says Vest. "The background is just an abstract pattern created from large wood type forms, creating a kind of plaid thing. The title of Sedaris's book was *Dress Your Family in Corduroy and Denim*, and somehow plaid seemed okay. I really wanted this poster to be a simple and classic design while still having a mysterious or experimental quality."

TITLE: Cat Power
CLIENT: Eleven Productions
SIZE: 14" x 22" (35.56 x 55.88 cm)
PRINTING PROCESS: Letterpress
INKS: Various
Are posters what you primarily do for this client? Yes

PROCESS

COMPS PRESENTED: 1
REVISIONS: 0
APPROVAL: Promoter
INVOLVEMENT WITH FINAL PRINTING:
Printed by Hammerpress

Working on the poster for Cat Power proved to be a bit of an epiphany for Vest and his crew. They created the background from "an assorted cluster of what was a very large metal plate that we had for another project and then cut down into these tiny little pieces, and the linoleum cut image from some old pulp Westerns I had," says Vest. The poster used the refuse of other projects but also inspired two more on its own. After spending a lot of time "tinkering obsessively, moving and shifting type and ornaments until they hit just the right spot," Vest was so happy with the layout that he built several projects from the template.

TITLE: Fabuloso
CLIENT: Hammerpress
SIZE: 6" x 9" (15.24 x 22.86 cm)
PRINTING PROCESS: Letterpress
INKS: Various
Are posters what you primarily do for this client?
We do everything.

PROCESS

COMPS PRESENTED: 1
REVISIONS: 0
APPROVAL: Hammerpress
INVOLVEMENT WITH FINAL PRINTING:
Printed by Hammerpress

Another of Vest's "miniature posters," the Fabuloso print shows how radically a template can be altered even when working with similar elements. By using humorous copy and imagery with a sly grin and a tight crop that references a swankier environ than their residence in the heartland of America, the piece gives recipients a good feel for the studio's personality and sense of humor.

TITLE: Pantyraid
CLIENT: Pantyraid! Burlesque Troupe
SIZE: 13" x 20" (33.02 x 50.80 cm)
PRINTING PROCESS: Letterpress
INKS: Various
Are posters what you primarily do for this client? Yes

PROCESS

COMPS PRESENTED: 1
REVISIONS: 0
APPROVAL: Pantyraid!
INVOLVEMENT WITH FINAL PRINTING:
Printed by Hammerpress

While exhibiting their work, the Hammerpress designers met a member of Pantyraid!, a burlesque troupe based in Tennessee, who loved their post-card series featuring vintage photographs of Kansas City burlesque dancers from the 1920s to the 1950s. Vest explains, "The idea was to do a poster in the style of those postcards without duplicating them. We tried extra-hard to make it look French and sexy."

TITLE: Decemberists
CLIENT: Eleven Productions
SIZE: 14" x 22" (35.56 x 55.88 cm)
PRINTING PROCESS: Letterpress
INKS: Various
Are posters what you primarily do for this client? Yes

PROCESS

COMPS PRESENTED: 1
REVISIONS: 0
APPROVAL: Promoter
INVOLVEMENT WITH FINAL PRINTING:
Printed by Hammerpress

It is funny what can transpire when your work and the press are tied so closely together. Vest says, "This poster was actually started without a particular project in mind. I had the large circle pattern set up on press for another project we were working on and ran an extra 250 or so pieces. It sat around for about a month, and then we laid down a couple of the large background frame pieces. It then sat around for a couple of weeks until we came to the Decemberists show, which we were doing a poster for. The typography was pretty basic on top of the three or four layers we had already printed." All of that good karma did not last, though. "As luck would have it, a poster we essentially started a couple months in advance wouldn't dry in time for the show, so we had stacks of these things leaning against the walls in our shop on top of the heater vents so they would dry faster."

TITLE: Canadian Gala
CLIENT: Bungalow Creative
SIZE: 12" x 24" (30.48 x 60.96 cm)
PRINTING PROCESS: Letterpress
INKS: Various
Are posters what you primarily do for this client? Yes

PROCESS

COMPS PRESENTED: 1
REVISIONS: 0
APPROVAL: Creative director
INVOLVEMENT WITH FINAL PRINTING:
Printed by Hammerpress

"This poster was done as a commemorative piece to be sold at the Gala Chorus event in Montreal. Gala Chorus is an international gathering of mostly gay and lesbian choral groups," explains Vest. "The intent was to make a piece that might appeal to gay and lesbian sensibilities, explain the mission of the festival, and look really pretty and all that—without relying too heavily on stereotypical imagery and design." This is one of Vest's favorite pieces, but it didn't sell. "I don't think they sold more than about fifty or so. I just didn't get it. I thought this thing would sell like hotcakes."

★ PEDRAM **HARBY** ★

TEHRAN, IRAN

SOMETHING IS HAPPENING

Often the most amazing work is being done where you least expect it. In the United States, it may be in the garage down the street from your office where some kid is silkscreening band posters. Internationally, it has to be the work being done in Iran. A great deal of pressure is on Pedram Harby, though he is up to the task, as he stands in for an entire movement in his country.

The work of Maryam Enayati (page 244) is discussed in the Next Wave section, but honestly, an entire third of this book could have been taken up by the challenging work of Iran's young designers.

Over the last few years, Harby has led the charge, and Iranian posters—his in particular—continue to garner awards and medals internationally. He is also the proud winner of the Seventh Biennial of Iranian Graphic Designers. In Iran, "everyone is indebted to Morteza Momayez, the godfather of Iranian design," says Harby. Rene Wanner, the famous poster collector and blogger, champions the Iranian movement as well, exposing the designers to an international audience.

In Iran, Harby says, "we can communicate in three ways: poster, book cover, and logo. These three have the most cultural impact in Iran." While he works in all these media, the poster is his forte, mixing Farsi and English in his work for reasons surprising to most of us but not to the creative minds in a restrictive society: recognition and innovation. "As Iranian designers want to participate in international exhibitions, we predominantly use English in the designs so people outside of Iran can understand our work," explains Harby. In addition, he and his colleagues see themselves as part of a new wave of designers striving to create a new mixture in typography.

WOVEN TOGETHER

Most of these designers use the poster as their canvas, and their work is influential. Harby cites Majid Abbasi and Reza Abedini as major influences, and, internationally, Uwe Loesch. He also finds a great deal of inspiration in music and the words that accompany them. "Lyrics of songs have given a great deal of inspiration to my work." He weaves together a distinctive use of imagery and a masterful application of Persian typography, and something striking allows forms before the viewer's eyes.

Harby's journey with each poster is personal and much more than just an assignment or project. "I believe each person has an idea of himself in the framework of the poster," he says. "I think that my work is affected mostly by my religion [Islam], and I think the centrality of each image in my posters is similar to people doing their pilgrimage by circling the Ka'bah in Mecca. And if you see an unfocused image in my work, it is because in our religion, real images of our prophets should not be used and mostly are shown as unfocused images. I am not a real Muslim, but I love old traditions and customs."

Harby is starting a new tradition, one in which Iranian designers grace the world stage with increasing frequency.

"I believe each person has an idea of himself in the framework of the poster."

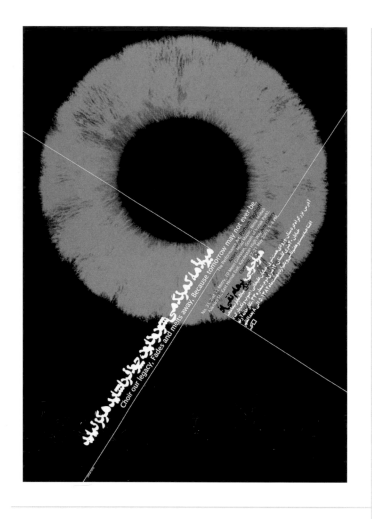

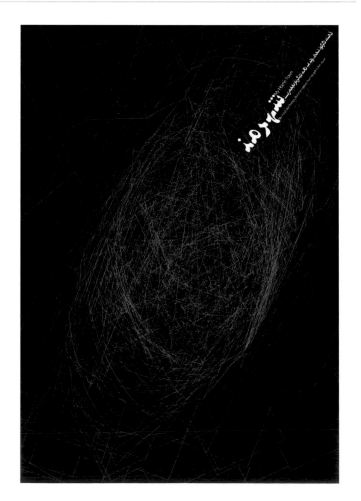

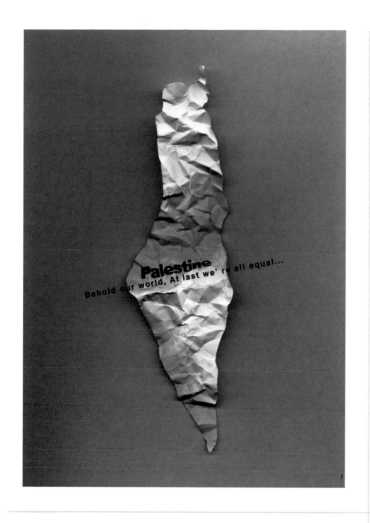

Palestine

Behold our world, At last we're all equal...

مذ فقط برای سایه خودم می نویسم

Choir our legacy, Fades and melts away, Because tomorrow may not ever be.

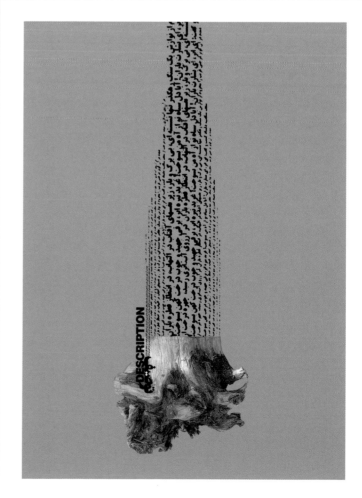

DESCRIPTION

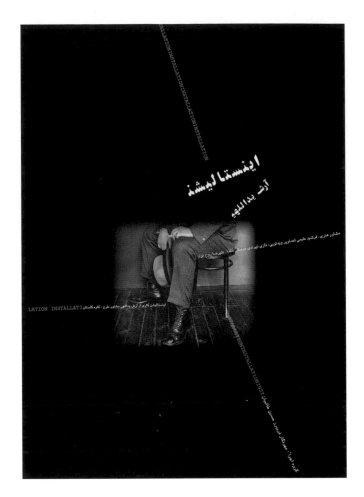

فصل هفتم
(فصل اول بخش دانشجویی)
تئاتر شهر با همکاری گروه‌های نمایشی برگزار می‌نماید:
عمری با نمایش نمایشنامه‌خوانی
بهار ۱۳۸۳، چهارشنبه‌ها بخش دانشجویی، پنج‌شنبه و جمعه‌ها بخش اصلی، کافه‌تریای سالن اصلی ساعت ۱۵

AN AFTERNOON WITH DRAMA

City Theatre presents: The 7th
Play reading
Spring 2004, Thursdays and Fridays, The main cafeteria **3pm** Chapter
www.charsoo-theatre.com - info@charsoo-theatre.com

TITLE: Kalhor
CLIENT: Ctrl+G Poster Exhibition
SIZE: 27.56" x 39.37" (70 x 100 cm)
PRINTING PROCESS: Digital
INKS: 4-color process
Are posters what you primarily do for this client? Yes

PROCESS
COMPS PRESENTED: 1
REVISIONS: 0
APPROVAL: Pedram Harby
INVOLVEMENT WITH FINAL PRINTING:
Prepared for production

Harby's poster for a gallery exhibition of one of his country's most recognizable artists has a decidedly modern twist. Kalhor is a well-known Iranian calligrapher. Creating an "encounter between modern design and Kalhor's old-fashioned personality is illogical to the viewer" and challenging to held notions.

TITLE: Conceptual Art (1)
CLIENT: Arteh Gallery of Tehran
SIZE: 19.69" x 39.37" (50 x 70 cm)
PRINTING PROCESS: Offset
INKS: 2 color
Are posters what you primarily do for this client? Yes

PROCESS
COMPS PRESENTED: 1
REVISIONS: 0
APPROVAL: Parham Tagihoff
INVOLVEMENT WITH FINAL PRINTING:
Prepared for production and press inspected

This piece for artist Parham Tagihoff's exhibit always makes Harby smile, who notes, "Most people think this is the shape of a pineapple, although in reality it is that of an eye." Intersecting Farsi and English copy at dramatic angles provides tension. As for color, Harby says his original plan was for red, "but I changed it to silver on press for greater impact."

TITLE: Violence
CLIENT: Mons Political Poster Exhibition
SIZE: 27.56" x 39.37" (70 x 100 cm)
PRINTING PROCESS: Digital
INKS: 1 color
Are posters what you primarily do for this client? Yes

PROCESS
COMPS PRESENTED: 1
REVISIONS: 0
APPROVAL: Exhibition organizer
INVOLVEMENT WITH FINAL PRINTING:
Prepared for production

It is amazing the impact that can be achieved with simple objects available at the local store. When Harby was given the subject *violence* for his submission to the prestigious Mons exhibit in Belgium, he looked to an odd source—the home furnishing store IKEA. "This photo is of a wooden doll that I purchased at IKEA and used to signify a cultural attack." The off-center typography, dramatic lighting, and stark black and white printing combine to form an arresting image.

TITLE: Trace
CLIENT: Pedram Harby
SIZE: 27.56" x 39.37" (70 x 100 cm)
PRINTING PROCESS: Digital
INKS: 2 color
Are posters what you primarily do for this client? Yes

PROCESS
COMPS PRESENTED: 1
REVISIONS: 0
APPROVAL: Pedram Harby
INVOLVEMENT WITH FINAL PRINTING:
Prepared for production

For this self-promotional piece in magenta and black, Harby set out to express clarity and instead leaves the viewer with ambiguity. The digital fingerprint motif is meant to convey a sense of identity, but Harby notes, "Most people think I have taken a certain direction in my life, but I really don't know." This uncertainty is reflected in the confused shapes operating in a mazelike fashion on the fingerprint.

TITLE: My Hometown
CLIENT: Ctrl+G Poster Exhibition
SIZE: 27.56" x 39.37" (70 x 100 cm)
PRINTING PROCESS: Digital
INKS: 2 color
Are posters what you primarily do for this client? Yes

PROCESS
COMPS PRESENTED: 1
REVISIONS: 0
APPROVAL: Pedram Harby
INVOLVEMENT WITH FINAL PRINTING:
Prepared for production

For a gallery exhibition, Harby decided to explore his city, Tehran, and its growth into something he hopes will blossom into much more. When he describes this "caterpillar" image as his interpretation of his hometown, it is obvious he views it in the cocoon stage.

TITLE: Palestine
CLIENT: First International Biennial of the Islamic World
SIZE: 27.56" x 39.37" (70 x 100 cm)
PRINTING PROCESS: Digital
INKS: 4-color process
Are posters what you primarily do for this client? Yes

PROCESS
COMPS PRESENTED: 1
REVISIONS: 0
APPROVAL: Pedram Harby
INVOLVEMENT WITH FINAL PRINTING:
Prepared for production

Visual problem solving comes easily to Harby, as in his striking interpretation of the political struggles of Palestine. However, designing in English has its limitations on occasion. "I was unable to properly express my viewpoint in the English text" that ended up on the final poster, says Harby. He may be disappointed, but he does not give nearly enough credit to his visual articulation.

TITLE: Hedayat
CLIENT: 5th Color Typography Exhibition Boot-E-Koor ("Blind Owl")
SIZE: 27.56" x 39.37" (70 x 100 cm)
PRINTING PROCESS: Digital
INKS: 1 color
Are posters what you primarily do for this client? Yes

PROCESS

COMPS PRESENTED: 1
REVISIONS: 2
APPROVAL: 5th Color
INVOLVEMENT WITH FINAL PRINTING:
Prepared for production

For Harby's interpretation of famed Iranian writer Hedayat (see Maryan Enayati's interpretation on page 243), he set out to mimic "the shape that Parisian artists produce on the street"—an outline based on viewing the person at a distance, then cut in silhouette out of paper. Harby made the technique his own by blurring the image, but not enough to dissolve the familiar shape of Hedayat's famous hat.

TITLE: Performance Art (II)
CLIENT: Khak Gallery of Tehran
SIZE: 19.69" x 39.37" (50 x 70 cm)
PRINTING PROCESS: Offset
INKS: 3 color
Are posters what you primarily do for this client? Yes

PROCESS

COMPS PRESENTED: 2
REVISIONS: 3
APPROVAL: Parham Tagihoff
INVOLVEMENT WITH FINAL PRINTING:
Prepared for production and press inspected

In creating an evocative promotional poster for artist Parham Tagihoff's exhibition, Harby pushed his use of Farsi into new arenas of typography. Lines of copy jut dramatically from the lone twisting Farsi letterform and were printed with a double hit of black ink to enhance the feeling. However, Harby could not believe the one thing that went wrong, given all of the attention to the type. "The worst part about this poster is that the date printed on it was incorrect," he laughs.

TITLE: Description
CLIENT: Pedram Harby
SIZE: 27.56" x 39.37" (70 x 100 cm)
PRINTING PROCESS: Digital
INKS: 4-color process
Are posters what you primarily do for this client? Yes

PROCESS

COMPS PRESENTED: 1
REVISIONS: 0
APPROVAL: Pedram Harby
INVOLVEMENT WITH FINAL PRINTING:
Prepared for production

Harby originally created this poster for a competition but changed his mind and let it languish, hoping to use it later as a self-promotional piece. We are fortunate to be the first to view it, and it is certainly worthwhile. The tree root base gives way to a Farsi explosion of varying point sizes and thicknesses to convey the cylindrical shape of the trunk, to astonishing effect. This poster showcases Harby's integration of typography and image.

TITLE: *An Afternoon with Drama, 8th Chapter*
CLIENT: City Theatre of Tehran
SIZE: 19.69" x 39.37" (50 x 70 cm)
PRINTING PROCESS: Offset
INKS: 2 color
Are posters what you primarily do for this client? No

PROCESS

COMPS PRESENTED: 2
REVISIONS: 3
APPROVAL: Theater officials
INVOLVEMENT WITH FINAL PRINTING: Prepared for production

For the following year's production of *An Afternoon with Drama*, Harby played with the image of a stool used on stage, placing the typography to dramatic effect in a phantom fourth leg and the corresponding rungs. The result is an interlocking of information and image.

TITLE: Installation
CLIENT: Barg Gallery of Tehran
SIZE: 19.69" x 39.37" (50 x 70 cm)
PRINTING PROCESS: Offset
INKS: 1 color
Are posters what you primarily do for this client? No

PROCESS

COMPS PRESENTED: 1
REVISIONS: 0
APPROVAL: Theater officials
INVOLVEMENT WITH FINAL PRINTING: Prepared for production and press inspected

Asked to design a poster for artist Arash Yadollahi's exhibition of work at the Barg Gallery, Harby, a fan of his work, jumped at the chance. This is his first real poster design and his first experience with offset printing. It is amazing how true Harby's vision is as his brilliant angled typography, direct yet obtuse imagery, blurred edges and obstructed figures, and clever mix of Farsi and English all make their first appearance.

TITLE: *An Afternoon with Drama, 7th Chapter*
CLIENT: City Theatre of Tehran
SIZE: 19.69" x 39.37" (50 x 70 cm)
PRINTING PROCESS: Offset
INKS: 2 color
Are posters what you primarily do for this client? No

PROCESS

COMPS PRESENTED: 1
REVISIONS: 5
APPROVAL: Theater officials
INVOLVEMENT WITH FINAL PRINTING:
Prepared for production and press inspected

Using a blurred figure as a gateway into the production of *An Afternoon with Drama*, Harby wedges the Farsi and English typography into the main image, effectively stopping the viewer in his tracks. He admits, "The color was a struggle with this printing, and we ultimately went with a color that differs from the one I chose."

★ JIANPING HE ★

BERLIN, GERMANY
WUXI, CHINA

THE BRIDGE

Few designers in the world so perfectly bridge Eastern and Western sensibilities as designer and educator Jianping He. From his upbringing in a rural farming village in China, where his parents were sent to work in fields hundreds of miles apart and his grandmother kept watch over him, to his immersion in the world of cutting-edge design in which he now resides in Berlin, He has emerged as something unexpected from his meager beginnings—unapologetically modern.

Educated under Heinz-Juergen Kristahn at the University of Arts in Berlin, He decided he had found a new home and never left. Here he combines his love of black and white imagery and his inventive typographical solutions, which treat Latin languages as instruments as well as words, and, most important, his immediate imagery. He does not mess around, despite the occasional whiff of fantasy or mystique in his work. His designs hit quickly and with power.

He is heavily influenced by Chinese culture and the social imagery to which he was subjected in his youth. A political sense pervades his choice of images and how he applies them. He often works by photographing objects that catch his eye and those in his immediate surroundings; then, when the right project to comes along, he returns to the images and manipulates them. This approach leads to photographs working in some fashion in several projects. The real key to this process is that he finds evocative images and captures them in a dramatic and simple fashion right from the beginning.

CHINA BY WAY OF BERLIN

Besides the obvious influences of the design history of China and the current climate in Berlin, He carries the teachings of Kristahn into his work as well as lessons learned from his own students. He also loves the work of Raymond Savignac, which he says he "hopes to understand better with each and every day." With respect to his sense of typography and the dreamlike surroundings of his images, he says, "I think the main influence for my work is traditional Chinese artwork as well as Chinese calligraphy and traditional woodcut work. I am also heavily influenced by Eiko Ishioka's costumes for theater and films." That quality of cinema or performance is reflected in the drama of his work.

The illusion of drama is one of the ways in which He boils down his philosophical decisions and symbolic imagery into one direct image with a multitude of interpretations. For He's work, viewers shape the final direction for the piece in that they must interact with, investigate, and interpret his executions.

GLOBAL VILLAGE

He cannot get enough of the large format available for a poster. "It is similar to how an artist approaches a large white canvas," he says. In order to make the most of that large format, you need "idea plus creativity plus aesthetic plus zeitgeist plus originality." He relishes the education he received in Berlin and wishes to impart as much of that as he can to the generation of designers trailing behind him.

He's work has won awards and acclaim all over the globe, including at the most prestigious poster competitions. However, although his work is featured in prominent collections and museums, he is really leaving his mark by means of his teachings and involvement with other international designers—especially those passionate about the poster, where he excels. Designers often cite He as their motivation to stretch their talents into another area. Now he is writing books that describe his work with his students, thus reaching beyond his rural village to the global village.

"Idea plus creativity plus aesthetic plus zeitgeist plus originality."

solidarity

屬民服務

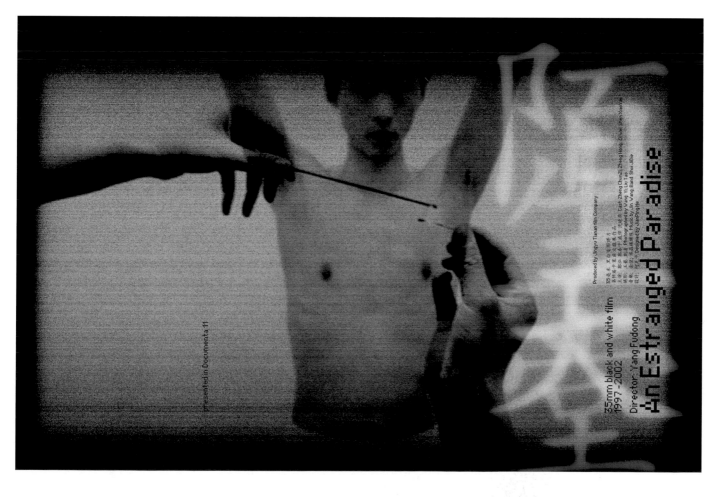

Attached to General Administration of Press and Publication. P.R.China. Published by Art and Design Publishing house: No.14, Fuchengmenwai Street, Xi Cheng District, Beijing. 00832 P.R.China. Designed by Jianping He 2003

艺术与设计
ART AND DESIGN
中国美术出版社

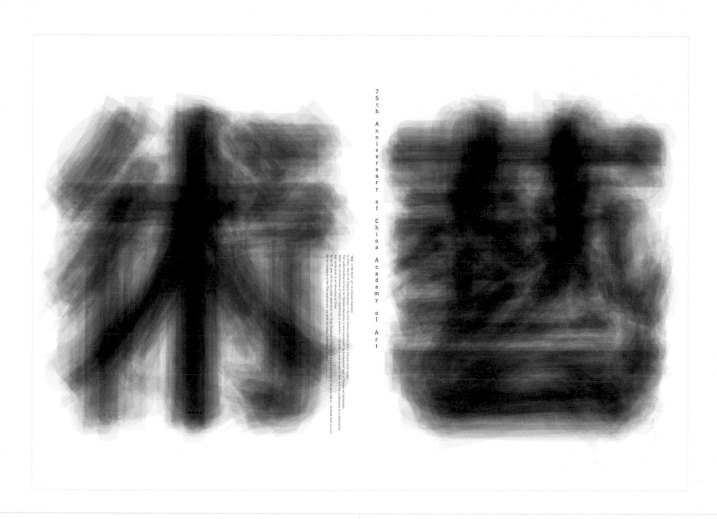

"術" in the word "art" is Chinese character.
In China, the art of Chinese characters is the fine artistic tradition many Chinese artists model.
During this concentration, we have the Chinese characters is also considered the traditional part of Chinese art philosophy, their indication is art-educating experience in China.
In our 75-year-old art-educating experience for China Academy of Art Art, it is worth pointing to this precept of "making ways in art".
At the tradition of the 75th anniversary, we hold the value combination of education.

100 beste Plakate 03
Deutschland Österreich Schweiz –
in China

德国奥地利瑞士
一百张最佳海报展
南京艺术学院 2005年4月17日至4月30日
开幕式4月16日下午2时30分
南京艺术学院美术学院展厅

TITLE: Solidarity 1
CLIENT: Association of Applied Graphic Art and Graphic Design, Prague, Czech Republic
SIZE: 33.1" x 46.8" (84.1 x 118.9 cm)
PRINTING PROCESS: Digital
INKS: 4-color process
Are posters what you primarily do for this client? Yes

PROCESS

COMPS PRESENTED: 1
REVISIONS: 0
APPROVAL: Curator
INVOLVEMENT WITH FINAL PRINTING: None

Created as a social response for a poster exhibition in the Czech Republic, He's simple photographs of arms take on new meaning as interlocking and overlaid images. Similarly, the layered type form the word *solidarity* in English. The average brown color is by no means a mistake.

TITLE: Hesign Studio Berlin
CLIENT: Hesign Studio Berlin
SIZE: 16.5" x 23.4" (42 x 59.4 cm)
PRINTING PROCESS: Silkscreen
INKS: Black
Are posters what you primarily do for this client? Yes

PROCESS

COMPS PRESENTED: 5
REVISIONS: 0
APPROVAL: Hesign Studio
INVOLVEMENT WITH FINAL PRINTING:
Prepared for production and press inspected

He brought his signature imagery, dreamlike and evocative, to this promotional poster for his Berlin studio. The same dreaminess pervades both his website and his typographical sensibilities, with solid letters seemingly anchored in the ether. Reflections of the misty valleys of Hangzhou, China, appear in a number of He's pieces.

TITLE: Hesign 2004
CLIENT: Hesign Studio Berlin
SIZE: 27.3" x 39" (70 x 100 cm)
PRINTING PROCESS: Offset
INKS: 4-color process
Are posters what you primarily do for this client? Yes

PROCESS

COMPS PRESENTED: 3
REVISIONS: 0
APPROVAL: Hesign Studio
INVOLVEMENT WITH FINAL PRINTING:
Prepared for production and press inspected

In the mystical setting of He's New Year's poster for his studio, the numbers 2004 peek through the clouds in a fashion more like bobbing in water than resting on treetops. It is left to the viewer to decide whether the numbers are emerging or sinking as the typography rains down the side of the page.

TITLE: *An Estranged Paradise*
CLIENT: Yang Fudong
SIZE: 27.3" x 39" (70 x 100 cm)
PRINTING PROCESS: Offset
INKS: 4-color process
Are posters what you primarily do for this client? Yes

PROCESS

COMPS PRESENTED: 1
REVISIONS: 0
APPROVAL: Director
INVOLVEMENT WITH FINAL PRINTING: None

This poster promoting the acclaimed film of Shanghai artist and filmmaker Yang Fudong, *An Estranged Paradise*, was shown as part of "Documenta 11." He aimed to portray the black and white 35-mm film's imperfect sense of human surroundings and the story of the protagonist's quest to find what ails him, as he seems to suffer a malaise—only to find that he is surprisingly overwhelmed by the quiet and peaceful life he had previously enjoyed.

TITLE: Klonen 2
CLIENT: Berlin University of the Arts
SIZE: 33.1" x 46.8" (84.1 x 118.9 cm)
PRINTING PROCESS: Offset
INKS: 4-color process
Are posters what you primarily do for this client? Yes

PROCESS
COMPS PRESENTED: 1
REVISIONS: 0
APPROVAL: Program director
INVOLVEMENT WITH FINAL PRINTING: None

Students at the University of Arts in Berlin held a seminar on "cloning, humans, and science," explains He. With this image that evokes numerous connotations beyond the obvious human and cow references, he underscores the concept of cloning with the masterful use of duplicate type running through the middle of the poster.

TITLE: *Art and Design* 1, 2
CLIENT: Art and Design Publisher
SIZE: 33.1" x 46.8" (84.1 x 118.9 cm)
PRINTING PROCESS: Silkscreen
INKS: Black
Are posters what you primarily do for this client? Yes

PROCESS
COMPS PRESENTED: 1
REVISIONS: 0
APPROVAL: Publisher
INVOLVEMENT WITH FINAL PRINTING: None

This poster for Beijing's *Art and Design* magazine is from a series of iconic forms created to promote the Chinese design scene and its innovators. This one showcases He's trademark typography and shading/blurring technique.

TITLE: 75th Anniversary of China Academy of Art 1, 2
Client: China Academy of Art
SIZE: 33.1" x 46.8" (84.1 x 118.9 cm)
PRINTING PROCESS: Silkscreen
INKS: Black
Are posters what you primarily do for this client? Yes

PROCESS
COMPS PRESENTED: 1
REVISIONS: 0
APPROVAL: Academy director
INVOLVEMENT WITH FINAL PRINTING: None

In celebrating the seventy-fifth anniversary of the Chinese Academy of Fine Arts, He had "the chance to reconsider my understanding of art, at least in the sense of Chinese art. In this series of two posters, I attempted to combine the heritage of art with the spirit of the times." He uses "computer characters in different fonts that overlap in a translucent manner, resulting in an effect that is comparable to the ambience of Chinese calligraphy." He asks, "Is the gradual dependence of art on technology the future direction of modern art, or is art simply driving its way into a blind alley?" He also allows nostalgic memories of the school in Hangzhou where he spent four years—"the wonderful heated discussions, independence, academic pursuit, and serenity"—to color his design.

TITLE: 100 Best Posters '03 in China
CLIENT: 100 Best Posters Association
SIZE: 27.3" x 39" (70 x 100 cm)
PRINTING PROCESS: Offset
INKS: 4-color process
Are posters what you primarily do for this client? Yes

PROCESS
COMPS PRESENTED: 1
REVISIONS: 0
APPROVAL: Association head
INVOLVEMENT WITH FINAL PRINTING: None

When the German design association 100 Best Posters needed to design a poster promoting an exhibit in Nanjing, China, who better to speak to both audiences than He? Continuing his experimentation with typography, he created an image for the number 100 that is entirely digital in makeup yet feels like a gouache calligraphic painting.

★ HENDERSON BROMSTEAD ART CO ★

WINSTON-SALEM, NORTH CAROLINA, USA

YOU WORK WHERE?

Some of the most exciting work being done in the United States during the past five years has come from a most unusual outpost. The Carolinas have begun a changeover from tobacco and farming country to the home of banking and energy concerns. This does not sound like a terribly creative environment, but perhaps that is the reason the work of HendersonBromsteadArtCo cries out for attention.

Hiding down in the Old South has not kept national clients from calling on them—but it has allowed the firm to grow and experiment without the pressure of the next hot young thing working a block away, as in New York or Seattle. The result is a singular vision and artsy sense evident that is particularly in their imaginative poster work.

This artsy sense is easy to trace to Hayes Henderson's late switch of college majors to design and his early days toiling as an illustrator and suffering many a disappointment, even when working with the hottest designer in the world at the time. He recalls, "I got into illustration because I liked image making but got into design because I was pissed at how poorly my illustrations were being treated by designers and art directors. I also saw the potential to make a better living. Not quite the same muse, eh? I always got tearsheets back and was disappointed. I couldn't even get David Carson to do something cool with the work I did with him. Okay, there was a Tony Hawk piece, but that's it. Maybe it was me. He must have liked them, though; he never gave the work back."

"I CAN DO THAT"

It became obvious that establishing his own firm was in the cards as Henderson sat around thinking, "I can do that." He also wanted to control his own destiny because he was dismayed by past clients asking for colors and solutions used in previous illustrations. He was crying out to avoid "coming up with something good and then doing it over and over. You just become a bad imitation of yourself after a while. You have to be uncomfortable to do something original—whatever the hell *original* is." Henderson adds, "My little rant should be a cautionary tale for designers to keep their creative process open and flowing and let others things come in and change the course, like someone else's opinion, or a new thought along the way. Protectionism limits scope of thinking. I've learned the potential of that as a director

of other designers. It's cool to realize that I have five designers working with me so I have six potential solutions instead of one. That, and if their solution is better than mine, I still get to put my name on their work because it's my company. Cool."

Most of what he has been putting his name on lately has been posters. "We do a lot of poster work, and it seems like over the last few years, there's more consideration of the lowly poster as part of a multitiered marketing campaign. A while back, it felt like offering it as part of a marketing solution seemed antiquated and behind the times, but not anymore. I think people are now grasping that there is an image-building quality that belies its niche-ish shortcomings in a society that's used to getting mass-marketed to. It is more personal and helps connote quality or hipness, possibly feeding off its own roots by representing an underground or street-smart sensibility and lending credibility to the thing it's hawking." Henderson continues, "Basically, I think people still want to see posters. Despite the advancement and broad-based ability of information transfer, people are still drawn to big, pretty pictures on an individual basis. You can get what you need from many media, but you *want* posters. There may be a quaintness to the poster, a nostalgia, but the tactile quality, the art-object ability, is something other media can't achieve due to the inherent personal detachment of digital media—more information and less emotional attachment."

His artistic side finds an affinity for likeminded designers and illustrators, past and present, enjoying and reveling in "Ivan Chermayeff's technique, Paul Rand's simplicity, Saul Bass's range, Paula Scher's coolness, Brad Holland's brain. I was a fine arts major with one semester left and changed majors to applied arts because I liked work that I saw from Matt Mahurin and Marshall Arisman and Brad Holland and Gary Kelly and Gary Panter." Henderson also admits to another draw to his pathway into a design career: "My future wife was a design major."

"People are still drawn to big, pretty pictures on an individual basis. You can get what you need from many media, but you want posters."

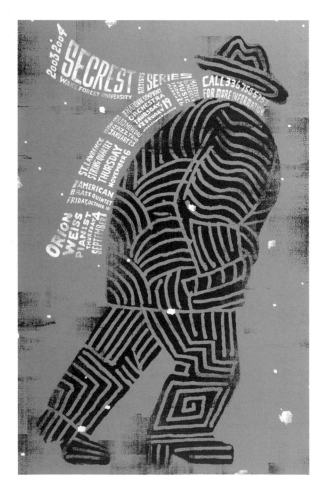

winston-salem symphony 2000/2001 season

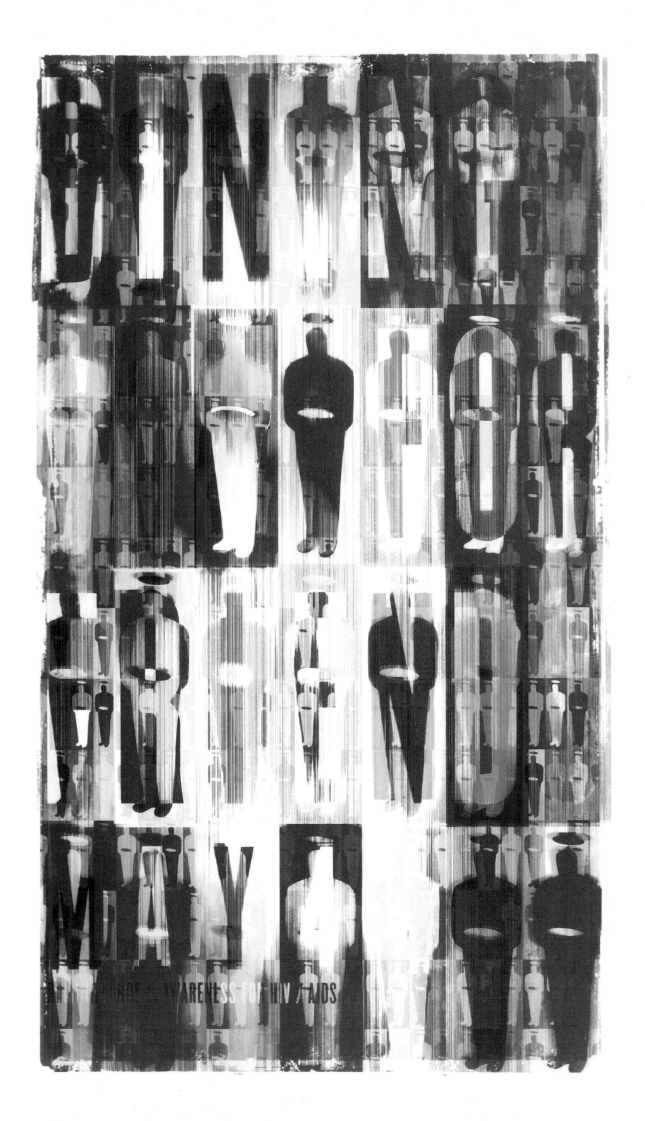

TITLE: Dining for Friends 2003
CLIENT: Triad Health Project
SIZE: 24" x 36" (60.96 x 91.44 cm)
PRINTING PROCESS: Silkscreen
INKS: 1 color
Are posters what you primarily do for this client? Yes

PROCESS

COMPS PRESENTED: 7–8
REVISIONS: Not many
APPROVAL: Small group of caring clients
INVOLVEMENT WITH FINAL PRINTING: Production

HBA prides itself on doing what is best for the project no matter the job title. Henderson recounts, "We had several good ideas to present to the Triad folks for this year's event, but Brent Piper nailed it when he came up with this solution. Usually, I'm not a big fan of taking familiar icons and doing the clever twist thing, but this just seemed to be the one. One of those 'Why didn't I think of that?' pieces. This was a good example of the fluidity that the studio has when need be. I've always been impressed with our studio's designers because there's always been this great sense of a common purpose. People pick up and help wherever it's needed. No sense of office politics or hierarchy. There seems to be no ego, at least with them, and no task is too menial if someone needs help. Brent and I switched roles here. He came up with the concept and design, and usually at this point I'll jump in and start putting my fingers all over it, but the best use of my time on this was to become Brent's illustrator. He was art director and designer, working through the type treatment and layout, while I got the hands to his liking. He was pretty good to work for."

TITLE: Secrest Artists' Series 2000–01
CLIENT: Wake Forest University
SIZE: 24" x 33" (60.96 x 83.82 cm)
PRINTING PROCESS: 4 color
INKS: Process
Are posters what you primarily do for this client? Yes

PROCESS

COMPS PRESENTED: 3
REVISIONS: 4–5
APPROVAL: Series director
INVOLVEMENT WITH FINAL PRINTING: Production

Long relationships with clients build up an immense level of trust that is often rewarded with amazing work. As Henderson remarks, "My client is cool on this project. We've been working together for years, and she puts up with a lot of shit at this point because the relationship has gotten so casual. We typically get together three to five times over the course of the project. These meetings go from March through early June. It's extended because the client travels a lot. It's nice, though, that she recognizes more time means more thought and also preferential scheduling, because I can plot the course of the project well in advance. The nice thing is that I still need to stay on my toes. She'll pose critical questions that I usually find helpful when I really dig." If you can develop such a relationship with a client, Henderson recommends, "Hang onto it. At least that's what I'm banking on."

TITLE: Secrest Artists' Series 2001–02
CLIENT: Wake Forest University
SIZE: 20.5" x 34.5" (52.07 x 87.63 cm)
PRINTING PROCESS: 3 color
INKS: Red, blue, black
Are posters what you primarily do for this client? Yes

PROCESS

COMPS PRESENTED: 3
REVISIONS: 4–5
APPROVAL: Series director
INVOLVEMENT WITH FINAL PRINTING: Production

With his illustration background, Henderson can find himself caught up in a style and unsure of a poster's reception. "This one, in hindsight, felt like I was just pushing a technique I was interested in it more than what worked best for the Music Series. It seemed like a well-received piece, although I think a lot of the Wake folks wondered what the hell it meant. Looking back, the theme seemed a little editorial, which is really the reason I developed this collage technique in the first place. The concept was supposed to be about transcending the earthbound pressures and obligations and just taking the time out to sit and listen to something that feeds the spirit—a little escapism. This piece was completed in August of 2001. Creating a red, white, and blue piece about escaping the harsh realities of life, right before 9/11, seemed like a crazy coincidence to me. I don't think anyone else got that, though."

TITLE: Secrest Artists' Series 2003–04
CLIENT: Wake Forest University
SIZE: 18.5" x 28.5" (46.99 x 72.39 cm)
PRINTING PROCESS: 3 color
INKS: Blue, darker blue, yellow
Are posters what you primarily do for this client? Yes

PROCESS

COMPS PRESENTED: 2
REVISIONS: A lot
APPROVAL: Event director
INVOLVEMENT WITH FINAL PRINTING: Production

Henderson reveals that for this year's Secrest poster "the final art was done on a sticky note as I'm sitting on the phone with the client setting up the meeting to actually kick off the project. It popped in my head and I went through different concepts and more rendered illustrations of this same concept, only to hate them all and scan the sticky note. Billy Hackley got hold of this one too and made it look better. We back-and-forthed this one a lot," creating a timeless image from a tiny little sketch.

TITLE: Secrest Artists' Series 2002–03
CLIENT: Wake Forest University
SIZE: 24.5" x 34.5" (62.23 x 87.63 cm)
PRINTING PROCESS: 4 color
INKS: Process
Are posters what you primarily do for this client? Yes

PROCESS

COMPS PRESENTED: 1
REVISIONS: 1 bazillion
APPROVAL PROCESS: Event director
INVOLVEMENT WITH FINAL PRINTING: Production

Reminiscing about this poster, Henderson spins a yarn like his old grandpa, "only without the denture smell and spastic colon." Admitting that the idea came about at the end of the process, he "had been shooting blanks for a couple of weeks, and the night before I'm sitting on the front porch with a sketchbook, filled with a few personality enhancers, looking at a big maple tree in my front yard and thinking about the series happening in fall and winter and how much that tree changes from season to season, and that's where the idea came from." Designer Bill Hackley helped bring it to life, and they rushed it over to the client.

TITLE: Secrest Artists' Series 2004–05
CLIENT: Wake Forest University
SIZE: 18" x 28" (45.72 x 71.12 cm)
PRINTING PROCESS: 4 color
INKS: Process
Are posters what you primarily do for this client? Yes

PROCESS

COMPS PRESENTED: 1
REVISIONS: Oodles
APPROVAL: Event director
INVOLVEMENT WITH FINAL PRINTING: Production

After all of these years on this project, Henderson says, "This will be my last year of flying primarily solo on concept development for Secrest. As the group has expanded over the years, the formula for creating work has developed to accommodate that, except for the Secrest Series poster. I've selfishly hoarded this project because I always wanted to do it, as well as my client balking at bringing in other folks. Save my collaborations with Billy to make the design and illustrations look better, I've kept it as my personal project for years."

TITLE: Symphony 2000–2001 Season
CLIENT: Winston-Salem Symphony
SIZE: 19" x 37" (48.26 x 93.98 cm)
PRINTING PROCESS: 4 color
INKS: Process
Are posters what you primarily do for this client? Yes

PROCESS
COMPS PRESENTED: 8
REVISIONS: 4
APPROVAL: Marketing director and
symphony conductor
INVOLVEMENT WITH FINAL PRINTING: Production

For the poster, designer Bill Hackley "did the art completely by mouse. Wow! Who needs pencils? Not us! It also is suppose to look like one continuous line. Guess what? It's not! Anyone anal enough to look for the disconnects deserves to find a few. That's my philosophy," says Henderson. Working with clients in a creative field can be fraught with peril at times, but Henderson navigates the minefield: "The client was one of those dangerous creative types with a musical background and some marketing classes, so of course that naturally extends into giving expert input on how to design. We weathered that process, and the poster was a big success."

TITLE: BOOM
CLIENT: American Institute of Graphic Arts
SIZE: 17" x 36" (43.18 x 91.44 cm)
PRINTING PROCESS: 2 color
INKS: Black and orange
Are posters what you primarily do for this client? Yes

PROCESS
COMPS PRESENTED: 1
REVISIONS: 0
APPROVAL: Marketing chair
INVOLVEMENT WITH FINAL PRINTING: Production

Remembering this poster for the American Institute of Graphic Arts (AIGA) event, Henderson reflects, "The name of the show is BOOM, and when it was launched in the late 1990s it pertained to the boom of the dot.com economy. When we created the poster in 2003, that word had vastly different connotations. We focused on what happens if you don't let it out, creatively and otherwise. The whole suppression of expression theme seemed relevant and timely. Still does." Designer Billy Hackley worked so fast he literally "slapped this together in about twenty minutes. Just kidding. It was fifteen."

TITLE: Cyberspace Symposium
CLIENT: Wake Forest University
SIZE: 20" x 37" (50.80 x 93.98 cm)
PRINTING PROCESS: 3 color
INKS: Black, 485 red, yellow
Are posters what you primarily do for this client? Yes

PROCESS
COMPS PRESENTED: 3
REVISIONS: 1
APPROVAL: Client
INVOLVEMENT WITH FINAL PRINTING: Production

Working for a husband-and-wife client with backgrounds in publishing and journalism struck the HBA team as an odd dynamic. Henderson notes that the husband was organizing the event but left the poster to his wife. "Both were interestingly detached from the project. Image creation didn't seem that important to them." Not so for Henderson, who says "the piece was created by cutting out hundreds of little fragments of information from magazines and then running them through a copier several times for density. The only legible information is on the outer edge of the blunted figure." The secret: "The fragments make for an interesting read, as they all have some relationship to the design concept regarding the Internet. Ironically, the best way to produce this piece for a cyberspace symposium was through an analog, traditional paste-up approach."

TITLE: Have a Heart
CLIENT: United Way
SIZE: 16" x 35" (40.64 x 88.90 cm)
PRINTING PROCESS: 1 color
INKS: 175 red
Are posters what you primarily do for this client? Yes

PROCESS
COMPS PRESENTED: 8
REVISIONS: 3
APPROVAL: 4–5 marketing chairs
INVOLVEMENT WITH FINAL PRINTING: Production

The sheer number of great concepts created for this project prods Henderson into revealing, "One thing that's possibly our secret sauce, and I've learned this by when it's happened as well as when it hasn't, is that we never stop looking at options until we're absolutely running up on the deadline. I know it drives the designers nuts sometimes. But we tweak stuff to death. Even when we know we have something good out of the gate, we will bang it around, completely change it, and look at it forty different ways just so we know we looked at it every way we could imagine. Typically, this exercise takes us full circle and reinforces that we had the right idea in the first place, but it helps to confirm that initial intuition." In this case, designer Michelle White had several good ideas, "but she really sunk her teeth into this one and created hordes of variations after we had a pick from the concepts we presented." He also describes the trying aspect of pro bono work: "This was one of those presentations where they couldn't decide between a couple of the ideas, so they started trying to combine what they liked about each. Since it was free, we said no. Tough love, really."

TITLE: Dining for Friends 2002
CLIENT: Triad Health Project
SIZE: 22.25" x 36" (56.52 x 91.44 cm)
PRINTING PROCESS: 4 color
INKS: Process
Are posters what you primarily do for this client? Yes

PROCESS
COMPS PRESENTED: 6
REVISIONS: Lots
APPROVAL: Event committee
INVOLVEMENT WITH FINAL PRINTING: Production

Henderson remarks, "The clients we work with at Triad have always been great, incredibly appreciative people. The individuals have changed over the years, but the enthusiasm and genuine appreciation has always remained consistent. The Dining for Friends event is their biggest fund-raiser as well as a respite from constantly facing the realities of their cause [AIDS]." He adds, "The poster is always supposed to be a balance between informational and something that folks hang onto as an event memento. This one, designed with Bill Hackley, pushed the decorative envelope as well as their comfort zone, but ended up being a popular year." When presenting for this project, "we typically have eight or ten workable ideas but usually only show a couple. In previous years, we've shown all we did just to show off our range, but it's felt better the last few years just to show the ones we really care about most."

TITLE: Feed the Monster
CLIENT: American Advertising Federation
SIZE: 23.5" x 34" (59.69 x 86.36 cm)
PRINTING PROCESS: 3 color
INKS: Black, blue, fluorescent orange
Are posters what you primarily do for this client? Yes

PROCESS
COMPS PRESENTED: 2
REVISIONS: 0
APPROVAL: None
INVOLVEMENT WITH FINAL PRINTING: Production

Enjoying a chance to tweak the awards process, Henderson set out to create "a collage piece with little smart-ass giblets sprinkled throughout. The local ADDY organization asked us to do the piece because we had been getting some press nationally and we had actually won the ad show the year before with a design piece. I think it was basically received with a 'What tha fuh!?' It wasn't what the local big-headline-and-radio-spot crowd was expecting for an advertising show, particularly because it was essentially making fun of advertising and contests."

★ FONS HICKMANN (M23) ★

BERLIN, GERMANY

UNAPOLOGETICALLY MODERN

The maniacal circus music that greets you when you enter Fons Hickmann's website provides insight to his skewed worldview. His work has a sense of irony and playfulness while being unapologetically modern. The hand-drawn or found image or bit of type and the technologically sophisticated application of these elements intersect in an unexpected marriage that becomes stronger than its individual parts. His unique perspective and adept execution have garnered universal acclaim and broad exposure.

Perhaps the biggest compliment that can be paid is that his style is such an unusual and challenging assemblage that it is difficult to mimic because it changes with each piece, yet stays amazingly current and fresh.

Hickmann is quick to pull back the curtain on the thinking that has led to his astounding collection of work. You can almost taste his willingness to make risky decisions and to reap the rewards. "Learn all you can. Try all you want. See what there is to see. Explore and experiment. Make mistakes. Climb vast peaks and plunge to hidden depths. Be decent, be depraved, be boring, be radical. Fall in love, wallow in hate. Smell like a flower, stink like a fish. Laugh and cry. And then forget it all and find your own way—to create."

FILLING A BLANK SPACE

Hickmann expresses undying affection for the poster and the unique challenge it presents. "No other medium shows the mastery of a designer more clearly than the job of filling a blank space of particular size and format. With posters, it's all about distilling the message down to its essence, to its core. Which doesn't mean a poster has to be bland or prudish. It can easily be kitschy or even playful if that's the best way to support the message being put across." He also sees the parallels with another passion—the written word. "The poster requires a certain concentration. It permits no wavering. Interestingly, similar laws govern writers for the production of a quality text.

Only that which needs to be said is said. The information should be clear and unequivocal. It is better to be precise than waffly. The designer has to successfully hit the given mark within the scope and possibilities open to him. If he doesn't, the whole is thing is a sad patchwork, neither one thing nor the other—a wasted space."

Hickmann appreciates those that have gone down this path before him. "Everything we do is nothing without knowing the past heroes: Hans Hillmann, Shigeo Fukuda, Armin Hofmann, Saul Bass, Grapus." He also knows that the poster cannot be stopped as an art form, much in the way that rock and roll will never die.

THE IDEA

m23 serves as a collection of like minds for Hickmann. The staff members are dedicated to the mental aspect of creation and expression, whether they are designers, musicians, architects, theoreticians, or athletes. Hickmann himself is so dedicated to the pursuit of thought that he is now a university professor, a job that has taken him as far as China to speak and teach. For Hickmann, design is all about "the idea." He says, "As a child, I was always jealous of the scabs and bruises that my older brothers got from their football games. Their wounds were proof to me that fun is worth suffering for." We can all be thankful he is willing to endure that suffering so we may reap the spoils.

"Smell like a flower, stink like a fish. Laugh and cry. And then forget it all and find your own way—to create."

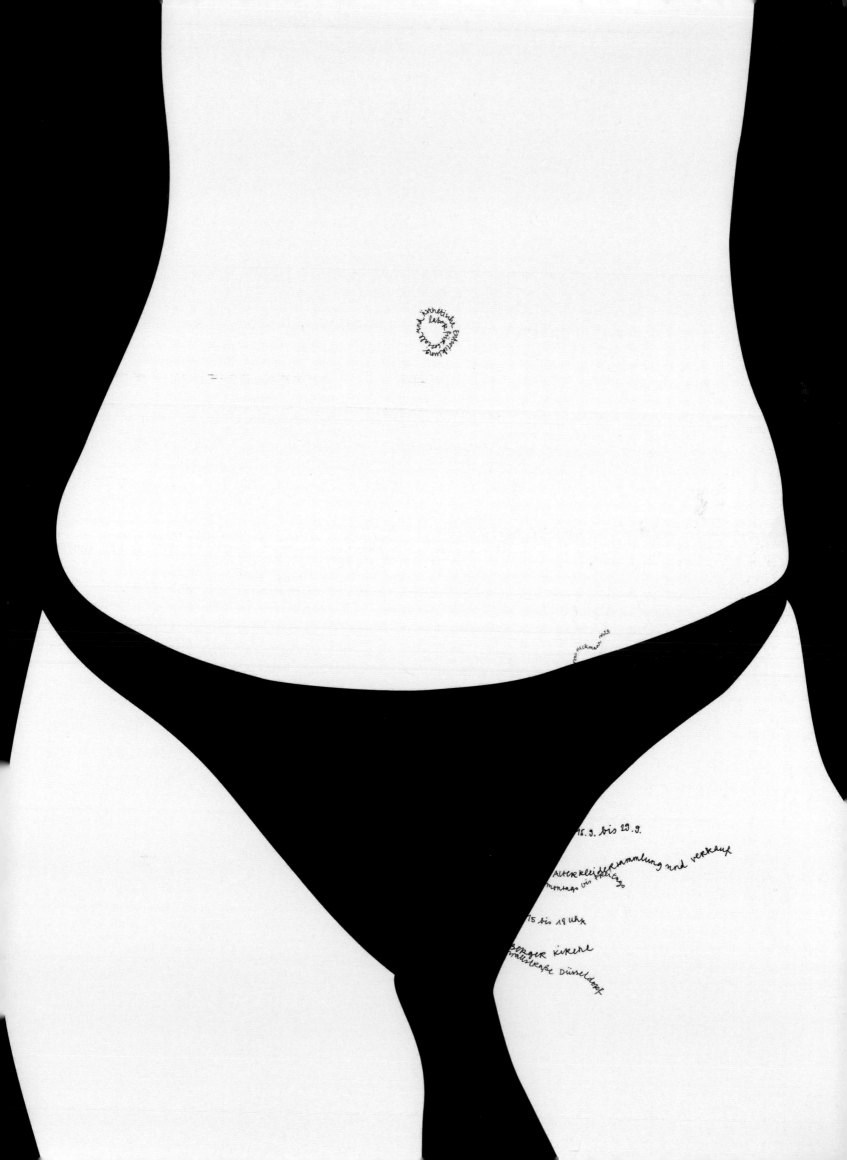

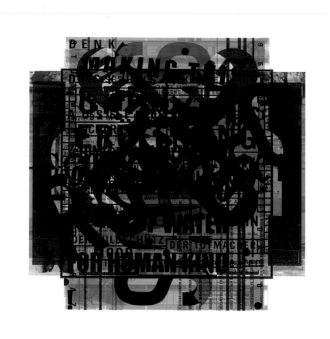

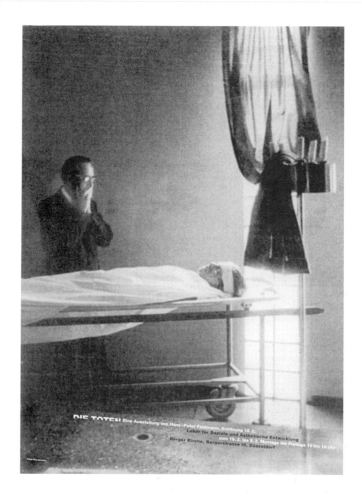

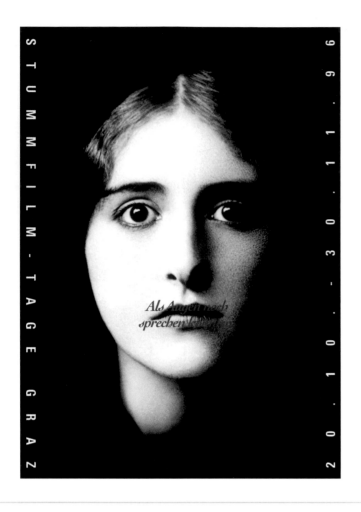

AN ALLE
HÄUSER DIE
OHREN HABEN

Diakonie

Eine geistliche Rede mit Megaphon
von Thorsten Nolting

Innere Mission

Donnerstag, 12.8. 13 Uhr
Düsseldorf-Garath, Fritz-Erler-Straße,
Ecke Thomas-Dehler-Straße

Donnerstag, 16.9. 13 Uhr
Vodafone Hochhaus, Mannesmannufer

TITLE: Clothing Collection
CLIENT: Laboratory for Social and Aesthetic Development
SIZE: 47.24" x 33.07" (120 x 84 cm)
PRINTING PROCESS: Silkscreen
INKS: Black
Are posters what you primarily do for this client? Yes

PROCESS
COMPS PRESENTED: 1
REVISIONS: 2
APPROVAL: Center head
INVOLVEMENT WITH FINAL PRINTING: No

This simple, cheeky poster, designed with Gesine Grotrian-Steinweg, seems perfect when you hear Hickmann detail the inherent comedy in the church rummage sale it promoted. "The ritual of putting old clothes into bags and donating them to the church or Red Cross is familiar enough. For this, the pastor decided to sort the garments into a color scheme and arrange them in different piles on the church floor. The result was a sea of color that visitors and buyers could immerse themselves in. After repeatedly fishing items out, trying them on, and putting them to one side, the clothing slowly merged into an orgiastic tumult of color." Hickmann says their effort and "the proceeds were donated to a good cause." This did not prevent them from focusing on the funny concept of someone lacking in clothes either ready to be dressed or generous enough to have donated everything but their tiny briefs.

TITLE: Young and Social
CLIENT: Diakonie
SIZE: 47.24" x 33.07" (120 x 84 cm)
PRINTING PROCESS: Silkscreen
INKS: Gold, cyan, magenta, black
Are posters what you primarily do for this client? No

PROCESS
COMPS PRESENTED: 1
REVISIONS: 2
APPROVAL: Diakonie manager
INVOLVEMENT WITH FINAL PRINTING: No

This poster was designed with Barbara Bättig. Hickmann calls the approach a "new design for an old theme. Diakonie wanted to encourage young people to formulate social ideas and to put them into practice. We made posters and flyers aimed at teenagers and invited them to send in their ideas." He adds, "Design can be politically or socially relevant only when it takes up a position and communicates content. Everything else is just decoration." Modern design and typography mix with the obvious Christ figure and the declaration of caring in the touched heart from which the title emanates.

TITLE: Should I Stay or Should I Go?
CLIENT: www.fonshickmann.com
SIZE: 47.24" x 33.07" (120 x 84 cm)
PRINTING PROCESS: Offset
INKS: 4-color process
Are posters what you primarily do for this client? n/a

PROCESS
COMPS PRESENTED: 1
REVISIONS: 0
APPROVAL: Ourselves
INVOLVEMENT WITH FINAL PRINTING: Yes

Hickmann loves the poster so deeply that he produced one to promote his new website. He paired scrawled typography with Simon Gallus's strange cropping of trees and then tilted the whole thing on its side (or did he?). The image draws the curious further into their web.

TITLE: All My Posters
CLIENT: MoMa Toyama
SIZE: 47.24" x 33.07" (120 x 84 cm)
PRINTING PROCESS: Silkscreen
INKS: CMYK
Are posters what you primarily do for this client? Yes

PROCESS
COMPS PRESENTED: 1
REVISIONS: 0
APPROVAL: MoMA Toyama
INVOLVEMENT WITH FINAL PRINTING: No

Hickmann's subtle humor comes across with this poster entitled "All My Posters," created exclusively for an exhibition at the Museum of Modern Art in Toyama. All the posters he had designed over the previous four years were superimposed using transparent ink. Hickmann says, "The design was dedicated to anyone who didn't have enough time to visit the exhibition, giving them a chance to see the complete poster collection in one go."

TITLE: Die Toten Poster Series
CLIENT: Laboratory for Social and Aesthetic Development
SIZE: 39.37" x 33.07" (100 x 84 cm)
PRINTING PROCESS: Silkscreen
INKS: CMYK
Are posters what you primarily do for this client? Yes

PROCESS
COMPS PRESENTED: 1
REVISIONS: 1
APPROVAL: Center head
INVOLVEMENT WITH FINAL PRINTING: No

Hickmann used artist Hans-Peter Feldmann's photos to promote the Die Toten art exhibit, where he "presented magazine photographs of people killed by RAF terrorism. These iconic images—etched into our collective memory—showed the victims and perpetrators side by side, with no attempt at offering any evaluation," says Hickmann. "More than a hundred dead were arranged in a circle, forming a kind of hemline around the Laboratory. The only information accompanying each picture was the relevant name and date of death. The church was converted into a morgue, triggering reactions from the visitors of an intensely conflicting nature."

TITLE: When Eyes Could Still Speak
CLIENT: Silent Movie Festival
SIZE: 33.07" x 23.62" (84 x 60 cm)
PRINTING PROCESS: Silkscreen
INKS: Black and red
Are posters what you primarily do for this client? Yes

PROCESS
COMPS PRESENTED: 1
REVISIONS: 1
APPROVAL: Festival head
INVOLVEMENT WITH FINAL PRINTING: No

Hickmann designed four posters to promote a silent film festival and took the opportunity to examine his own feelings about film. "The emergence of film is an attempt to capture life and take it deeper into newfound realms of beauty and horror. The history of film is predominantly a drive for perfection. Nevertheless, the charm of film partly springs from mistakes and imperfection. The poster series explores the aesthetics of mistakes in contrast with the perfect portrait. The poster also plays with the way information is coded and decoded in the development of our communication."

TITLE: Substantial
CLIENT: Hauschka
SIZE: 47.24" x 33.07" (120 x 84 cm)
PRINTING PROCESS: Offset
INKS: 4-color process
Are posters what you primarily do for this client? Yes

PROCESS
COMPS PRESENTED: 2
REVISIONS: 1
APPROVAL: Hauschka
INVOLVEMENT WITH FINAL PRINTING: No

Working with designer Barbara Bättig, Hickmann tackled this unusual music project for Hauschka. They disassembled a piano, then bent the strings to form the word *substantial*. This approach was meant to reflect the manner in which the original piano music was recorded and then manipulated in the computer.

TITLE: Acid Bath in Mai
CLIENT: Laboratory for Social and Aesthetic Development
SIZE: 33.07" x 23.62" (84 x 60 cm)
PRINTING PROCESS: Offset
INKS: Black
Are posters what you primarily do for this client? Yes

PROCESS
COMPS PRESENTED: 1
REVISIONS: 1
APPROVAL: Center head
INVOLVEMENT WITH FINAL PRINTING: No

This poster is part of a series organized by the pastor at the City Church in Düsseldorf, which Hickmann says "instigated a season of events in the Berger Church: concerts by DJs, an exhibition to which visitors brought their own exhibits, a twenty-four-hour social experiment, art film evenings, clothing collections, an Internet exhibition, open discussions and video speeches, communal meals with creative artists, the homeless and normal members of the public, collective partaking of Christmas pastries, a talk by theorist Bazon Brock, and the transformation of the Berger Church into a chill-out zone on Saturdays." Bringing it all together, he says, is "clarity: black/white, the Protestant impact of Helvetica, minimalism, and the distinctly conceptual approach." Using that simplicity, this piece promotes a DJ concert with type and image off register to create a blurry, trippy effect that mirrors the evening's musical experience.

TITLE: To All Buildings That Have Ears
CLIENT: Diakonie
SIZE: 33.07" x 23.62" (84 x 60 cm)
PRINTING PROCESS: Offset
INKS: 4-color process
Are posters what you primarily do for this client? No

PROCESS
COMPS PRESENTED: 1
REVISIONS: 2
APPROVAL: Diakonie manager
INVOLVEMENT WITH FINAL PRINTING: No

Working with designer Barbara Bättig, Hickmann set out to promote "Inner Mission," a spiritual and social event. He explains the program: "Using the general principle of compassion as a starting point, activists aim to shape their own inner lives and the inner life of the city's social environment. The Church Welfare in Düsseldorf wanted to provide support, so a program was set up to focus on the inner world. The idea was to use events and social exercises to ascertain and test the potential for shaping inner life." m23 used a graphic "sign" to call attention to the program and soothing white to make a safe set of enclosed walls that signify the inner aspect.

★ JEWBOY CORPORATION ★

TEL AVIV, ISRAEL

AN UNLIKELY YET HIGHLY EFFECTIVE MIX

In some ways, the work of Jewboy Corporation shifts meaning when you have just the right touch of background. Yaron Shin has a master's degree from Utrecht School of Arts in the Netherlands, but it's his degree in controls and robotics that really brings his work into focus. This perplexing mix of technologies perfectly sums up his design aesthetic, which is even odder when you take into account that he comes from the unlikely outpost of Tel Aviv.

It's not just the work that has a postmodern flair; the firm does as well. It's not really even a business. The truth is, "Jewboy Corporation was never officially built. It is a project, not a company." In actuality, all of his work is not even done under this guise. Shin himself says, "Many people know Jewboy, but few know the person behind it. Sometimes even those folks I work for."

Formed during his studies in the Netherlands, Jewboy is now an unstoppable force. The exhibition and publication of Shin's work in Spain, Germany, Australia, Mexico, Italy, and at home in Israel attest to that. This exposure has made a huge impact on his life. "It made me famous! Well, actually, I'm not that famous, but I am a very good designer. Actually, I don't know if I'm that good, but I do make a great potato soup. Actually, my girlfriend doesn't even agree with that." As you can see, fame hasn't deadened his wit one iota.

SHOOT—DON'T TALK
It's a quick pull of the trigger (literally, in one of his pieces) that brings Shin's work to life. Paraphrasing Eli Wallach, he says, "In posters as in life, if you need to shoot—shoot, don't talk."

Shin fires out a potent mix of images inspired by his techy background mixed with a love affair with the atmospheric work of the 4AD record label and the software capabilities of Adobe After Effects, not to mention models and online pornography. Just look at some of this stuff! When questioned, Shin notes that his main influences include past masters in the vein of Factory Records–era Peter Saville: "The style has no connection to what I do, but the zone—oh, the zone! I think it's very much the same." We trust Shin does not deliver his promotional posters the night of the event, as Saville once famously did!

Enamored with the large format of the poster and the possibilities inherent in that scale, Shin also admits a dislike for most other poster designs. He does not shy away from offending either his viewers or his family. Members of his family are buried in his images, and viewers are likely better served by not guessing which are blood relatives. In spite of living in a region of nearly constant turmoil, he still keeps a smile. Well, at least a smirk. While discussing his design philosophy, Shin noted in all seriousness, "People of planet Earth. Enjoy! At least try to."

"In posters as in life, if you need to shoot—shoot, don't talk."

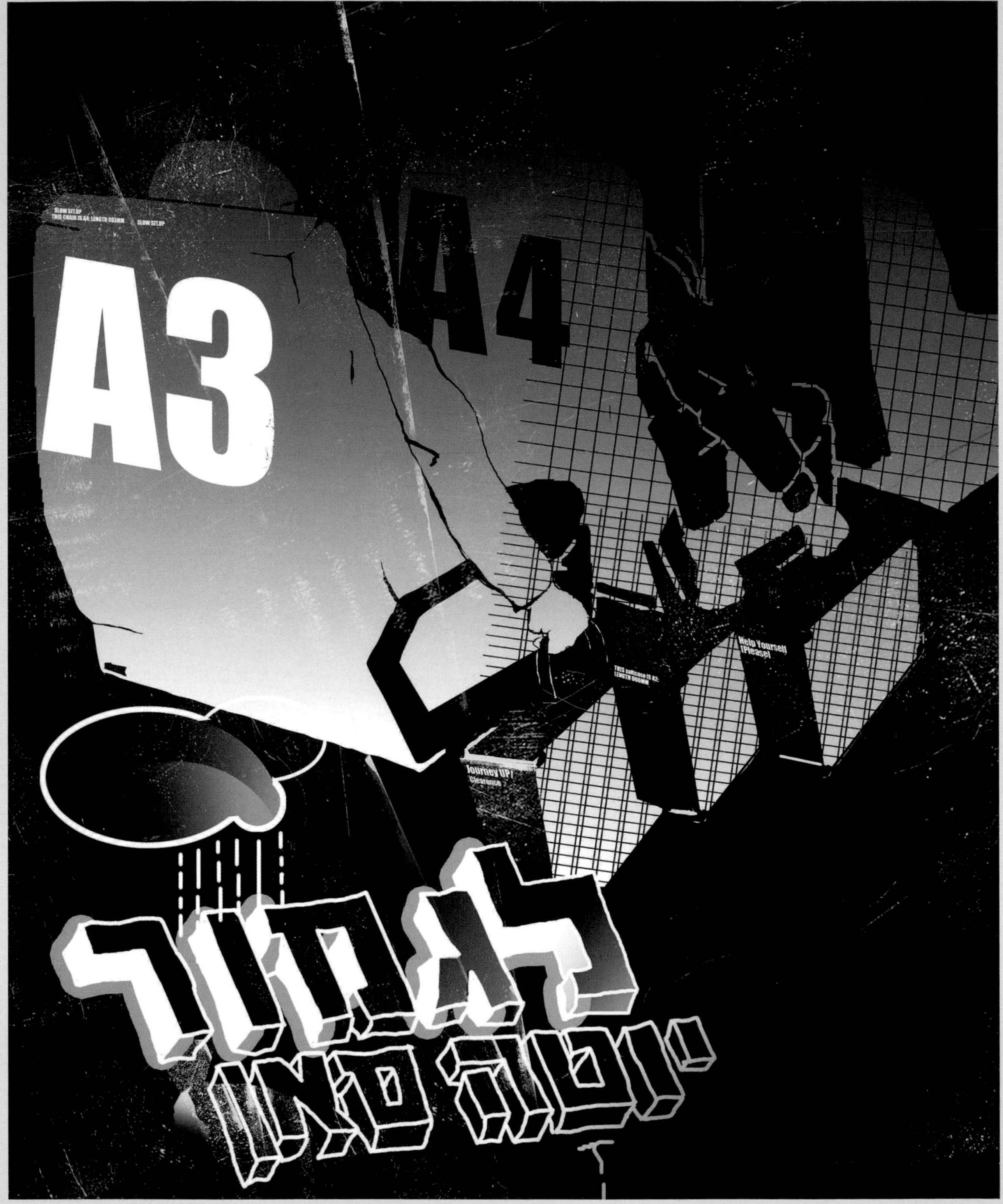

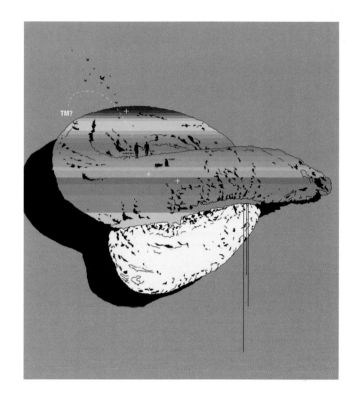

TITLE: War Loves You Back
CLIENT: *Belio* Magazine
SIZE: 39.37" x 27.56" (100 x 70 cm)
PRINTING PROCESS: 4 color
INKS: Process
Are posters what you primarily do for this client? No

PROCESS
COMPS PRESENTED: 1
REVISIONS: 0
APPROVAL: *Belio* magazine
INVOLVEMENT WITH FINAL PRINTING: None

Asked by the Spanish magazine *Belio* to react to the war in Iraq, Shin designed what he felt was the obvious solution: "Pointing a gun at anyone is actually pointing it at yourself." The image contains a personal reference. "This gun is based on images of a real gun we had at my brother's home. That gun eventually fell into disrepair, and now no one knows where or how it disappeared."

TITLE: Promotion Poster for Launch Party for the Release of a New Sitra Ahra Book
CLIENT: Sitra Ahra Book Publishers
SIZE: 39.37" x 27.56" (100 x 70 cm)
PRINTING PROCESS: 4 color
INKS: Process
Are posters what you primarily do for this client? No

PROCESS
COMPS PRESENTED: 1
REVISIONS: 0
APPROVAL: Sitra Ahra manager
INVOLVEMENT WITH FINAL PRINTING: Jewboy Corporation

Shin takes chances in his work and doesn't let up on the smirks. He also steals imagery from himself literally. "The writer was troubled with the dick image, claiming it might create expectations. All in all, too many questions about it. I *can* reveal it's a kind of self portrait. The rest of the images are made of bits of files going back to the early 1990s and up to the end of 2004." Taking little bits of his own work made perfect sense, given the book being promoted. "The book is made up of small fragments of text jumping back and forth, childhood, youth, and adulthood. It is actually pieces of the author's life, and so it is defined as a diary. It tells ten small stories about frustration, with no beginning and no end."

TITLE: The Columbia Journey
CLIENT: Kosmonaut Clun
SIZE: 39.37" x 27.56" (100 x 70 cm)
PRINTING PROCESS: 4 color
INKS: Process
Are posters what you primarily do for this client? Yes

PROCESS
COMPS PRESENTED: 1
REVISIONS: 0
APPROVAL: Sitra Ahra manager
INVOLVEMENT WITH FINAL PRINTING: Jewboy Corporation

Designing a promotion to provide "a short review of an explosive house party with fireworks and light effects using Internet and TV/video images with graphic manipulation," Shin again courted controversy. "Israel sent an army hero and icon, Mr. Ilan Ramon (RIP), on the [doomed] Columbia [space shuttle] mission. Oh boy! What a comeback did he make. I just had to connect it to this fireworks special party. I will burn in hell. I know."

TITLE: Body Parts
CLIENT: Reign Productions
SIZE: 39.37" x 27.56" (100 x 70 cm)
PRINTING PROCESS: 4 color
INKS: Process
Are posters what you primarily do for this client? Yes

PROCESS
COMPS PRESENTED: 2
REVISIONS: 0
APPROVAL: Reign Productions crew
INVOLVEMENT WITH FINAL PRINTING: Jewboy Corporation

Shin used a combination of scans and original photography to create this piece for an exhibition in which the client requested a very specific vibe. He recalls, "They said it should be nasty, sexy, and vulgar, but not offensive. Well, it is impossible to see anything intimate in this. I just feel it is there."

TITLE: Shortcut House Party
CLIENT: Shortcut Post Productions
SIZE: 39.37" x 27.56" (100 x 70 cm)
PRINTING PROCESS: 4 color
INKS: Process
Are posters what you primarily do for this client? No

PROCESS
COMPS PRESENTED: 3
REVISIONS: 0
APPROVAL: Shortcut manager
INVOLVEMENT WITH FINAL PRINTING: Jewboy Corporation

Drawing—literally—on his talent for computer animation and illustration, Shin implements the philosophy of "life is short, so get naked" in this promotional poster for the Shortcut Annual Party. Unfortunately, not everyone in Tel Aviv shares his philosophy. He laments the eventual fate of the posters: "When they were hung up, religious people destroyed them.... So, to my dismay, they had a short street life."

TITLE: Bomb Attack
CLIENT: Saloona Art Exhibition
SIZE: originally: 39.37" x 27.56" (100 x 70 cm)
PRINTING PROCESS: 4 color
INKS: Process
Are posters what you primarily do for this client? No

PROCESS
COMPS PRESENTED: 1
REVISIONS: 0
APPROVAL: Exhibition curators
INVOLVEMENT WITH FINAL PRINTING: Jewboy Corporation

The idea for this promotional poster was "Let's get nuked!" Shin selected an image from the exhibition "right after the tsunami disaster that references the parallel destruction of humanity from the nuclear bombing of Nagasaki. Both disasters contain a horrible beauty. The image shows how a designer can make the best of this horror and make it sexy or appealing almost naïve." The combination of hand-drawing and computer illustration manipulating shapes, forms, drawings, and cheap, free, freehand icons certainly made the rounds. Shin recalls, "This image was also presented in the exhibition and found itself on lightboxes as well as on a postcard and in a graphic design magazine. In short, this image is a whore."

TITLE: Mr. Yuta San
CLIENT: Sitra Ahra Book Publishing
SIZE: 39.37" x 27.56" (100 x 70 cm)
PRINTING PROCESS: 4 color
INKS: Process
Are posters what you primarily do for this client? No

PROCESS

COMPS PRESENTED: 1
REVISIONS: 0
APPROVAL: Sitra Ahra management crew
INVOLVEMENT WITH FINAL PRINTING:
Jewboy Corporation

To Done With It! is a book that mixes fictional items and real experiences into short stories, so Shin fed off of the design he had produced for the book cover and tapped into a personal remembrance for this promotional poster. Sadly, he notes, "The writer committed suicide two years ago. I had to come up with something respectful for the family, yet not compromising the way he was." The title of the book alludes to "the connection between image and name he is taking a journey on a symbolic plane with a symbolic suitcase, never to return." The author also "loved A3 and A4 papers to work on," so references were woven into the piece.

TITLE: Dan Shaham's B-day Grand Party
CLIENT: Mr. Dan (Crazykiller) Shaham
SIZE: 39.37" x 27.56" (100 x 70 cm)
PRINTING PROCESS: 4 color
INKS: Process
Are posters what you primarily do for this client? Yes

PROCESS

COMPS PRESENTED: 3
REVISIONS: 0
APPROVAL: Dan Shaham and his crew
INVOLVEMENT WITH FINAL PRINTING:
Jewboy Corporation

This poster was all about the well-known Dan Shaham, a Tel Aviv nightlife celebrity. As Shin explains; "He is a megalomaniac, and he needed something that covered his whole life. He enjoys deer-hunting as a hobby. That is the kind of person he is." Thankfully, the deer in the poster are shown alive so as not to frighten the partygoers. At least until they arrive.

TITLE: Shitty Day for Some
CLIENT: Ascolla Graphic Design Exhibition
SIZE: 39.37" x 27.56" (100 x 70 cm)
PRINTING PROCESS: 4 color
INKS: Process
Are posters what you primarily do for this client? Yes

PROCESS

COMPS PRESENTED: 1
REVISIONS: 0
APPROVAL: Ascolla graphic design
department manager
INVOLVEMENT WITH FINAL PRINTING:
Jewboy Corporation

Promoting a T-shirt exhibition in which all of the shirt designs were made under the briefing of "say something," Shin's image also used for a shirt is "based on something I found at my doorstep. It wasn't really dog shit but human! This made me think about how people cannot control their ego— for example, killing penguins or hunting for fun, and on the other hand they cannot control their body and hide the shame of being a lousy drunk junkie."

TITLE: *Man*
CLIENT: Sitra Ahra Book Publishing
SIZE: ORIGINALLY: 39.37" x 27.56" (100 x 70 cm)
PRINTING PROCESS: 4 color
INKS: Process
Are posters what you primarily do for this client? No

PROCESS

COMPS PRESENTED: 1
REVISIONS: 0
APPROVAL: Sitra Ahra manager
INVOLVEMENT WITH FINAL PRINTING:
Jewboy Corporation

Shin designed a promotional poster for a book based on the cover art he had produced earlier. The book tells the story of "a completely anonymous man who makes the journey to the big city with the intention of becoming famous." When this plan falls apart, "he makes a deal with the devil." Shin was able to accentuate the power of the image and interject some dark humor in describing the basis for the illustration. "The man silhouetted is my dad. No, Daddy! Not with the iron cord!" I prefer to focus on the rainbow portion of the image.

★ ANDREW LEWIS DESIGN ★

VANCOUVER ISLAND, CANADA

BIG NUMBERS

From his outpost in British Columbia, Andrew Lewis has been quite a poster-making machine over the years. With a portfolio that includes nearly 500 posters and print runs of nearly one million copies distributed around the world, he is a long way from the limited-edition madness of the current movement in the United States. This high level of activity has seen his posters find homes in galleries, museums, and collections all over the globe. From France to New York to Guadalajara to Beijing, his prints are on display.

Lewis has even begun to pare down his poster work. He had been doing "theater posters, gastronomic or hospitality venues—a little of everything" and now is much more selective. He also strives "not to repeat myself as a designer or illustrator, hence my ever-evolving styles."

He also has become something of a champion of the form. "I have always, in every article, interview, or conference that I have been involved with, talked about the poster as a viable, vibrant medium. My bias has been more toward the poster biennials in Mexico, Europe, the United States, and Asia, where you quickly can see trends or movements. China is an emerging superforce in poster design and production because of the recent development of advertising there and also due to the simple body count of designers. There are over 400 design universities in China! You can imagine the percentage of designers currently working on posters." You can hear Lewis's excitement at the prospect of a nation of reinforcements shoring up the poster field.

THE TEST OF TIME

Lewis's work is driven by a love of "the many past poster masters I admire, such as Leonetto Cappiello, Jules Chéret, and the Push Pin Group. Where image, text, message, and purpose were paramount in the creation of their posters, they all were responsible for pushing the medium and the public's reaction to seeing the new works. They have an influence on my posters, as does the international travel I get in during a typical year."

The other driver is his concern with repetition. "When I drive my car, I go through the fifty-odd radio stations and marvel at the diversity of what I am hearing. Ska, techno, jazz, country—each is great in its own warped way. To me, the same is true of designing posters—not having one concrete viewpoint or style but rather a collection of mindsets or perspectives. I find it mind-numbing to see a designer with one style, one viewpoint, and really one solution to all problems."

For Lewis, a successful poster must "be able to last the test of time, not to date itself with fashionable visuals, and to rely on a seemingly simple idea at first that tends to eventually take on its own life." Posters should contain "many levels of information that, when digested, create a single image that causes a reaction in a single moment in time." Capturing that moment is the challenge. "My best posters, may I say, seemed to have appeared from the ether without much gray matter or effort applied. I have little explanation for them, but I am grateful for their surprise visits."

MORE LIKE WORK

Despite his long-held appreciation of the poster, especially when printed in a large format, Lewis still finds the process of designing them "painful and more like work. The results may look positive, hopefully fresh and innovative, but the process, for me, is basic misery, full of self-doubt." Luckily for the rest of us, he continues to rise to the challenge.

" I find it mind-numbing to see a designer with one style, one viewpoint, and really one solution to all problems. "

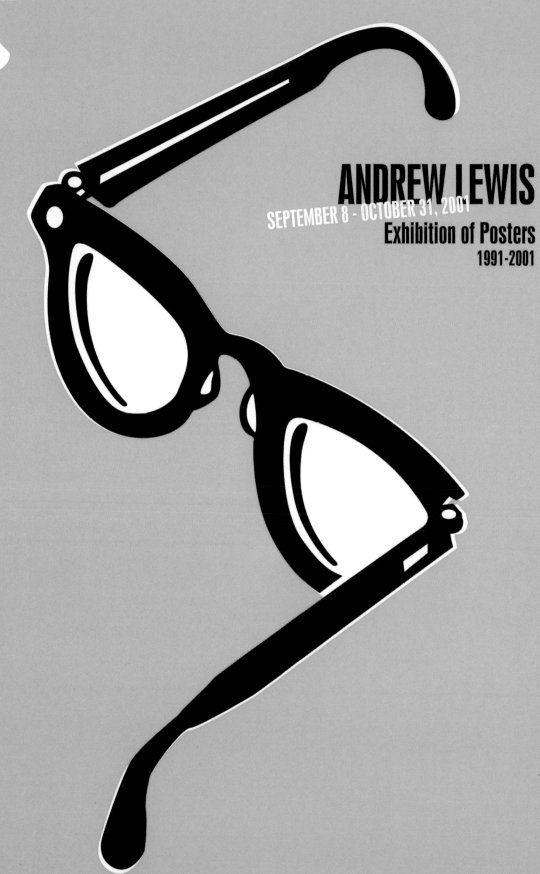

ANDREW LEWIS
SEPTEMBER 8 - OCTOBER 31, 2001
Exhibition of Posters
1991-2001

417 W. Magnolia, Fort Collins, Colorado, USA 80521 (970) 221-6735

Printed in Canada by

The exhibition is sponsored by Colorado State University, The Fort Collins' Lincoln Center, Poudre School District, The Fort Collins Chamber of Commerce and the Fort Collins Convention and Visitors Bureau. Funding is also provided by the Colorado Council on the Arts, The City of Fort Collins Fort Fund and by Toma and Associates. Design: Andrew Lewis Design

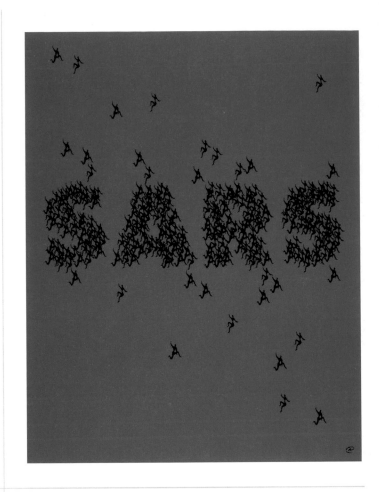

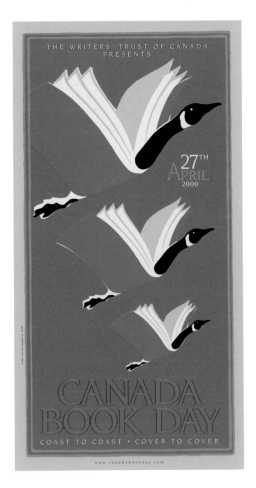

Bienal Internacional del Cartel en México
MUSEO FRANZ MAYER
del 25 de Octubre de 2004
al 30 de enero de 2005

TRAMA VISUAL
Alvaro Obregón 73, col. Roma, México, D.F. 06700

CARTELES CONTRA LA
IMPUNIDAD

TRIBECA
PERFORMING ARTS CENTER
Borough of Manhattan Community College

P R E S E N T S

JJ McCOLL'S

we're
still
hot!

THE MUSICAL

January 15-30
Tribeca Performing Arts Center
Tickets: 212.220.1460

199 Chambers Street
New York City

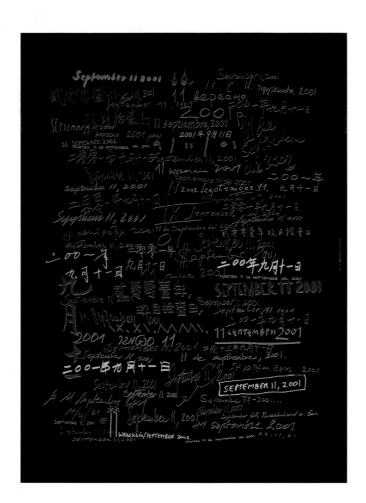

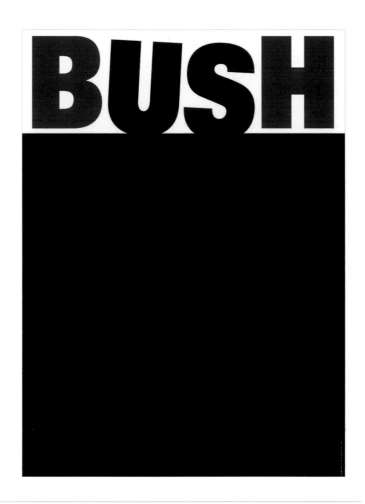

TITLE: Andrew Lewis Exhibition of Posters
CLIENT: Colorado International Invitational Poster Exhibition
SIZE: 18" x 26" (45.72 x 66.04 cm)
PRINTING PROCESS: Offset
INKS: 2 color
Are posters what you primarily do for this client? Yes

PROCESS
COMPS PRESENTED: 32
REVISIONS: 1
APPROVAL: Andrew Lewis Design
INVOLVEMENT WITH FINAL PRINTING:
Prepared for production and press inspected

For the Colorado International Invitational Poster Exhibition, Lewis was entrusted with designing the event's promotional poster. It seemed an easy task, given his vast experience in the medium. However, he himself was the invited exhibitor, and "designing a poster for your own exhibition is much more difficult than it looks," he laments. Numerous ideas were vetted internally; Lewis jokingly says he "met with myself and argued." The notion of "illustrating the viewing of posters, which we perceive as visuals and thoughts," soon framed his final image of glasses looking in both directions at once.

TITLE: Museo Taurino
CLIENT: La Maestranza Cantina
SIZE: 24" x 44" (60.96 x 111.76 cm)
PRINTING PROCESS: Silkscreen
INKS: 3 color
Are posters what you primarily do for this client? Yes

PROCESS
COMPS PRESENTED: 1
REVISIONS: 0
APPROVAL: Owner
INVOLVEMENT WITH FINAL PRINTING: None

For a cantina in Guadalajara, Mexico, Lewis put together an engaging poster "to be used internally and externally to promote both the cantina and the adjacent museum dedicated to the corrida, or bullfight," supporting his woodcut style with the aid of his trusty computer. There was only had one hitch: He had to convince the owner his services were needed. Luckily, he succeeded.

TITLE: SARS
CLIENT: Government of China, Health Authority
SIZE: 26" x 40" (66.04 x 101.60 cm)
PRINTING PROCESS: Screen print
INKS: 2 color
Are posters what you primarily do for this client? Yes

PROCESS
COMPS PRESENTED: 1
REVISIONS: 0
APPROVAL: Chinese government official
INVOLVEMENT WITH FINAL PRINTING: None

"In the summer of 2003, the epidemic of SARS hit China and, oddly, Toronto, Ontario, with devastating consequences," says Lewis. Feeling a strange connection between the occurrences in China and Canada, when the Chinese government requested poster submissions addressing this issue, Lewis had his pen ready. "After all of the submissions were received, this one was selected for internal use and as an awareness campaign in China."

TITLE: The Hunt for Perfect Coffee
CLIENT: Starbucks Coffee
SIZE: 24" x 36" (60.96 x 91.44 cm)
PRINTING PROCESS: Offset
INKS: 4-color process
Are posters what you primarily do for this client? No

PROCESS
COMPS PRESENTED: 2
REVISIONS: 6
APPROVAL: Starbucks Toronto and Seattle offices
INVOLVEMENT WITH FINAL PRINTING: None

Sometimes the smallest player can make the biggest impact. Navigating a process that included working with not only the Starbucks Toronto and Seattle offices but also their Toronto advertising agency, Lewis was asked to design "a poster for the promotion of new store openings—specifically, those opening in the fall." Brainstorming for imagery and execution, he settled on "the scratchboard illustration using the hunting image to play on the coffee as a fox image."

TITLE: Canada Book Day
CLIENT: Writers' Trust of Canada
SIZE: 24" x 44" (60.96 x 111.76 cm)
PRINTING PROCESS: Offset
INKS: 4-color process
Are posters what you primarily do for this client? Yes

PROCESS
COMPS PRESENTED: 3
REVISIONS: 0
APPROVAL: Jean Baird and the Board of Directors
INVOLVEMENT WITH FINAL PRINTING:
Prepared for production and press inspected

While working on a redesign for an annual event, Lewis wanted to find a deeper connection between specific imagery for his country and the concept. He wound up illustrating with a book and Canadian goose image," executed with a scratchboard technique, as he "focused on the schools as an audience, from kindergarten to high school. This image was so successful that the Writers' Trust of Canada used it as the corporate brand logo, and a series of three more posters were commissioned."

TITLE: Posters Against Impunity
CLIENT: International Poster Biennial of Mexico
SIZE: 26" x 40" (66.04 x 101.60 cm)
PRINTING PROCESS: Screen print
INKS: 2 color
Are posters what you primarily do for this client? Yes

PROCESS
COMPS PRESENTED: 1
REVISIONS: 0
APPROVAL: Biennial organizer
INVOLVEMENT WITH FINAL PRINTING:
Prepared for production and press inspected

Lewis was asked to help advertise a poster exhibition in Mexico by Xavier Bermundez. The "Posters Against Impunity" exhibition "addresses the social effects of crimes that are unpunished in Central and South American countries," says Lewis. To get the point across, "the poster illustrates this endless concession of fear and needless aggression of person upon person." And it does so in an incredibly bold graphic manner.

TITLE: *We're Still Hot: The Musical*
CLIENT: Out to See Productions
SIZE: 24" x 42" (60.96 x 106.68 cm)
PRINTING PROCESS: Screen print
INKS: 2 color
Are posters what you primarily do for this client? No

PROCESS

COMPS PRESENTED: 3
REVISIONS: 9
APPROVAL: Producer, director, and the PR firm
INVOLVEMENT WITH FINAL PRINTING: None

Armed with his pen, Lewis tackled a "poster for a new off-Broadway musical on the theme of menopause." Taking but a second to fully think about the subject matter, he came up with the perfect images. "The fire extinguisher and bra, I felt, summed up the hot flashes and the heat of the production."

TITLE: September 11, 2001
CLIENT: Brno International Poster Biennial
SIZE: 38" x 54" (96.52 x 137.16 cm)
PRINTING PROCESS: Digital
INKS: 4-color process
Are posters what you primarily do for this client? Yes

PROCESS

COMPS PRESENTED: 1
REVISIONS: 0
APPROVAL: Andrew Lewis Design
INVOLVEMENT WITH FINAL PRINTING:
Prepared for production and press inspected

The poster has always been much more than just paper to Lewis. At times, it has felt like his only outlet. "Two days after the 9/11 attacks, I put out an email request to over eighty international poster designers to provide in their handwriting the words *September 11, 2001*. The response was awesome." Soon he was assembling the poster as with the seventy-eight files that were emailed back. "The first one was from Milton Glaser—just two hours after I sent out the request!"

TITLE: BUSH
CLIENT: Colorado State University "Graphic Response" Exhibition
SIZE: 26" x 40" (66.04 x 101.60 cm)
PRINTING PROCESS: Digital
INKS: 4-color process
Are posters what you primarily do for this client? Yes

PROCESS

COMPS PRESENTED: 1
REVISIONS: 0
APPROVAL: Exhibition curator
INVOLVEMENT WITH FINAL PRINTING:
Prepared for production and press inspected

"'Graphic Response' was an exhibition in conjunction with the International Poster Exhibition on responding to current social issues," says Lewis. For his response, Lewis knew where he to direct his attention—a little south of the Canadian border. "George W. Bush was busy invading oil-rich countries, and this was a response illustrating that the need for oil is destroying the United States. It is executed using the simple motifs of red blood, black oil, and typography."

TITLE: SHMODKA
CLIENT: Southwest Missouri State University
SIZE: 26" x 40" (66.04 x 101.60 cm)
PRINTING PROCESS: Screen print
INKS: 1 color
Are posters what you primarily do for this client? Yes

PROCESS

COMPS PRESENTED: 1
REVISIONS: 0
APPROVAL: Professor of the Design Department
INVOLVEMENT WITH FINAL PRINTING: Prepared for production and press inspected

Lewis still finds time to be not only the teacher but also the student. "After teaching a workshop at the Central Academy of Fine Art in Beijing, China," Lewis says, he was "asked by [Southwest Missouri State University design professor and international poster giant] Cedomir Kostovic to prepare an assignment on the new alcoholic drink Shmodka." The parameters given to Lewis "included point-of-purchase posters as well as packaging and advertising media applications." Once he completed his design using ink, scratchboard, and Canadian vodka, "twenty-four students followed a brief I created using these guidelines and specifications."

TITLE: KYOTO
CLIENT: Andrew Lewis Design
SIZE: 26" x 40" (66.04 x 101.60 cm)
PRINTING PROCESS: Screen print
INKS: 2 color
Are posters what you primarily do for this client? Yes

PROCESS

COMPS PRESENTED: 1
REVISIONS: 0
APPROVAL: Andrew Lewis Design
INVOLVEMENT WIH FINAL PRINTING:
Prepared for production and press inspected

Lewis found himself perplexed by the Kyoto Accord. Not knowing where to turn, he looked to an old friend: the poster. "Following a summit in Canada on the Kyoto Accord environmental bill, I created this as a response to the vague resolve by this international committee." Lewis created the shortsighted beam of light using ink and a toothbrush.

★ LITTLE FRIENDS OF PRINTMAKING ★

MADISON, WISCONSIN, USA

UNTIL COVERED IN INK DO US PART

Upon graduating from the University of Wisconsin with their degrees in printmaking, this husband-and-wife team decided to stay put. After all, they had already begun to make a name for themselves as the Little Friends of Printmaking. Despite the heavy influence of a humorous visual language in James and Melissa Buchanan's work, their fine art background screams through in the details of their design and the craft of their printing.

This controlled looseness and an affinity for the process has allowed their young firm to draw a great deal of attention on the national stage. Their work has made its way into several collections and exhibitions in just three short years and has gone on a cross-country tour with their Canadian neighbors, Seripop (featured on page 154).

Young upstarts that they are, the Buchanans are more than happy to take on the main point of criticism levied at the underground poster movement in the United States. "Designers we know deride the kind of poster art Little Friends does because of the frequent lack of hard direction from a client, and because we have an unusual amount of control over the content and the level of information that goes on the poster. The thing is that a blank piece of paper can be absolutely terrifying. No feedback! No direction! It's not all it's cracked up to be. It takes either a massive ego or a prodigious artistic talent to fill that blank piece of paper, and then it takes something still beyond that to fill it with something that really communicates," says Melissa Buchanan. We'll put them in the artistic talent category.

MATERIAL CULTURE
The Buchanans are well versed in both past and contemporary art, but it is tough to identify their greatest influences. They do concede that Cuban poster artist Muñoz Bachs is a "favorite in our household." It is clearer that they are "pathetically, desperately nuts for the material culture of the mid-twentieth century. It's hard to even imagine now a time when a package of meat or motor oil or *whatever* was covered with wild and energetic illustrations and hand-set type. What the hell happened to American visual culture? We love John and Faith Hubley and the whole UPA [United Productions of America; the reference is to a new wave of animation in film], or any cartoon that's so cheaply made that things scuttle sideways. George Grosz, Saul Steinberg, James Jarvis, Todd James." Combine a healthy dose of television, 1970s pop radio, and British acid folk music with weekly visits to the zoo, plus the tech savvy to design in Flash rather than an illustration software program, and you have the heady brew that is the Little Friends.

The Buchanans are inching closer to merging their commercial and fine art worlds as, "the design rags are paying a little more attention to posters than usual, and in the worlds of fine art and art history, there's an increased interest in material culture in general, in all historical periods, *as art*. This has led to a larger appreciation of illustrators and graphic designers who were, up to now, nothing more than minor cult figures in the history of art," says Buchanan.

UNLIMITED POSSIBILITIES
"Even at our most isolated, it's hard not to consider Little Friends part of a movement," says Buchanan. "We certainly look at a huge volume of contemporary work, and that's got to have some effect on our work; and if not our work, our desire to push the work further. We've done a lot of proselytizing on behalf of concert posters over the years, by speaking and by going out on the road with our Little Friends/Seripop touring exhibition, and we'll continue to do so in the future. We're less concerned with the poster movement as a social club than the poster as an art form with unlimited possibilities, but the community aspect has allowed us to meet a lot of interesting designers."

The poster has kept the Buchanans oddly in tune with technology and closer as a couple. James suffered a "horrific career-ending injury" to his wrist. He still wanted to be able to work on the same art as Melissa, and through trial and error they found he could draw using an old analog mouse on Flash MX software. In some ways, it is perfect that they use a program most often associated with glitzy interactive media for the most low-tech of tasks—drawing.

The Little Friends love the power of the poster. "It ought to look great from 20 feet but still reward a viewer's close inspection with something extra to look at once you've got it in your hands. It's got to be a big, bold statement that works for the entire audience. A good concert poster needs to speak to not only current but to all potential fans of the band. A poster is no place for in-jokes or design conceits. I mean, our background is fine art. We do our best to make a good silkscreen, and if it turns out to be a nice poster, well, bonus for us. We don't pretend to know a lot about design, but it's easy for even us to see when a poster just doesn't work." Don't worry, Little Friends—yours work.

"A poster is no place for in-jokes or design conceits."

ALAMO DRAFTHOUSE PRESENTS

THE FLAMING LIPS'
ZAIREEKA

JULY 23 · 8PM
OLD SETTLERS
· · PARK · ·
ROUND ROCK, TX

4x
MUSIC &
VIDEO

DEATH FROM ABOVE 1979

CONTROLLER.CONTROLLER & YOUNG BODIES
WED. APRIL 13 9PM CLUB 770 FREE!

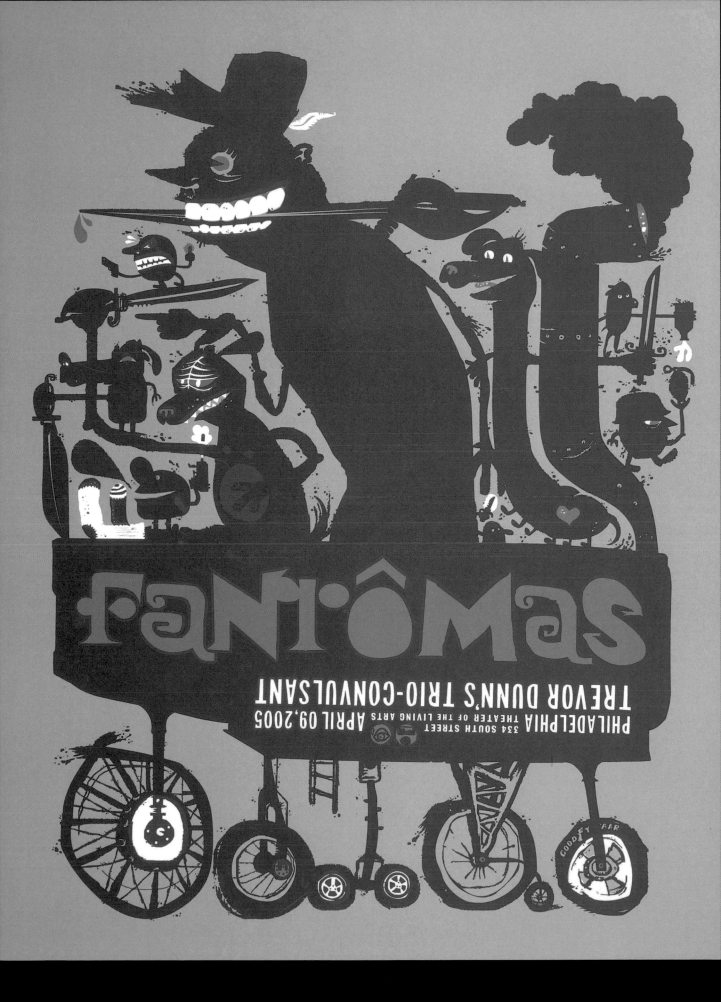

TITLE: The Flaming Lips' *Zaireeka*
CLIENT: Alamo Drafthouse
SIZE: 18" x 25" (45.72 x 63.50 cm)
PRINTING PROCESS: Silkscreen
INKS: 4 color
Are posters what you primarily do for this client? Yes

PROCESS
COMPS PRESENTED: 1
REVISIONS: 0
APPROVAL: Promoter
INVOLVEMENT WITH FINAL PRINTING:
Printed by Little Friends

When this job showed up on the Friends' doorstep, the instructions were, "Don't worry. Do whatever you want. Do that thing that you do." Melissa Buchanan says, "I really have no idea what they could possibly be referring to. Their enthusiasm ought to put me at ease, but instead it usually puts me in a cold, clammy sweat." The venue didn't help either. "It was an unusual event for us because it wasn't a concert, strictly speaking. It was a freak-out in the desert, and the Flaming Lips weren't going to play, they were just going to show up and have a beer and toddle around as the people flipped out. Our initial plan for this poster was to remake a Wayne Coyne poster [The lead singer of the group was once a highly regarded silkscreen poster artist in his own right] in our own illustration style, but we found that impossible." So they ended up with "that layer of cute shit in our artwork that just barely conceals an undercurrent of violence and dread. A good match for the band."

TITLE: Death from Above 1979
CLIENT: Wisconsin Union Directorate
SIZE: 12" x 19" (30.48 x 48.26 cm)
PRINTING PROCESS: Silkscreen
INKS: 4 color
Are posters what you primarily do for this client? Yes

PROCESS
COMPS PRESENTED: 1
REVISIONS: 0
APPROVAL: Promoter
INVOLVEMENT WITH FINAL PRINTING:
Printed by Little Friends

Coming out of their "Do More With Less" period, the Little Friends "felt like our game was sufficiently tightened up that we could go back to using a wider palette with more confidence." Applying four colors to a maniacally laughing figure, they received "a lot of messages after this poster hit the streets, some kindly, some less so, about posters with faces on them that might have inspired this design. We normally take this kind of stuff pretty seriously, but a person's face has got to be the most frequently used subject matter ever, in any medium," notes Buchanan. Just ask Dave Plunkert (featured on page 170).

TITLE: VHS or Beta
CLIENT: The Conservatory
SIZE: 11.5" x 18" (29.21 x 45.72 cm)
PRINTING PROCESS: Silkscreen
INKS: 2 color
Are posters what you primarily do for this client? Yes

PROCESS
COMPS PRESENTED: 1
REVISIONS: 0
APPROVAL: Promoter
INVOLVEMENT WITH FINAL PRINTING:
Printed by Little Friends

Returning from a cross-country tour of split exhibitions with Seripop (featured on page 154), the Little Friends "felt a bit like hack cartoonists." During the tour, "the response to our work had been very positive, but the contrast in method and style between Seripop and Little Friends cast the strengths and weaknesses of our respective work in pretty sharp relief. There was a lot of soul-searching in the van that led to a conscious effort to "design" their work more. With the familiar black figure, the poster shows "our underprinting at its most self-indulgent. To have underprinting beneath black may seem like—and in fact it may be—a ridiculous and self-defeating impulse, but it was our solution to the problem of refining the focus and scope of our poster designs," they say. "This was about the time that we started trying to dirty up our look a bit. Being totally incapable of doing these things the easy way, and needing to exert control over every square inch of our poster, we ended up drawing each individual bit of splatter, which is about as stupid and tedious as it sounds. There is nothing about hand-drawn splatter that is makes it more interesting than regular splatter, and we certainly do not mean to imply an increased sense of value or craft. This is more an insight into our psychoses than our technique."

TITLE: Slutfest
CLIENT: Wisconsin Union Directorate/Slutfest
SIZE: 19" x 25" (48.26 x 63.50 cm)
PRINTING PROCESS: Silkscreen
INKS: 3 color
Are posters what you primarily do for this client? Yes

PROCESS
COMPS PRESENTED: 3
REVISIONS: 4
APPROVAL: Event organizer
INVOLVEMENT WITH FINAL PRINTING:
Printed by Little Friends

The University of Wisconsin puts on an annual hard-core music festival every spring. One year, the Little Friends "caught wind that a number of women's health seminars and skill-shares had been added to the event and that it was to be renamed Slutfest. This was a shock to us because we mainly knew Hardcore Fest as two days in a darkened room with greasy boys in slightly damp navy blue hoodies whose breath smells faintly of sour milk. This is hardly a setting conducive to ladies and their lady antics. Most of our early comps had something to do with this odd new scenario—the introduction of girls to a largely male-attended event, the punk rock booty call." After going a few rounds with the client, they settled on "the transsexual pony dog. It's cute," say the Buchanans.

TITLE: Melt Banana/Breather Resist
CLIENT: Wisconsin Union Directorate
SIZE: 12" x 19" (30.48 x 48.26 cm)
PRINTING PROCESS: Silkscreen
INKS: 2 color
Are posters what you primarily do for this client? Yes

PROCESS
COMPS PRESENTED: 1
REVISIONS: 0
APPROVAL: Promoter
INVOLVEMENT WITH FINAL PRINTING:
Printed by Little Friends

Striving for "big fat chunky monster" lettering, the kind you might see adorning an old cover of *Famous Monsters of Filmland* magazine or *Nightmare* magazine, to complement their angry spirits and stern figure, the Buchanans worked tirelessly on the typography. When that was complete, the poster came together quickly with the familiar "black figures" illustration style and the Little Friends sense of humor. The Buchanans concede that chunky typography "is one of our favorite recurring motifs in our concert posters."

TITLE: The Blow/Y.A.C.H.T.
CLIENT: Wisconsin Union Directorate
SIZE: 12" x 19" (30.48 x 48.26 cm)
PRINTING PROCESS: Silkscreen
INKS: 3 color
Are posters what you primarily do for this client? Yes

PROCESS

COMPS PRESENTED: 1
REVISIONS: 0
APPROVAL: Promoter
INVOLVEMENT WITH FINAL PRINTING:
Printed by Little Friends

While touring the country, the Little Friends stayed at a multimedia art space and hostel in Anacortes, Washington, called the Department of Safety. "We wanted to show our appreciation for the hospitality of the folks in the Northwest," say the Buchanans. "Also, while we were on tour we'd been to see Beautiful Losers [an art exhibit inspired by skateboarding culture] in San Francisco and got to see in person a lot of Mike Mills stuff that had exerted a great deal of influence on us back in the mid-1990s. Now, admittedly, coming from a fine art background, we have some difficulty resolving issues of, uh, *influence*—found images, borrowed imagery, etc. At the time we made this poster, we didn't think anything at all of quoting Mills's speakers and wires, but as time went on we felt increasingly guilty about it until it became our number-one priority to track down the images we thought we'd ripped off. To our relief, it turned out that they didn't look much alike." The result is a blend of subtle overprinting with the humorous effect of showing the "inner workings" of the bear as he "plays" music on his computer.

TITLE: Wilco/Deerhoof
CLIENT: Last Coast/True Endeavors
SIZE: 18" x 24" (45.72 x 60.96 cm)
PRINTING PROCESS: Silkscreen
INKS: 3 color
Are posters what you primarily do for this client? Yes

PROCESS

COMPS PRESENTED: 1
REVISIONS: 0
APPROVAL: Promoter
INVOLVEMENT WITH FINAL PRINTING:
Printed by Little Friends

When Deerhoof's show was moved to a slot opening for Wilco, Little Friends ended up doing the poster for that event instead. "The challenge here was to create a poster that would appeal to two such distinct and disparate audiences," say the Buchanans. "This poster represented a serious paring-back of all the tiny details and visual overload we used to put into posters. We felt like it was time to change things." Unsurprisingly, producing a single image was difficult. "The burden of proof was on us to get this thing as clear and pitch-perfect as possible. We were both used to getting our way to some extent previously, and suddenly there wasn't even room for one point of view. Of all the posters we've made, this is the one that caused us to fight the most. This was the breech birth of posters."

TITLE: Dan Sartain
CLIENT: The Conservatory
SIZE: 16.5" x 21.75" (41.91 x 55.25 cm)
PRINTING PROCESS: Silkscreen
INKS: 3 color
Are posters what you primarily do for this client? Yes

PROCESS

COMPS PRESENTED: 1
REVISIONS: 0
APPROVAL: Promoter
INVOLVEMENT WITH FINAL PRINTING:
Printed by Little Friends

Promoting a show where several touring artists were playing together for only one night, the Buchanans fretted, "There wasn't a single thread that you could follow from one act to the next and pick up on visually. Dan Sartain was definitely the headliner, but the other groups were so distinctive that they couldn't be totally disregarded. Our solution was to try to evoke a lazy Saturday in the dormitory, listening to records and staring out the window. All sorts of different stuff might pass over the turntable. It was late spring, we were about to graduate from college, and were maybe getting a touch sappy and sentimental about it." When putting together the dorm room, they "snuck all sorts of stuff in there from our apartment: James's North Stars pennant, posters, a bunch of cool records and toys, and our cat."

TITLE: Fantômas/Trevor Dunn's Trio-Convulsant
CLIENT: Fantômas
SIZE: 19" x 25" (48.26 x 63.50 cm)
PRINTING PROCESS: Silkscreen
INKS: 3 color
Are posters what you primarily do for this client? Yes

PROCESS

COMPS PRESENTED: 1
REVISIONS: 0
APPROVAL: Fantômas
INVOLVEMENT WITH FINAL PRINTING:
Printed by Little Friends

Melissa Buchanan enthusiastically states, "This is probably the only poster we ever did where I really felt like we nailed it. This was sort of the logical conclusion of the black figure thing, even though we still continue to do it. Here, color and line start to creep in more, and it works. I like how we let the overlapping of silhouettes get a little ambiguous. I hope that's as appealing to other people as it is to us." An old friend from their artwork slips in as well. "I think this is one of the first appearances of the knife motif in our posters, which had been a big part of our regular artwork for years. I also really like the comparative specificity of some of the more drawn details and the general reemergence of line drawing." When asked to do this, she thought, "Oh yeah, we can totally do this. No problem." The frenzied madness that sends Fantômas from noise rock to cartoon themes was a perfect fit.

LUBA LUKOVA

NEW YORK, NEW YORK, USA

AN OPPORTUNITY TO CREATE

Although it would be a mistake to place too much significance on the early stages of Luba Lukova's career and her childhood in the shadow of Bulgarian communism, her upbringing in a restrictive society has indeed had an undeniable influence on her work. Oppression—and the battle creativity wages against it—are evident in nearly everything she touches. She puts her heart into each and every illustration, and the clarity and conciseness of her vision belie the conviction of an artist who relishes the opportunity to create.

However, the qualities that make Lukova's work so special are part of her, not just her background. Training at the Academy of Fine Arts in Sophia may have informed her sense of typography and imagery, but it takes only a few minutes of talking with her before you realize that the accent that has remained strong more than a decade after her decision to remain in New York during a trip to the United States cannot mask a deeply thoughtful person. It is curiosity, compassion, and, most important, empathy with her subjects that form the almost iconically simple images that grace her work. The humanity of the images transcends their black-and-white plainness.

Lukova is perhaps the most successful of current designers at speaking to an audience with direct simplicity wrapped in a sophisticated package. Her sturdy yet delicate images have drawn comparisons to everyone from the German expressionists to Picasso. Her admirable reputation in the illustration world has plum assignments coming into her studio daily. Her work has appeared in nearly every publication of significance and worldwide in the collections of the Museum of Modern Art, the Library of Congress, Japan's Museum of Modern Art, the Bibliothèque Nationale de France, and others. She is also the recipient of a Gold Medal at the International Poster Biennial in Mexico and the ICOGRADA Excellence Award from the Festival Internationale d'Affiches in Chaumont, France.

KINDRED SPIRITS

Though Lukova's images have justifiably won rave reviews for themselves, her posters are where her work shines brightest. Perhaps this is because the medium is perfect for her favored strong central imagery. It is also a grand opportunity for her to display her secret weapon: a beautiful and sophisticated sense of typography that is hidden in straight illustration. As suspected, she reveals that she "very much likes Polish poster design from the 1970s." Lukova's work is kindred to that amazing decade of posters, mirroring the power of its fascinating conceptual images and tightly executed hand-drawn type. Her designs, like those of past masters, go beyond the statement of information to invoke thought and investigation.

She also finds inspiration from expected sources. "My influences are definitely from fine art, literature, and theater—artists such as Picasso, Goya, Rembrandt, Käthe Kollwitz, folk art, Shakespeare, and Chekhov." Not to mention her Bulgarian influences, such as "Alexander Poplilov, Asen Stareishinski, and Iliya Beshkov," and some that are more personal, like "the films of Charlie Chaplin, and my grandmother, who was an artist."

CONNECTION

Lukova loves the opportunities presented by the poster. "The poster has to be accessible and visible because the viewer has only seconds to grasp its meaning." She has a theory explaining its rebirth: "Posters bring a kind of humanness and emotion that the screen-based media can't provide yet." She may be selling her own talents short in that regard. She has the ability to convey a connection that few others can. It is no coincidence that she may be the only designer mentioned in the same breath as Picasso these days. Of course, that ability to communicate intimately with the viewer has an odd side effect: theft. Lukova mentions she "enjoys everything about designing posters, but especially when someone steals them from the theater lobby."

She might still have a spark of rebellion against an oppressive society left in her.

"Posters bring a kind of humanness and emotion that the screen–based media can't provide yet."

La MaMa E.T.C. presents Seven

74 East 4th Street, New York, NY 10003
Box Office 212-475-7710

May 19–June 13, 2004

NEA, DCA, NYSCA,
THE FORD FOUNDATION,
THE TROY FOUNDATION,
FRANK CARUCCI,
DONALD CAPOCCIA,
HAROLD & MIMI STEINBERG CT

Seven: Antigone Mythos Oedipus Seven Against Thebes Dionysus Filius Dei Medea Trojan Women Electra

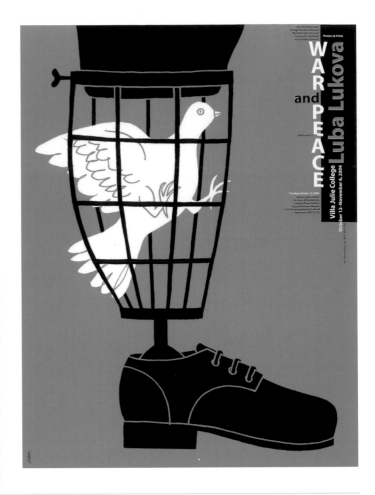

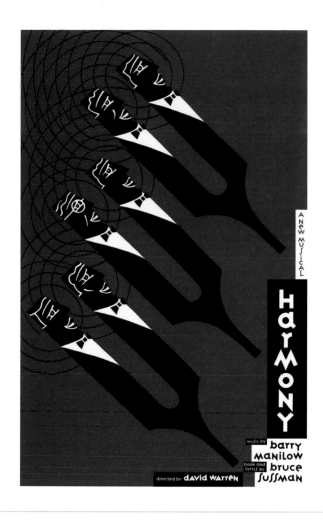

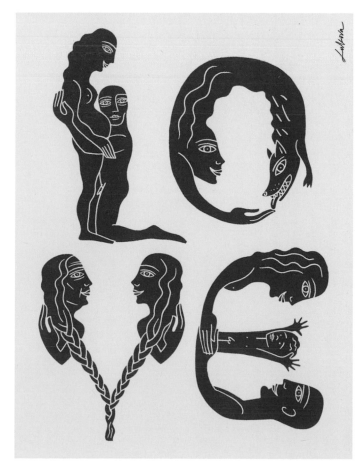

SHAKESPEARE'S THE TAMING OF THE SHREW

OCTOBER 27 NOVEMBER 8 1998

ANDREI DIRECTED BY SERBAN

CENTER FOR THEATRE STUDIES AT COLUMBIA UNIVERSITY

LA MAMA E.T.C.

Water

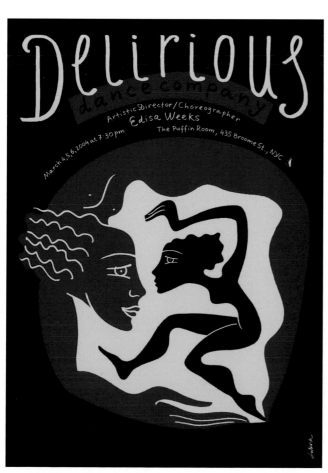

TITLE: Seven
CLIENT: La MaMa e.t.c.
SIZE: 27" x 39" (68.58 x 99.06 cm)
PRINTING PROCESS: Offset
INKS: 4-color process
Are posters what you primarily do for this client? Yes

PROCESS
COMPS PRESENTED: 3
REVISIONS: 1
APPROVAL: Stage director
INVOLVEMENT WITH FINAL PRINTING:
Prepared for production and press inspected

Lukova was challenged with creating a poster for a Greek play festival at La MaMa e.t.c. in New York. "It was called 'Seven' because of the seven different productions. For me, it meant I had to design one poster uniting all of them. I chose to do so using a classical Greek woman's face in profile and hand-lettered text intertwined in her hair."

TITLE: War Is Not the Answer
CLIENT: AIGA Orlando
SIZE: 27" x 39" (68.58 x 99.06 cm)
PRINTING PROCESS: Offset
INKS: 4-color process
Are posters what you primarily do for this client? Yes

PROCESS
COMPS PRESENTED: 1
REVISIONS: 0
APPROVAL: Self
INVOLVEMENT WITH FINAL PRINTING:
Prepared for production and press inspected

While creating a poster for her lecture at the AIGA, Orlando, current events were weighing heavily on Lukova's mind. "That was just before President Bush announced the war on Iraq. Like many others, I hoped that this is not going to happen, so I decided to make an antiwar poster instead of the usual designer talk announcement." This is not surprising, given her background, nor is her lament that "unfortunately my poster did not change the events that followed."

TITLE: War and Peace
CLIENT: Villa Julie College
SIZE: 27" x 39" (68.58 x 99.06 cm)
PRINTING PROCESS: Offset
INKS: 4-color process
Are posters what you primarily do for this client? Yes

PROCESS
COMPS PRESENTED: 1
REVISIONS: 0
APPROVAL: Self
INVOLVEMENT WITH FINAL PRINTING:
Prepared for production and press inspected

Even when creating work for her own promotion, Lukova is unable to keep herself from discussing the plight of others. She recalls, "This is a poster for an exhibition of my posters at Villa Julie College. The show was called 'War and Peace.' I wanted to convey a message about the price we pay for peace. The idea for this poster came after watching a film about handicapped U.S. soldiers returning from the battlefields."

TITLE: *Romeo and Juliet*
CLIENT: Ahmanson Theatre
SIZE: 27" x 39" (68.58 x 99.06 cm)
PRINTING PROCESS: Offset
INKS: 4-color process
Are posters what you primarily do for this client? Yes

PROCESS
COMPS PRESENTED: 1
REVISIONS: 0
APPROVAL: Stage director
INVOLVEMENT WITH FINAL PRINTING:
Prepared for production and press inspected

Some projects come with a little added pressure, Lukova admits. "It is not easy to design posters for such well-known plays as *Romeo and Juliet*. It is even more difficult when the director is someone as important as Sir Peter Hall, the founder of the Royal Shakespeare Company in London. I usually show at least three sketches to my clients. In this case, I produced more than 40 drawings until I came to this image, which I thought could work. It was the only piece I showed to the company, and luckily it became the poster for this production."

TITLE: Censorship
CLIENT: American Friends Service Committee
SIZE: 27" x 39" (68.58 x 99.06 cm)
PRINTING PROCESS: Offset
INKS: 4-color process
Are posters what you primarily do for this client? Yes

PROCESS
COMPS PRESENTED: 1
REVISIONS: 0
APPROVAL: Program director
INVOLVEMENT WITH FINAL PRINTING:
Prepared for production and press inspected

Lukova knows a powerful illustration when she sees it and is not above using it again for the right cause. "The image for this poster was first published on the cover of the Sunday *New York Times* Arts and Leisure section. It illustrated an article about how the Taliban regime censored music." The message stuck with her and later showed up on this poster for the American Friends Service Committee, a Nobel Prize–winning humanitarian organization.

TITLE: *Harmony*
CLIENT: Barry Manilow
SIZE: 27" x 39" (68.58 x 99.06 cm)
PRINTING PROCESS: Offset
INKS: 4-color process
Are posters what you primarily do for this client? Yes

PROCESS
COMPS PRESENTED: 1
REVISIONS: 0
APPROVAL: Stage director
INVOLVEMENT WITH FINAL PRINTING:
Prepared for production and press inspected

In creating a poster for a Broadway production of Barry Manilow's musical *Harmony*, Lukova wanted to delve into the subject manner in a unique way. The play, she says, "tells the real story of a band of six musicians called the Comedian Harmonists. They worked back in 1920s in Germany and were banned after the fascists took power in Europe, because not all of them were Aryans. Because it was a Broadway show, I was asked to stay away from politics, so I decided to transform the six performers into tuning forks. The idea was that despite their personal differences and the historical turbulences, they were able to create harmony."

TITLE: Kids Unique
CLIENT: Kids Unique
SIZE: 27" x 39" (68.58 x 99.06 cm)
PRINTING PROCESS: Offset
INKS: 4-color process
Are posters what you primarily do for this client? Yes

PROCESS
COMPS PRESENTED: 5
REVISIONS: 0
APPROVAL: Chairman of the organization
INVOLVEMENT WITH FINAL PRINTING:
Prepared for production and press inspected

While designing a poster for a nonprofit organization helping disadvantaged urban youth, Lukova was stricken by a common sight in the city. "I quite often see young trees being planted in sidewalks in New York City. Two posts and a rope are used to support the tree. I thought this would be an appropriate poetic metaphor for my poster. The child became a tree protected from the dangers of the street."

TITLE: Peace
CLIENT: War Resisters League
SIZE: 27" x 39" (68.58 x 99.06 cm)
PRINTING PROCESS: Offset
INKS: 4-color process
Are posters what you primarily do for this client? Yes

PROCESS
COMPS PRESENTED: 1
REVISIONS: 0
APPROVAL: Editor
INVOLVEMENT WITH FINAL PRINTING:
Prepared for production and press inspected

Lukova is not the only one who can spot a powerful image—or agree with a worthy cause. She says, "This was first published as a black-and-white illustration on the *New York Times* Op-Ed page. It was illustrating an article discussing the American involvement in the Balkan conflict. To my surprise, a couple of days later I saw my image made into a poster and posted on the streets in Brooklyn. It was a cheap Xerox reproduction done without my knowledge by the War Resisters League. I contacted them and proposed making a real poster replacing the black background with blue—which I thought emphasized the irony of the image."

TITLE: Love
CLIENT: Scheufelen
SIZE: 27" x 39" (68.58 x 99.06 cm)
PRINTING PROCESS: Offset
INKS: 4-color process
Are posters what you primarily do for this client? Yes

PROCESS
COMPS PRESENTED: 1
REVISIONS: 0
APPROVAL: Art director
INVOLVEMENT WITH FINAL PRINTING:
Prepared for production and press inspected

Lukova was asked to participate in "a promotional poster for the German paper manufacturer Scheufelen. Twelve international designers were asked to create a poster inspired by an ancient Tibetan parable about the most important things in life." The parameters of the problem led to this illustration of four powerful letterforms sympathetic to one another, almost like four individual posters.

TITLE: *The Taming of the Shrew*
CLIENT: La MaMa e.t.c., Columbia University
SIZE: 27" x 39" (68.58 x 99.06 cm)
PRINTING PROCESS: Silkscreen
INKS: 2 color
Are posters what you primarily do for this client? Yes

PROCESS
COMPS PRESENTED: 5
REVISIONS: 0
APPROVAL: Stage director
INVOLVEMENT WITH FINAL PRINTING:
Prepared for production and press inspected

In discussing her approach to the design for a poster for the classic Shakespeare comedy, Lukova says, "I have seen many posters for *The Taming of the Shrew* that represented in a tacky way the battle of the sexes, and I wanted to stay away from such a solution. To me, the idea behind the show is about the taming of ourselves, how we have to learn to temper our anger. I pictured an invisible muzzle we have to carry around to be able to survive in this society."

TITLE: Water
CLIENT: Union Theological Seminary
SIZE: 27" x 39" (68.58 x 99.06 cm)
PRINTING PROCESS: Silkscreen
INKS: 3 color
Are posters what you primarily do for this client? Yes

PROCESS
COMPS PRESENTED: 1
REVISIONS: 0
APPROVAL: Self
INVOLVEMENT WITH FINAL PRINTING:
Prepared for production and press inspected

Lukova knows the power of an image so well that she holds onto the rejected in hopes they will shine another day. "Initially, this was supposed to be a UNESCO poster about climate change, but the client selected another idea of mine," says Lukova. "A couple of months later, the Union Theological Seminary of New York invited me to show my work at their gallery. So as it often happens to me, I reused the rejected idea as a poster for my show. I thought it was appropriate, as the fish is also a symbol of faith, and it suggests the spiritual drought society faces today."

TITLE: *Delirious*
CLIENT: Delirious Dance Company
SIZE: 27" x 39" (68.58 x 99.06 cm)
PRINTING PROCESS: Offset
INKS: 4-color process
Are posters what you primarily do for this client? Yes

PROCESS
COMPS PRESENTED: 10
REVISIONS: 0
APPROVAL: Choreographer
INVOLVEMENT WITH FINAL PRINTING:
Prepared for production and press inspected

Designing for a production of New York choreographer Edisa Weeks, Lukova was amazed by the show. "She performed on stage with her shadow. The shadow was manipulated digitally, and it moved independently, projected on a big screen behind the dancer. I found this theatrical metaphor and the grace of the performer inspirational. We chose this image after discussing many sketches. It hopefully speaks about someone in a passionate dialogue with her inner self."

METHANE STUDIOS

ATLANTA, GEORGIA, USA

MARK'S GARAGE

Robert Lee and Mark McDevitt, former Columbus College of Art and Design students reunited by a love of poster design, formed Methane Studios in 1998. While the studio has grown into a full-service firm, they started out solely producing posters for Robert's band in Mark's garage, and posters remain the bulk of what they do. That won't change anytime soon, as McDevitt notes they "enjoy the boldness and the large format and great big areas of color available with poster design."

Methane often polishes off their work with a little humor as well; note their marketing lines "Farm Fresh Methane" and "Put a Little More Methane in Your Life."

That humor masks a lot of hard work, though. McDevitt cautions, "Silkscreen posters have to be thought out. Prepress work is very important. We have to consider color, size, and audience as well as the technical aspect." Their work ethic shapes the entire process. Methane's "design philosophy is to sketch and concept our asses off on the front end. Research the material and explore a number of ideas before settling on one. We have stacks and stacks of sketches from the last 15 years." They also try to get started early, "visiting the assignment before it comes down to being due the next day," so that time constraints don't force them to settle on a solution they are unhappy with.

HAND IN HAND

Lee has noticed the change in the poster scene in recent years. With the computer's help, production speed and access to knowledge has increased, but he believes plenty of posters have always been out there. "I just think designers are starting to look at them as a bit more exciting than the annual reports of days past. Poster designers can take more chances and push the envelope." Methane also notes that the connection between fans and a collectable visual connection to music is even more desired now that the record has disappeared and the CD seems to be following in its footsteps, leaving fans little in the way of a visual badge. McDevitt notes, "Art and music go hand in hand," and fans crave the interpretation of the music available through gig posters.

Lee and McDevitt admit a love of designs from "all the old albums from the fifties and sixties, and Saul Bass, David Stone Martin, Jim Flora." But you can also see the heavy influence of pop culture from their childhoods. "We love Wacky Packs, those novelty stickers from the seventies that parody food and product labels, *Mad* magazine's amazing illustrations, Christmas-themed stop-motion animation, board games, *The Six Million Dollar Man, Planet of the Apes*, Bugs Bunny, Hanna-Barbera, *H.R. PufnStuf*, eighties soap operas, B-movies like *The Warriors, The Omega Man, Porky's, Losin It*—the list goes on and on." That doesn't touch on the passion for "music of all kinds—Merle Haggard to Pavement to Louvin Brothers to Serge Gainsbourg to Led Zeppelin." You can hear the yearning to get back to their stereos in the way they list each artist.

Through their funky eye-catching design, Methane are now inspiring a new generation of designers who did not experience the 1970s firsthand, much in the way the famous painter whose work adorns so many classic jazz albums, David Stone Martin, flavors their work.

TEN YEARS FROM NOW

From day one in Methane history, McDevitt says "We have always done posters for personal enjoyment first, and always hoped we would eventually be able to at least pay for the printing." Those days are long behind them. All they know is that business gets better each year and all the hard work seems to be paying off—aside from "blowing our spending money on music." Making their mark nationally and adding to the local flavor in Atlanta, they aren't sure about a poster movement currently taking place, as "it's hard to see a movement until it passes." But, McDevitt adds, "I sure hope we can say we were part of it when looking back ten years from now."

"Poster designers can take more chances and push the envelope."

THE VON BONDIES AUF DERMAR 09/19/04 THE EXIT-IN

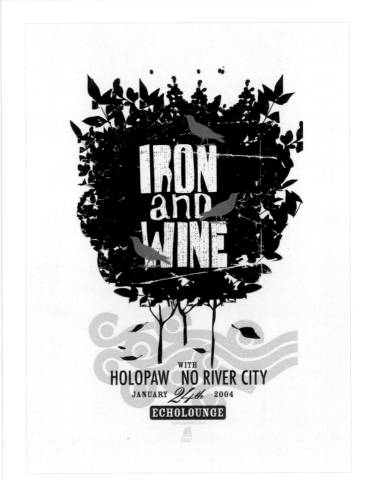

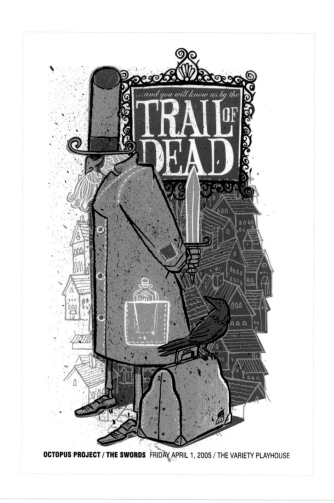

OK PRODUCTIONS PRESENTS
FRCNCH KICKS

THE ORANGES BAND / CALLA / THURS. 9:30 MARCH 24, 2005 / THE EARL
EAST ATLANTA VILLAGE, ATLANTA GA. / BADEARL.COM

TITLE: The Von Bondies
CLIENT: Exit Inn
SIZE: 19" x 25" (48.26 x 63.50 cm)
PRINTING PROCESS: Silkscreen
INKS: 3 color
Are posters what you primarily do for this client? Yes

PROCESS
COMPS PRESENTED: 1
REVISIONS: 0
APPROVAL: Promoter
INVOLVEMENT WITH FINAL PRINTING:
Prepared for final production

"Who doesn't like an image of giant mouth eating spoonfuls of chocolate?" asks McDevitt. He liked it enough to retain for a brief time, as "this poster was intended for another band, but I think it works better for the Von Bondies anyway." The scene isn't all fun and chocolate, though. "The mouth is influenced by a combination of Polish and Russian posters, very different from each other." The final piece was big success in all quarters. "The bass player's mom— at least she said she was—even purchased one for her daughter."

TITLE: New Pornographers
CLIENT: The Echolounge
SIZE: 19" x 25" (48.26 x 63.50 cm)
PRINTING PROCESS: Silkscreen
INKS: 2 color
Are posters what you primarily do for this client? Yes

PROCESS
COMPS PRESENTED: 1
REVISIONS: 0
APPROVAL: Promoter
INVOLVEMENT WITH FINAL PRINTING:
Prepared for final production

McDevitt confesses, "I'm influenced by the early German graphic designer Lucian Bernhard and his simple but powerful images with minimal use of color." With that in mind, he "was working on this late on a summer evening, using a simple image of a lantern, when I noticed the moths on my window attracted from my light, and literally a light went off in my head like a cartoon and everything clicked. How many times have I seen moths flying around lanterns at campsites in the past? I added the moths as type elements and added the sexy image of the girl, as Neko Case, who is in the band and is very sexy herself." This final addition "helped tie in another element of attraction to the design."

TITLE: Fiery Furnaces
CLIENT: Exit Inn
SIZE: 19" x 25" (48.26 x 63.50 cm)
PRINTING PROCESS: Silkscreen
INKS: 4 color
Are posters what you primarily do for this client? Yes

PROCESS
COMPS PRESENTED: 1
REVISIONS: 0
APPROVAL: Promoter
INVOLVEMENT WITH FINAL PRINTING:
Prepared for final production

Lee first took the easy road with "rather obvious furnace references with the smokestacks," but he was far from finished. Drinking in the band's music, he "wanted to give it a slightly psychedelic Beatles feel, since the Furnaces' music teeters on the bizarre and surreal." With a Sgt. Pepper–style figure of a man wearing a derby and playing the tuba, he certainly captured that feeling.

TITLE: Wilco
CLIENT: Sasquatch Music Festival
SIZE: 19" x 25" (48.26 x 63.50 cm)
PRINTING PROCESS: Silkscreen
INKS: 4 color
Are posters what you primarily do for this client? Yes

PROCESS
COMPS PRESENTED: 1
REVISIONS: 0
APPROVAL: Promoter
INVOLVEMENT WITH FINAL PRINTING:
Prepared for final production

For Wilco's appearance at a music festival in the Pacific Northwest, McDevitt "wanted to have fun, since it was for the Sasquatch Music Festival." So he seized the moment to use the obvious central image, because "who knows when I'll have another chance to draw Bigfoot?" He wanted to try something new, noting that "a lot of the posters for Wilco I had seen were a little dry. I was going for a 1930s Fleischer Studio look and wanted to keep the colors simple, much like early animation, not to mention that this approach it made it easier to print," which was helpful, as time was running short. "This version almost didn't happen—I almost fell back on a design that has yet to see daylight—as I had to redraw it a few times to get it right, but I was coming up on a deadline and finally made it work." After sweating out the process, McDevitt loves the final product.

TITLE: Iron and Wine
CLIENT: The Echolounge
SIZE: 19" x 25" (48.26 x 63.50 cm)
PRINTING PROCESS: Silkscreen
INKS: 3 color
Are posters what you primarily do for this client? Yes

PROCESS
COMPS PRESENTED: 1
REVISIONS: 0
APPROVAL: Promoter
INVOLVEMENT WITH FINAL PRINTING:
Prepared for final production

Setting the mood, Lee chose a quiet scene, "but it is also a flood, so the image has a melancholy undertone" that suits the music of the band. This piece also showcases Lee's enjoyment of the printing process. He "overprinted the brown on top of the two orange birds so that they only show up in relief." The feel of that application of ink adds to the mood as well.

TITLE: Mission of Burma
CLIENT: The Echolounge
SIZE: 12" x 19" (48.26 x 63.50 cm)
PRINTING PROCESS: Silkscreen
INKS: 2 color
Are posters what you primarily do for this client? Yes

PROCESS
COMPS PRESENTED: 1
REVISIONS: 0
APPROVAL: Promoter
INVOLVEMENT WITH FINAL PRINTING:
Prepared for final production

For McDevitt, this poster is "another influenced by the great Lucian Bernhard." With his use of bold shapes, McDevitt was "striving for an image that would attract the viewer's attention." He admits, "There is nothing ironic about this poster but, given the current state of the world's conflicts, maybe there should have been."

TITLE: *Trail of the Dead*
CLIENT: Variety Playhouse
SIZE: 17" x 24" (43.18 x 60.96 cm)
PRINTING PROCESS: Silkscreen
INKS: 4 color
Are posters what you primarily do for this client? Yes

PROCESS

COMPS PRESENTED: 1
REVISIONS: 0
APPROVAL: Promoter
INVOLVEMENT WITH FINAL PRINTING:
Prepared for final production

Promoting a performance by the group And You Will Know Us By the Trail of the Dead, Lee was hoping for "a play on Jack the Ripper and Edgar Allan Poe." He established a "turn-of-the-century gothic" setting, "a dark alley where the killer lies in wait." In order to keep the dark feeling, Lee printed a great deal of the white ink over the darker colors.

TITLE: The Wrens
CLIENT: The Echolounge
SIZE: 12" x 19" (30.48 x 48.26 cm)
PRINTING PROCESS: Silkscreen
INKS: 2 color
Are posters what you primarily do for this client? Yes

PROCESS

COMPS PRESENTED: 1
REVISIONS: 0
APPROVAL: Promoter
INVOLVEMENT WITH FINAL PRINTING:
Prepared for final production

McDevitt finds inspiration when he least expects it. "This idea came to me one day while eating lunch in a park," he says. We can probably guess what inspired him. The technique of flies forming the words in the image is similar to the approach he used on the New Pornographers poster, but with a drastically different effect that plays up the frenetic buzzing pop of the band. Because "sexy" was not needed for the Wrens, he stepped into the leading role. "The figure in the jacket is me sans the head," he admits.

TITLE: The Unicorns
CLIENT: The Echolounge
SIZE: 19" x 25" (48.26 x 63.50 cm)
PRINTING PROCESS: Silkscreen
INKS: 3 color
Are posters what you primarily do for this client? Yes

PROCESS

COMPS PRESENTED: 1
REVISIONS: 0
APPROVAL: Promoter
INVOLVEMENT WITH FINAL PRINTING:
Prepared for final production

To create this "sweet and twisted scene—like some of their music," Lee drew on his love of old cartoons and animation for the band the Unicorns. This is "an obvious reference to the band name played out in the context of a twisted sweet children's story of the lengths a little girl would go to befriend a monster." He did say "sweet and twisted."

TITLE: My Morning Jacket
CLIENT: Exit Inn
SIZE: 16" x 25" (40.64 x 63.50 cm)
PRINTING PROCESS: Silkscreen
INKS: 3 color
Are posters what you primarily do for this client? Yes

PROCESS

COMPS PRESENTED: 1
REVISIONS: 0
APPROVAL: Promoter
INVOLVEMENT WITH FINAL PRINTING:
Prepared for final production

Lee says, "I grew up in Ohio, where there were all these barns with Mail Pouch chewing tobacco ads painted on them. The band had recorded a lot of their music in a grain silo on a farm, so I thought, why not?" Not content to leave the image at that stage, as the band's music is passionate, he decided to engulf the barn in flames. "The flames you see coming out of the barn are actually a scan of a woman's hairdo contrasted and turned upside down." To finish the scene, he "chose the script font at the bottom to resemble the grass and wheat you might find in a rural field."

TITLE: Lou Barlow
CLIENT: The Echolounge
SIZE: 19" x 25" (48.26 x 63.50 cm)
PRINTING PROCESS: Silkscreen
INKS: 2 color
Are posters what you primarily do for this client? Yes

PROCESS

COMPS PRESENTED: 1
REVISIONS: 0
APPROVAL: Promoter
INVOLVEMENT WITH FINAL PRINTING:
Prepared for final production

McDevitt says, "Lou Barlow's record is sort of quiet and folksy, and I wanted to reflect that feeling with the color of the paper and a loose feel with the ink drawing and hand-cut type. This was a popular style on jazz records back in the 1950s. I love doing this style, plus it was perfect design to feature my oldest son, Miles, and his trusty Red Rider BB gun scanning the wilderness for Black Bart and his band of nasties. Not very rock-and-roll, but there you have it."

TITLE: French Kicks
CLIENT: The Earl
SIZE: 19" x 25" (48.26 x 63.50 cm)
PRINTING PROCESS: Silkscreen
INKS: 3 color
Are posters what you primarily do for this client? Yes

PROCESS

COMPS PRESENTED: 1
REVISIONS: 0
APPROVAL: The Earl
INVOLVEMENT WITH FINAL PRINTING:
Prepared for final production

For the "sexy and bouncy music of the French Kicks," designer Lee delved into his reference material for movie posters from the 1960s. Capturing that appeal and even lifting a 1960s color palette, he then added what he refers to as "shiny happy boobies" and followed them up with a "dash of Monty Python." Result: our dancing girl.

★ MODERN DOG ★

SEATTLE, WASHINGTON, USA

CLASS VALEDICTORIAN

A lot has been written about the early days of Modern Dog and their role as the class clown at the design table since their founding in the 1980s by partners Robynne Raye and Mike Strassburger, so this profile narrows the focus to why they stand before you as a New Master while others of their generation are bypassed. Their work has been exhibited worldwide in prestigious museums and collections, and their main representation in those lofty environs is the simple and direct poster.

The firm started to make waves in the early days through funny and sometimes shocking designs for theaters and festivals. The posters proved so popular (and plentiful) that they were repurposed as playing cards and sheets of stamps, neatly tying in the firm's other claim to fame: innovative packaging. In the years to follow, Modern Dog felt the decline of the poster as projects became less and less frequent, but they never fully disappeared. More recently, however, posters have really picked up steam, and Modern Dog has reemerged as a leader and innovator of this form. The amusing part is that they have done so mostly by beating the young bucks at their own game: the gig or rock concert poster.

The studio had continued doing posters for speaking engagements and local events, but now they were reinvigorated with work for today's rock stars. They were poised for another big splash in the poster scene.

WHY NOT GET THE ORIGINAL?

Very quickly, venues saw that they need not hire a firm to give them that Modern Dog vibe when they could actually get the big dogs themselves. Keeping their business small over the years, the studio stands strong at four (not including various mutts and interns) and remains nimble, as everyone gets their hands dirty every day. Every piece has the personal, home-grown feel that is a hallmark of their work. The studio loves these projects for the "creative release" of "jamming out a gig poster with few artistic limitations. And to complete a poster in just a few hours feels really rewarding." It is this freedom they thirst for, but they add, "We still do lots of research and head-scratching, just like any other studio project."

Raye says of her poster process, "It feels more organic than for other projects and free of typical design restrictions. Personally, I turn on the waxer and get out the X-Acto blade. Then I just start by pulling out ideas that appeal to me on an emotional level. It's different for each person in the office, but one thing we all do consistently is try to relate to the subject in some way."

MUTUAL APPRECIATION SOCIETY

In the same way that they collect people's flotsam and jetsam for inspiration, they are true design lovers. Raye states, "There are so many past masters we admire. In college, Mike and I were really inspired by the great Polish poster artists of the 1950s, 1960s, and 1970s. The greats like Henryk Tomaszewski and Roman Cieslewicz remain inspirational to this day. We like the raw and highly illustrative problem solving done during that movement of poster history. Many years ago, a friend gave me a limited-edition book called *Corita*. The oversized book has several beautiful reproductions from Sister Corita Kent, a Catholic nun whose bright silkscreened posters were the all the rage during the 1960s. She designed the first Love stamp, as well as greeting cards, book jackets, and record covers. Her stuff still blows me away. Also, who doesn't love Saul Bass? The list could go on and on, so I better stop now." They also enjoy the current crop of poster mavens such as Methane (featured on page 124), Jewboy (featured on page 92), Sagmeister, Niklaus Troxler, Patent Pending (featured on page 140), as well as "the duo called Seripop [featured on page 154], because they continue to deliver the unexpected."

Modern Dog, as a firm, has remained the same size, but they haven't just gotten older—they have grown up a little (sometimes begrudgingly). As they matured a tad, they still remain well known for their "eighth-grade sense of humor" but also for so much technical know-how that they served as consultants on Adobe's software. This mix of keeping in touch with their raw emotional thinking about visual problem solving, pouring a little of themselves into each piece, and a savvy mature marketing sense and aesthetic makes them a hit with clients and allows them to leave their imitators in the dust.

"We still do lots of research and head-scratching, just like any other studio project."

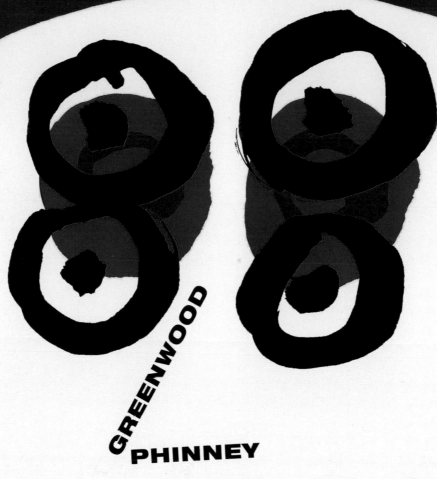

GREENWOOD
PHINNEY

7TH ANNUAL
ARTWALK
FRI MAY 10 6-9:30PM
SAT MAY 11 12-5PM

GREENWOOD AVENUE
FROM 65TH TO 87TH STREET
FOR MORE INFO: 206 684-4096

SPONSORED BY
GREENWOOD/PHINNEY CHAMBER OF COMMERCE
AND THE GREENWOOD ARTS COUNCIL

TITLE: Blondie
CLIENT: House of Blues
SIZE: 13" x 22" (33.02 x 55.88 cm)
PRINTING PROCESS: Screen print
INKS: 2 PMS
Are posters what you primarily do for this client? Yes

PROCESS
COMPS PRESENTED: 1
REVISIONS: 0
APPROVAL: Venue management
INVOLVEMENT WITH FINAL PRINTING: None

Like any red-blooded boy in the late 1970s/early 1980s, designer Mike Strassburger experienced Blondie as the perfect blend of overt sex appeal and skinny-tie rock and roll. Much later, working on Blondie's reunion tour poster, he had a chance to bring back some of that old magic. He says, "I used a current photo of Deborah Harry and manipulated the contrast until she looked more like the Deborah Harry I grew up with." He then tapped into his feminine side, as "all the typography is my version of girly."

TITLE: Naked Snowman
CLIENT: Advertising Federation of Fort Wayne
SIZE: 18" x 26" (45.72 x 66.04 cm)
PRINTING PROCESS: Offset
INKS: 4-color process plus 2 fluorescents
Are posters what you primarily do for this client? Yes

PROCESS
COMPS PRESENTED: 1
REVISIONS: 0
APPROVAL: None required
INVOLVEMENT WITH FINAL PRINTING: None

As unusual as the inspiration for this poster was, the fate of its production practically drowns in irony. Strassburger recounts his journey to Fort Wayne from one frigid day onward. "It was the one and only snowy day in Seattle, so I decided to highlight the cold day with a naked man with his pants down around his ankles next to a phone booth. I didn't know how conservative the audience would be, so I took it into Photoshop and blurred the hell out of it. The final effect with the crisp type and dirty marks is like you're looking through a printed window. When I arrived in Fort Wayne, much to my surprise the printer didn't have the software to open my file. I didn't find out until the day of my lecture. Not only was the poster not printed, but in the ad that they ran to advertise the show, the title of the show, including my name, got printed as a black box. So effectively, there was no advertising for this show at the Advertising Federation of Fort Wayne. They printed the poster later—after my lecture—and used it as a giveaway incentive."

TITLE: Furthur Your Creativity
CLIENT: Adobe Systems, Inc.
SIZE: 19" x 27" (48.26 x 68.58 cm)
PRINTING PROCESS: Offset
INKS: 4-color process plus 1 fluorescent
Are posters what you primarily do for this client? No

PROCESS
COMPS PRESENTED: 3
REVISIONS: 0
APPROVAL: Product marketing manager of InDesign
INVOLVEMENT WITH FINAL PRINTING: Prepared for production and press inspected

Strassburger was like a kid in a candy shop test-driving his client's new software. He found himself adding detail after detail to this poster, including the playfulness of the misspelling, which is "an intentional play off Ken Kesey's Magic Bus. This poster was the first thing I created in InDesign, and I had the feeling of being on drugs with all the freedom I had using the program. There's a giant 'QX' balanced on a tip of a triangle, representing the fall of Quark. Also, in the clouds it says 'Quark Sux,' and although it's almost impossible to see, we still couldn't tell the client before it went to press even though every designer knows it's the truth."

TITLE: ArtWalk 2005
CLIENT: Greenwood Arts Council
SIZE: 17.5" x 25" (44.45 x 63.50 cm)
PRINTING PROCESS: Screen print
INKS: 2 PMS plus black
Are posters what you primarily do for this client? Yes

PROCESS
COMPS PRESENTED: 1
REVISIONS: 0
APPROVAL: Arts Council committee
INVOLVEMENT WITH FINAL PRINTING: None

For some projects, the pressure to deliver an amazing piece doesn't always come from the client side. Designer Raye says, "I had a lot of self-imposed pressure placed on me due to the fact that this was the ArtWalk's tenth anniversary." Even so, she was able to experiment and allow the poster to take shape organically. "My favorite part—the butterfly wings turned kitty arms turned scarf—was a complete accident. I had cut them out for another project, and when I went to move them one of the wings floated down and landed on top of the cat art. I hesitated for a second, and that's my story."

TITLE: Air
CLIENT: House of Blues
SIZE: 14.5" x 22.5" (36.83 x 57.15 cm)
PRINTING PROCESS: Screen print
INKS: 1 PMS plus black
Are posters what you primarily do for this client? Yes

PROCESS
COMPS PRESENTED: 1
REVISIONS: 0
APPROVAL: Venue management
INVOLVEMENT WITH FINAL PRINTING: None

Raye knows that the life you live outside of the studio can have a bigger impact than the time you spend inside it. Such was the case for the Air poster. She says, "The weather was turning into BBQ season, I was grilling some chicken, and this idea popped into my head. I had several bee and wasp nests in my backyard and was stung a few times. It was the spring from hell. I went to sleep that night knowing what I was going to do, and when I woke up this was the poster."

TITLE: *Hedwig and the Angry Inch*
CLIENT: Crocodile
SIZE: 13" x 22" (33.02 x 55.88 cm)
PRINTING PROCESS: Screen print
INKS: 2 PMS plus black
Are posters what you primarily do for this client? Yes

PROCESS
COMPS PRESENTED: 1
REVISIONS: 0
APPROVAL: Venue management
INVOLVEMENT WITH FINAL PRINTING: None

In creating a poster for a local concert venue's New Year's Eve celebration featuring music from *Hedwig and the Angry Inch*, designer Vittorio Costarella decided to focus on the central figure in the play being showcased. "The main character is a drag queen, and I thought this would make an interesting image for the poster." When illustrating the portrait, he realized he "also wanted the face to be a question mark." Not quite finished yet, he added the third color that ties the image together—blue—only moments before he sent the poster to the printer.

TITLE: Damien Jurado
CLIENT: Crocodile
SIZE: 18" x 26" (45.72 x 66.04 cm)
PRINTING PROCESS: Screen print
INKS: 2 PMS
Are posters what you primarily do for this client? Yes

PROCESS

COMPS PRESENTED: 1
REVISIONS: 0
APPROVAL: Venue management
INVOLVEMENT WITH FINAL PRINTING: None

Costarella feels a connection with this artist's music. "Damien's music is from the heart. He writes about ordinary people and ordinary places." Costarella wanted to relate the image to his own "ordinary" days. "I work part time as a carpenter, and this is one of the things—getting a damn splinter stuck—that drives me nuts. It happens to me almost every day."

TITLE: The Vines
CLIENT: House of Blues
SIZE: 14" x 22" (35.56 x 55.88 cm)
PRINTING PROCESS: Screen print
INKS: 2 PMS
Are posters what you primarily do for this client? Yes

PROCESS

COMPS PRESENTED: 12 or so
REVISIONS: 0
APPROVAL: Venue management
INVOLVEMENT WITH FINAL PRINTING: None

Sometimes the artist you are featuring is not as close to your heart as others. This may require a little further exploration, says Costarella. "I don't think the Vines are incredibly original, but there's no doubt their music has a lot of nervous energy running through it. In the drawing, I tried to capture the many layers of their sound in a way that can best be described as textural. In some ways, I thought the vine and flower image was a cliché, but it's very natural to take them in this direction—or in one of the other twelve," he jokes. Because they are from Australia, he figured, "You've got to have a sheep or two in there as well."

TITLE: Dizzee Rascal
CLIENT: House of Blues
SIZE: 18" x 24" (45.72 x 60.96 cm)
PRINTING PROCESS: Screen print
INKS: 3 PMS and black
Are posters what you primarily do for this client? Yes

PROCESS

COMPS PRESENTED: 1
REVISIONS: 0
APPROVAL: Venue management
INVOLVEMENT WITH FINAL PRINTING: None

Designer Junichi Tsuneoka could not wait to work on the Dizzee Rascal poster. "Dizzee is from the U.K. garage rap scene, which is way outside of the mainstream U.S. rap world, and he's really different in that his musical influences are all over the place. He's also very young and had a life of small time crime before discovering his musical talent. So I tried to mix comics and the street cred—graffiti—to capture this raw energy. When he was in school, a teacher nicknamed him Rascal, so I made sure the poster had lot of chaotic line work, as if he was sitting in class scribbling away."

TITLE: Bettie Serveert
CLIENT: Crocodile
SIZE: 18" x 24" (45.72 x 60.96 cm)
PRINTING PROCESS: Screen print
INKS: 2 PMS
Are posters what you primarily do for this client? Yes

PROCESS

COMPS PRESENTED: 1
REVISIONS: 0
APPROVAL: Venue management
INVOLVEMENT WITH FINAL PRINTING: None

Tsuneoka is not unlike many young boys at a creative developmental stage. The outlets for expression that reach the masses inspire you the earliest and inform all of your work to follow. He says, "All my life I've loved comics, and I started drawing them at an early age, so now I get to incorporate two things I love: music and comics." He continues to challenge himself in trying new illustration styles. This poster was the debut of this particular method of drawing.

TITLE: Guster
CLIENT: House of Blues
SIZE: 13" x 22" (33.02 x 55.88 cm)
PRINTING PROCESS: Screen print
INKS: 1 PMS plus black
Are posters what you primarily do for this client? Yes

PROCESS

COMPS PRESENTED: 1
REVISIONS: 17
APPROVAL: Venue management
INVOLVEMENT WITH FINAL PRINTING: None

Sometimes a band's music takes on a personality almost like that of a living and breathing individual. For Tsuneoka, "Guster's music is like Bud Light and reminds me of school geeks. So Guster is a dork who carries pens in his pocket, but one leaked all over the place. The nametag is a warning to other people" and a rallying cry for fans.

TITLE: ArtWalk 2002
CLIENT: Greenwood Arts Council
SIZE: 18" x 25" (45.72 x 63.50 cm)
PRINTING PROCESS: Screen print
INKS: 2 PMS plus black
Are posters what you primarily do for this client? Yes

PROCESS

COMPS PRESENTED: 1
REVISIONS: 0
APPROVAL: Arts Council committee
INVOLVEMENT WITH FINAL PRINTING: None

Great event posters are often shaped by the personal experiences of the designers when they attended previously. Raye "was thinking of how my eyes feel after looking at a lot of art. I can only take so much until I have to sit down" when she came up with this image for the annual ArtWalk. The solution perfectly summarizes the amazing and plentiful display of work each year.

★ PATENT PENDING DESIGN ★

SEATTLE, WASHINGTON, USA

TWO STYLES, ONE MIND

The two men that make up the Patent Pending Design team are oddly similar yet very different—two great tastes that taste great together. The links are obvious in a physical sense, as they both clocked time working as art directors for Sub Pop Records, where Jeff Kleinsmith remains working on music packaging by day. An odd link in the current poster stratosphere can be formed through Kleinsmith's early days at the *Rocket* newspaper, where he learned a great deal working with the talented and challenging Art Chantry.

Kleinsmith now tries to bestow whatever knowledge he has gained on his current coworker at Sub Pop, Dustin Summers (who is also half of The Heads of State for poster work, featured on page 210.) The traveling part of the Patent Pending pair is Jesse LeDoux, who currently resides on the East Coast. Somehow it seems fitting the two would be at opposite ends of the country but of the same mindset at this stage in their partnership.

Kleinsmith's work, especially in the early stages, betrays the Chantry influence in his use of found imagery, but it also draws from the strongest elements of Chantry's work. Kleinsmith has incorporated into his own style amazing typography that is fully integrated into the poster concept and unapologetically used as a strong central image. LeDoux's work coincides with Jeff's at this point in the typography and the use of a central image. Most of LeDoux's work is rendered by hand and has a whimsical feel. With years of working closely together, these sensibilities began to bleed into one another, with Kleinsmith drawing more—he had always done so, but not as obviously—and in particular, drawing his typography. LeDoux, for his part, began to mess around with texture as well as roughen and bend his work in ways that Jeff had long since mastered. Years ago, the team experimented by printing their posters on top of one another, or trading images for a series. Now you will see a poster from the studio that the trained eye would swear is a collaboration of this type, but has been produced by only one hand.

Experimentation is a major part of their creative process. LeDoux notes, "Patent Pending does small runs, which means that the worst thing that can happen if an experiment goes wrong is that we have seventy-five stinkers lying around." Not having to worry about an economic safety net allows them to challenge and inspire the viewer with offbeat imagery and bold palettes. But the true strength of their work is a result of their love of the process. They labor mentally and physically over each work. Kleinsmith says excitedly, "It's equally the most challenging and rewarding thing I do. I don't get up for any other design problem like I do a poster, and I'm never as bummed out by the failure of a poor design as I am when I make a bad poster."

ELDER STATESMEN

Although their place is secure among current rock poster designs, it still is an odd perch. Kleinsmith mentions that he has been "making rock posters consistently for fifteen years, whereas the bulk of the poster makers these days started less than five years ago. When I started, there were really only a few doing this, as compared to what's going on now. So, while I consider myself part of the movement, I feel like more of an elder statesman." LeDoux adds, "We try to maintain a presence in the poster community" and have participated in lectures and taught classes to budding poster artists." Maybe helping out isn't a recipe for success, though. LeDoux laments, "The ever-increasing difficulty to get hired to do a good show is a definite downer. With more people making posters, it can become more challenging to be able to do the show of a band you're really into." However, he adds, "The surge in poster designers has brought more attention to poster design, thus raising the visibility of Patent Pending's stuff. It is even changing how folks view the bottom line, as Kleinsmith considers this purchasing boom a byproduct of a digital download culture, in which fans still want "something physical to associate with the bands."

It's no surprise that Kleinsmith and LeDoux list each other as influences. LeDoux says, "The people whose work I'm most inspired by are Ben Shahn, one of the most talented yet underrated masters, Stephan Britt, Tadanori Yokoo, Jeff Kleinsmith, Dan Clowes, and Mary Blair, though that's really just the tip of the iceberg. Influences can be found all around you. Everything can be inspiring. I've come up with some of my best ideas while doing the dishes or sitting on the bus. If you keep your eyes and mind open, good ideas and flakes of inspiration will naturally just float on in." Kleinsmith notes, "My love of music is a huge influence in general. For direct influences, I'd have to say, in chronological order, Ed Thrasher, Hipgnosis, Raymond Pettibon, Winston Smith, Jasper Johns, Kurt Schwitters, Andy Warhol, Art Chantry, and Saul Bass. My partner Jesse has really influenced me to draw more typography. Just to name a few." You can start adding the name Patent Pending to most young designers' list of strong influences.

"I don't get up for any other design problem like I do a poster."

THU APRIL 10 GRACELAND

ALL AGES

THE SOUNDTRACK OF OUR LIVES

PLUS SPECIAL GUESTS

Design by Jeff Kleinsmith (Patent Pending). Printed by Patent Pending Press.

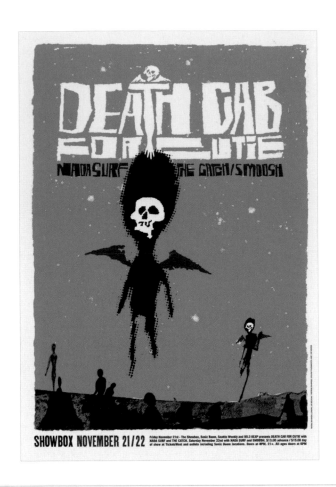

WITH CALEXICO + WHY? JULY 2 SHOWBOX

$13.00 ADV AT TICKETSWEST AND ALL OUTLETS. $15.00 DAY OF SHOW AND AT THE DOOR. DOORS AT 9PM. ALL AGES.

TITLE: Soundtrack of Our Lives
CLIENT: House of Blues
SIZE: 13" x 24" (33.02 x 60.96 cm)
PRINTING PROCESS: Screen print
INKS: 4 spot color
Are posters what you primarily do for this client? Yes

PROCESS
COMPS PRESENTED: 1
REVISIONS: 0
APPROVAL: Production company
INVOLVEMENT WITH FINAL PRINTING:
Patent Pending Press

For a Swedish psychedelic-tinged rock band, Kleinsmith gave himself specific parameters to work within. He says, "The starting point was two some-what disparate images that I challenged myself to put together. I knew I wanted a kind of psychedelic feel for the poster, but not in the traditional sense—more in a Monty Python kind of way." The playful and evocative image somehow perfectly suits a band with little in the way of horns.

TITLE: Death Cab for Cutie
CLIENT: Showbox Theatre
SIZE: 16" x 24" (40.64 x 60.96 cm)
PRINTING PROCESS: Screen print
INKS: 4 spot color
Are posters what you primarily do for this client? Yes

PROCESS
COMPS PRESENTED: 1
REVISIONS: 0
APPROVAL: Venue management
INVOLVEMENT WITH FINAL PRINTING:
Patent Pending Press

This poster was the fourth the firm did for the band, so Kleinsmith wanted to work on the base of the first three. He explains, "The first Death Cab poster Patent Pending did was by Jesse in late 1999. It depicted a fish girl floating happily and eerily under water. I went on to design three more, and I wanted to explore a number of styles but also move the sub-ject matter from deep under water to deep in space. Number two is a woman above water. Number three is a moving from Earth to outer space, and this, the fourth, is in space. Each one is eerie and dark—totally unlike the band, which is also intentional."

TITLE: Melvins
CLIENT: Melvins
SIZE: 22" x 34" (55.88 x 86.36 cm)
PRINTING PROCESS: Screen print
INKS: 5 spot color
Are posters what you primarily do for this client? Yes

PROCESS
COMPS PRESENTED: 1
REVISIONS: 0
APPROVAL: Band
INVOLVEMENT WITH FINAL PRINTING: None

Participating in a tour series featuring many other poster artists for the same band, Kleinsmith felt he had to "step it up a bit. I also wanted to make a 'rock' poster. That was my starting point. Now, I personally think a poster is a poster and it's either good or it isn't, and the idea of it being designated 'rock' or not is dumb, but I understood the challenge. Anyway, I found this image of a circle of dead and dying soldiers and the first thing I thought of was a penis—a giant death-dealing pink phallus from another planet. It seemed to satisfy my challenge and fit the Melvins at the same time."

TITLE: Bright Eyes
CLIENT: Showbox Theatre
SIZE: 12" x 24" (30.48 x 60.96 cm)
PRINTING PROCESS: Screen print
INKS: 4 spot color
Are posters what you primarily do for this client? Yes

PROCESS
COMPS PRESENTED: 1
REVISIONS: 0
APPROVAL: Venue management
INVOLVEMENT WITH FINAL PRINTING:
Patent Pending Press

Creating a poster for a musician well known for his earnest and emotional music detailing the darker corners of consciousness, Kleinsmith strove "to see if I could make an evil yet beautiful poster. I wanted to evoke the feeling of something painful and deep coming out from within." He did so with the hand-drawn type for the band's name.

TITLE: Interpol
CLIENT: Showbox Theatre
SIZE: 16" x 24" (40.64 x 60.96 cm)
PRINTING PROCESS: Screen print
INKS: 4 spot color
Are posters what you primarily do for this client? Yes

PROCESS
COMPS PRESENTED: 1
REVISIONS: 0
APPROVAL: Venue management
INVOLVEMENT WITH FINAL PRINTING:
Patent Pending Press

Being tapped into the rock poster scene, you can occasionally be inspired to avoid the other designs in the marketplace for a given recording artist. Such was the case for Kleinsmith. "Interpol has had many posters made for them, and they all tended to be red, white, and black. I have seen very few with anything other than that color scheme on their albums—but I knew that going into this I wasn't going to go that way. I made myself a personal challenge to create an Interpol poster that didn't use that color scheme but yet would evoke the dry, desperate, otherworldli-ness of their music."

TITLE: Clinic
CLIENT: Showbox Theatre
SIZE: 16" x 24" (40.64 x 60.96 cm)
PRINTING PROCESS: Screen print
INKS: 3 color
Are posters what you primarily do for this client? Yes

PROCESS
COMPS PRESENTED: 1
REVISIONS: 0
APPROVAL: Venue management
INVOLVEMENT WITH FINAL PRINTING:
Patent Pending Press

Even when you have an idea of where you want to go, getting there isn't always easy, explains LeDoux. "This poster was an uphill personal battle every stretch of the way. First off, I did the ground cracking open to spell *Clinic*, which I was quite happy with. From there, I tried a million different things floating out of the cracks, and nothing was floating my boat. Finally, I made the cloudy outline of the creature, and it felt like I was back on the right track. Then, it took me a million different tries to come up with something to fill up the cloudy shape. It wasn't until I was halfway done with the million-and-first try that I drew a creepy hand that I really liked, and instantly decided that it should just be *all* creepy hands. From there, the rest fell into place with relative ease."

TITLE: Franz Ferdinand
CLIENT: Showbox Theatre
SIZE: 18" x 24" (45.72 x 60.96 cm)
PRINTING PROCESS: Screen print
INKS: 3 color
Are posters what you primarily do for this client? Yes

PROCESS
COMPS PRESENTED: 1
REVISIONS: 0
APPROVAL: Venue management
INVOLVEMENT WITH FINAL PRINTING:
Patent Pending Press

The existing artwork for an artist can heavily inform a designer's direction for a concert poster, even if it sends him in the opposite direction, notes LeDoux. "The covers on Franz Ferdinand's album and singles are exact, angular, and clean. While this fits their music well, I wanted to approach the art for this poster in the complete opposite direction. The result is the messy ink drawing of a faceless yet good-looking lad—you know he's attractive because he's wearing a collared shirt, see?—who is most likely on his way to the Franz Ferdinand show right around the corner."

TITLE: Up Records Tenth Anniversary
CLIENT: Up Records
SIZE: 18" x 24" (45.72 x 60.96 cm)
PRINTING PROCESS: Offset and screen print
INKS: 4-color process, 4 spot color
Are posters what you primarily do for this client? No

PROCESS
COMPS PRESENTED: 1
REVISIONS: 0
APPROVAL: Record label owner
INVOLVEMENT WITH FINAL PRINTING: None

When LeDoux heard the breakdown for the schedule of a new poster he was working on, he knew just what to do. "This poster is actually a series of five posters to celebrate the tenth anniversary of the fabulous Up Records. To celebrate, they had shows five consecutive nights in Seattle featuring nearly all the bands who have released records on the label over the decade. I was asked to do a poster for each of the shows to commemorate the event and one to promote the series of shows. The result was a series of four screen-printed posters for each of the individual shows (I combined the two shows where Built to Spill headlined onto one poster) and one offset poster to hang around town to promote the festivities. It's not until you put the four individual posters together that you can see that they make the shape of Up's logo."

TITLE: Electric Six
CLIENT: The Crocodile Cafe
SIZE: 18" x 24" (45.72 x 60.96 cm)
PRINTING PROCESS: Screen print
INKS: 4 spot color
Are posters what you primarily do for this client? Yes

PROCESS
COMPS PRESENTED: 2
REVISIONS: 0
APPROVAL: Venue management
INVOLVEMENT WITH FINAL PRINTING:
Patent Pending Press

The internal struggle can be tougher than dealing with the client. LeDoux recalls that he really wanted to take inspiration from the band's name and their huge hit in the U.K., "Danger. High Voltage!" He started out with a robot, but it just was not working. However, he liked the type he had created for the robot and then set out to create a new image around the typographical solution. Finally, he added the over-the-top lightning bolts that tied the piece together.

TITLE: Mum
CLIENT: Showbox Theatre
SIZE: 18" x 24" (45.72 x 60.96 cm)
PRINTING PROCESS: Screen print
INKS: 4 spot color
Are posters what you primarily do for this client? Yes

PROCESS
COMPS PRESENTED: 1
REVISIONS: 0
APPROVAL: Venue management
INVOLVEMENT WITH FINAL PRINTING:
Patent Pending Press

When a band's music is more evocative than lyrical, the designer faces a peculiar challenge. How do you make the poster feel like an abstract artist sounds? For Kleinsmith, this poster's "imagery evokes moodiness like the band's music. I liked the idea of a godlike hand holding the mind's eye" and the cool factor it brings as a central figure.

TITLE: Mogwai
CLIENT: Showbox Theatre
SIZE: 16" x 24" (40.64 x 60.96 cm)
PRINTING PROCESS: Screen print
INKS: 2 spot color
Are posters what you primarily do for this client? Yes

PROCESS
COMPS PRESENTED: 1
REVISIONS: 0
APPROVAL: Venue management
INVOLVEMENT WITH FINAL PRINTING:
Patent Pending Press

LeDoux strove for a simple way to solve a complex problem. "Mogwai's music is hard to pin down. Sometimes it's really noisy. Sometimes it's really quiet. Like the lines that make up the poster, the music goes in every which direction. In addition, they're an instrumental band. The lack of words in a song forces the listener to create a story from just the notes played. I've attempted to illustrate this by not having an actual image on the poster. The lines become the image, much like Mogwai's notes become their words."

TITLE: Destroyer
CLIENT: The Crocodile Cafe
SIZE: 24" x 18" (60.96 x 45.72 cm)
PRINTING PROCESS: Screen print
INKS: 3 spot color
Are posters what you primarily do for this client? Yes

PROCESS
COMPS PRESENTED: 1
REVISIONS: 0
APPROVAL: Venue management
INVOLVEMENT WITH FINAL PRINTING: n/a

Knowing your way around the printing process can allow you to offer a unique look. LeDoux explains that "typically, the order the colors get printed goes from the lightest going down first and the darkest printing last. This poster does the opposite. I wasn't trying to be different—I just thought it looked better that way. Due to the layers of information buried beneath each other, it's a bit of a slow unloader [a term coined by photographer Lee Friedlander for an image that makes more sense to viewers the longer they look at it]. I'd consider Destroyer's music a slow unloader as well. With every album they've released, I listen a times before I realize how great it is."

★ SANDSTROM DESIGN ★

PORTLAND, OREGON, USA

MY FIRST REAL BREAK

You may know the name Sandstrom Design, but it's not likely you equate it with posters. They have had numerous successes and high-profile projects in the design field. In particular, their beverage packaging has won accolades around the globe. Their portfolio is full of pieces that have earned features in publications and collections worldwide. So what are they doing here surrounded by twenty-nine other "New Masters"?

Before forming his own firm with two partners, "coincidentally named Sandstrom Design," Steve Sandstrom had a rich history of poster work from his early days in-house at Nike as well as with earlier partnerships. "I actually got my first real break in the profession designing posters and promo materials for a progressive rock radio station in Portland. They were great to work with, and I had a significant influence over the entire twelve- to twenty-five-year-old male population in town," recalls Sandstrom. That was the beginning of a love affair with the poster and its gigantic brother, the billboard. Using dimensional objects and extensions, unusual shapes, and electronic and neon components, Sandstrom was an innovator in outdoor marketing. Wistful over having "a scale you rarely get to design to," he found himself back at square one trying to excite a slightly older audience with one tool—the poster. This time, however, he surrounded himself with a powerhouse creative staff to help.

STEPPENWOLF

Despite residing in "not the friendliest poster town," Sandstrom Design has always done posters and has partnered with their city's finest theater group, Portland Center Stage. They also use posters as point-of-purchase support for their product design—of which many wonderful examples exist, although their work for Tazo Tea may be the most familiar—and these are often awe-inspiring for a highly commercial genre. However, it was work for a prominent theater in another town that made the world realize how incredibly good they are at the poster game and made their inclusion inevitable. Sandstrom relishes "single-image power, or typographic power" in a poster. His work for Steppenwolf Theater in Chicago is rewarding on both fronts. It gives the productions soul—and also provides collectible posters that are still the talk of the city.

RARE DESIGN

As for poster assignments, Sandstrom laments, "They still don't come around as often as I'd like, so it's a refreshing assignment to get to do. I like to distill things into one powerful message or visual, with some scale to give it presence or attitude." In attempting to capture that presence or attitude, he swears, "Everything is an influence!" He does have a passion for other poster designers and enjoys "so many. Russian. Dutch. Toulouse-Lautrec. WPA. Saul Bass. Paul Rand. *All* forms of signage. Hatch Show Print. Art Chantry. I consider James Victore a modern master of poster design." It is interesting but unsurprising to hear some of the traditional masters on his list. A fascinating aspect of Sandstrom's poster work is the timelessness of the execution.

For the Steppenwolf Theater work, budget constraints forced Sandstrom to do everything with what he had on hand—no photography or digital assistance, which they could not bill for, from the youngsters in the office. But I know he is being modest, and the timeless nature of the posters is much more likely to be the result of his classic design sense.

It is a rare designer who can master both the scarce inch-to-inch ratio of a tiny consumer product as well as a gigantic display of artistic messaging. Sandstrom Design is the rare firm that can do it all and smile while they polish off the job and shake your hand. Classic.

"I like to distill things into one powerful message or visual."

The Time of Your Life

STEPPENWOLF
MAINSTAGE | THEATRE
CHICAGO
SEPT 12 – NOV 3, 2002
(312) 335-1650
WWW.STEPPENWOLF.ORG

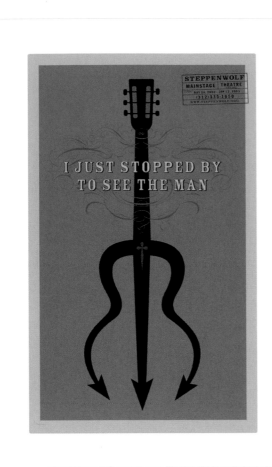

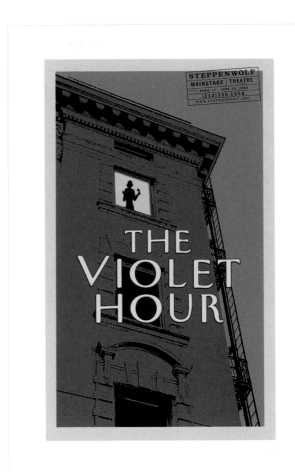

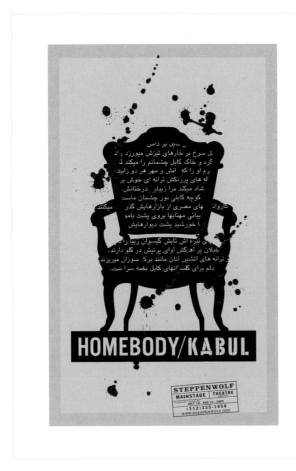

TITLE: *The Time of Your Life*
CLIENT: Steppenwolf Theatre
SIZE: 24" x 36" (60.96 x 91.44 cm)
PRINTING PROCESS: Offset
INKS: 5 color
Are posters what you primarily do for this client? Yes

PROCESS

COMPS PRESENTED: 1
REVISIONS: 1
APPROVAL: Agency creative director, marketing director, artistic director, executive director, and the play's director
INVOLVEMENT WITH FINAL PRINTING:
Prepared for production

This play is set in a Depression-era waterfront saloon where "the melancholy lives of a hard-luck bar's patrons are played out—as love and hope still seem possible through a slightly drunken haze." Sandstrom depicts that little bit of optimism through a filter of reality. "The upside-down heart is the last drip of alcohol, a teardrop, and a symbol for troubled romance," he laments.

TITLE: *I Just Stopped By to See the Man*
CLIENT: Steppenwolf Theatre
SIZE: 24" x 36" (60.96 x 91.44 cm)
PRINTING PROCESS: Offset
INKS: 5 color
Are posters what you primarily do for this client? Yes

PROCESS

COMPS PRESENTED: 1
REVISIONS: 1
APPROVAL: Agency creative director, marketing director, artistic director, executive director, and the play's director
INVOLVEMENT WITH FINAL PRINTING:
Prepared for production

Sandstrom tried to channel "Jesse, a blues legend presumed dead for twenty years, who hides out in the Mississippi Delta, having given up the Devil's music for gospel hymns," in *I Just Stopped By to See The Man*. "A British rock star finds Jesse by piecing together clues from old lyrics and tries to lure him back to performing the blues, putting the old man's soul in jeopardy," explains Sandstrom. "The pitchfork in the poster is in the shape of Jesse's retired Martin guitar and a symbol of the Devil's music."

TITLE: *The Violet Hour*
CLIENT: Steppenwolf Theatre
SIZE: 24" x 36" (60.96 x 91.44 cm)
PRINTING PROCESS: Offset
INKS: 5 color
Are posters what you primarily do for this client? Yes

PROCESS

COMPS PRESENTED: 1
REVISIONS: 1
APPROVAL: Agency creative director, marketing director, artistic director, executive director, and the play's director
INVOLVEMENT WITH FINAL PRINTING:
Prepared for production

Set in post–World War I New York, *The Violet Hour* portrays "a conservative young publisher from a wealthy family who struggles to decide which of two manuscripts to publish," says Sandstrom. "One is written by a talented close friend from college who desperately needs the break. The other is by a remarkable black singer (and his secret lover) with a fascinating life story. Each has deep personal implications. If he could see the future, would it help his decision?" The poster depicts that question with "a scene from the play involving the singer that takes place during the violet hour—the uniquely New York moment when the day becomes the night."

TITLE: *Homebody/Kabul*
CLIENT: Steppenwolf Theatre
SIZE: 24" x 36" (60.96 x 91.44 cm)
PRINTING PROCESS: Offset
INKS: 5 color
Are posters what you primarily do for this client? Yes

PROCESS

COMPS PRESENTED: 1
REVISIONS: 1
APPROVAL: Agency creative director, marketing director, artistic director, executive director, and the play's director
INVOLVEMENT WITH FINAL PRINTING:
Prepared for production

"An eccentric British woman has romantic notions of visiting Kabul, Afghanistan, from reading outdated travel guides," explains Sandstrom. "Her husband and daughter follow her to Kabul, only to be told of her brutal murder. Their disbelief and continued search lead them into a web of political deceit and dangerous associations." Relaying a sense of contradictions, Sandstrom used a chair from the woman's London home, embroidered with a "pattern that is an Arabic translation of a poem she read about Kabul," inspiring her trip.

TITLE: *Man from Nebraska*
CLIENT: Steppenwolf Theatre
SIZE: 24" x 36" (60.96 x 91.44 cm)
PRINTING PROCESS: Offset
INKS: 5 color
Are posters what you primarily do for this client? Yes

PROCESS

COMPS PRESENTED: 1
REVISIONS: 1
APPROVAL: Agency creative director, marketing director, artistic director, executive director, and the play's director
INVOLVEMENT WITH FINAL PRINTING:
Prepared for production

"A middle-aged man awakens in a panic late one night," explains Sandstrom about *Man from Nebraska*. "He is struggling with his religious beliefs and questioning who he really is. He leaves home and family to live in London on a mission of self-discovery." To capture this, Sandstrom used a "graphic showing a man standing in a symbolic Midwest landscape, with body language that questions the heavens as the horizon appears to cut off his head."

TITLE: *Wedding Band*
CLIENT: Steppenwolf Theatre
SIZE: 24" x 36" (60.96 x 91.44 cm)
PRINTING PROCESS: Offset
INKS: 5 color
Are posters what you primarily do for this client? Yes

PROCESS

COMPS PRESENTED: 1
REVISIONS: 1
APPROVAL: Agency creative director, marketing director, artistic director, executive director, and the play's director
INVOLVEMENT WITH FINAL PRINTING:
Prepared for production

With a "falling cupid to represent lost love and the Confederate flag within the silhouette to represent racial tension in the South," Sandstrom illustrates the sad tale of "the hopeful plans of a secret love affair between a poor black woman and a lower middle-class white man that fails to survive social and family racial pressures in South Carolina."

Title: Portland International Film Festival
CLIENT: Northwest Film Center/Portland Art Museum
SIZE: 26 x 40" (66.04 x 101.60 cm)
PRINTING PROCESS: Offset
INKS: 5-color process
Are posters what you primarily do for this client? No

PROCESS

COMPS PRESENTED: 2
REVISIONS: 0
APPROVAL: Northwest Film Center director
INVOLVEMENT WITH FINAL PRINTING:
Prepared for production and press inspected

"The film festival is one of Portland's bigger cultural events in terms of attendance and interest. Portland is a good city for appreciating film and filmmaking, including animation, experimental films and shorts. It's also a haven for animators and writers, and a few good directors and cinematographers have sprung from Portland," says Sandstrom. In recent years, poster concepts for the festival have made some connection with the international nature of the films featured and the city where the festival is held. Portland has a reputation for rain, coffee and tea consumption, environmental leadership, outdoor recreation, and quirky individualism, and it is known as the "city of roses" for its immense International Rose Garden and annual Rose Festival every June. Working with creative director Jon Olsen and photographer Mark Hooper each year, the Sandstrom team for these projects, including Greg Parra, Kristin Anderson, Starlee Matz, Ann Riedl, Kelly Bohls, and Spike Selby, have formed ideas around some of the characteristics and clichés about the city.

PAINTING IN BULK

At Concordia University, Chloe Lum and Yannick Desranleau intentionally dodged design courses in favor of those in video, performance, and bookmaking. They never considered a career in design, much less specializing in design for rock bands. During their studies, many of their performances included the action of wheat-pasting posters with bogus slogans. Soon their devotion to their own noise rock band called for those skills as they began collaborating on posters to promote their shows.

They quickly found themselves making a concerted effort to do innovative work that the bands, their fans, and the shows promoters could truly enjoy. They began to view the poster as a way of "painting in bulk." This vegan, cat-loving art school couple began to dream big. They wanted to "create a public dialog through rock poster art."

Their lack of formal training may help explain the wild abandon with which they explore typography. Theirs is not so much a case of breaking the rules as it is not knowing the rules to begin with. It is also why they view themselves as outside any current poster movement. "We consider ourselves part of a 'people who make weird junk' movement. Many of our peers make posters, but just as many do not. We do align ourselves with likeminded artists/designers/weirdos and have a particular interest in printed two-dimensional matter, but not limited to posters. We are more interested in aesthetic and accessibility than format."

QUEBEC AESTHETIC

One of the artists who interest them is local. "Here in Quebec, Vittorio Fiorruci is a cultural icon for his illustrations and branding work. Few people know his name—sadly, no book has been published on his life's work—but almost everyone in Montreal would recognize his monster creatures, which are prevalent in his poster/illustration work. His posters are a mix of bold, whimsical illustrations and savage wit, all in very bright primary colors with lots of black. In our opinion, his work defined a Quebec aesthetic in posters and graphics that was especially strong in the 1970s and 1980s. The work he created is, to our knowledge, the only commercial art in Quebec that did not rely heavily on existing trends from the United States or Europe. He is probably the first graphic artist either of us was aware of and is probably our biggest influence."

That is far from the end of their influences. Everything from Archie comic books translated into French to Bollywood movies to Expo 67, the 1976 Olympics, Mayan, Aztec, and Eskimo art, and numerous artists and filmmakers make their way into the visual blender. Not to mention gig poster designers from Art Chantry to the Little Friends of Printmaking (profiled on page 108). Throw classic rock, noise rock, and punk rock into the mix, and you are ready to roll.

SHY AND NEUROTIC

Chloe and Yannick have come to love the freedom of making posters, which allows them to "make their own schedules, design without pants on, spend time together." However, they find themselves "looking like hobos, as everything we own gets covered in printing stains." They also find it can be a solitary existence, as "we often go days without seeing anybody else. We are both shy and neurotic by nature, so the isolation suits us well."

When they do venture out, they "are people who enjoy walking in the city and looking at everything: posters that are peeling, boarded-up shop windows, discarded strip club flyers, cigarette butts, people, buildings, public art, billboards, graffiti, road signs." They find themselves "peering into stores and residences, exploring empty buildings and back alleys. Having our own work as part of the urban landscape that other people look at with delight/revulsion/indifference/curiosity excites us very much. We like being part of everyday life, in the background."

Seripop says, "We will be happy to make a million posters before we die. And we want to own a house and a pony some day."

"We consider ourselves part of a 'people who make weird junk' movement."

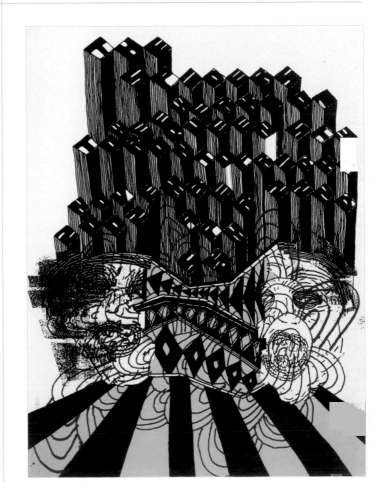

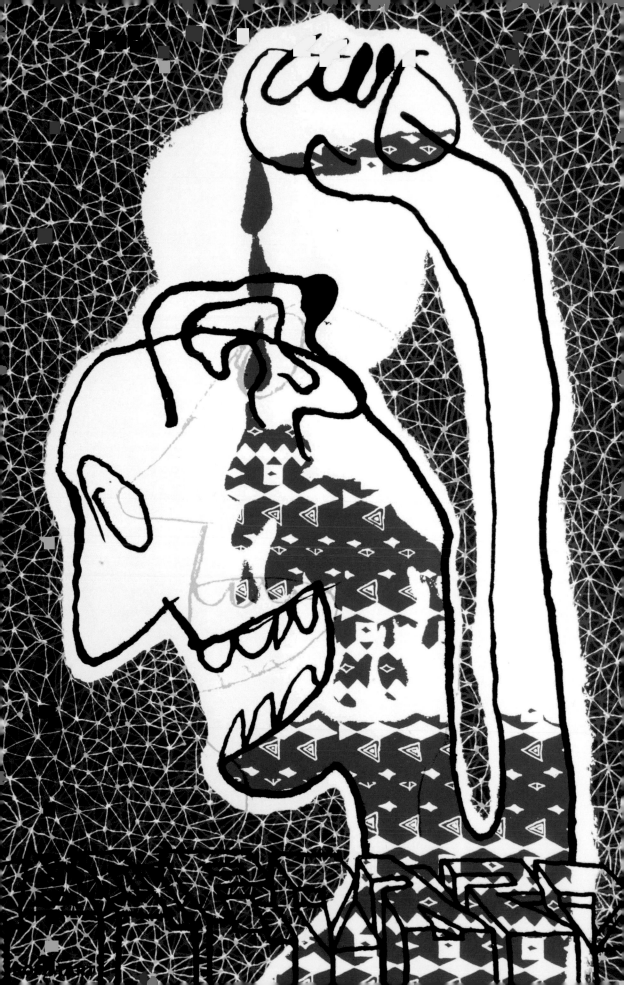

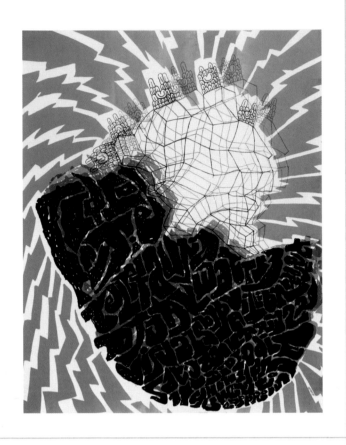

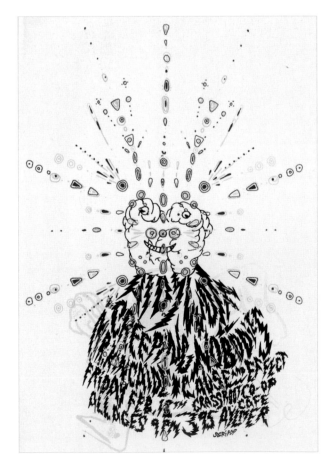

TITLE: AIDS Wolf/Les Angles Mortis Gig Poster
CLIENT: AIDS Wolf
SIZE: 12" x 18" (30.48 x 45.72 cm)
PRINTING PROCESS: Screen print
INKS: Latex paint
Are posters what you primarily do for this client? No

PROCESS
COMPS PRESENTED: 1
REVISIONS: 0
APPROVAL: None
INVOLVEMENT WITH FINAL PRINTING:
Printed by Seripop

Putting together a promotion for their own band, Seripop took an almost Dadaist approach. Intertwining patterns, small type, tonal color, and an "empty" face all amount to what the couple calls "ugh, pyramid face." Placing odd elements together is their specialty, hoping viewers will "see our band as a crazy band— so we did a crazy poster."

TITLE: Loosers Gig Poster
CLIENT: Loosers
SIZE: 18" x 18" (45.72 x 45.72 cm)
PRINTING PROCESS: Screen print
INKS: Latex paint
Are posters what you primarily do for this client? Yes

PROCESS
COMPS PRESENTED: 1
REVISIONS: 0
APPROVAL: None
INVOLVEMENT WITH FINAL PRINTING:
Printed by Seripop

Things don't always go as planned in rock and roll. "Originally, we were hired by Loosers to do a poster for a show they were playing with Damo Suzuki. We ended up doing a huge portrait of Damo with his name radiating from his eyes and the other bands and information smaller." A band member soon emailed the bad news that Damo was no longer playing on the bill. "So we just cranked up our Loosers disc and busted this out in a few hours."

TITLE: Japanther/USA Is a Monster Gig Poster
CLIENT: Mandatory Moustache
SIZE: 18" x 24" (45.72 x 60.96 cm)
PRINTING PROCESS: Screen print
INKS: Latex paint
Are posters what you primarily do for this client? Yes

PROCESS
COMPS PRESENTED: 1
REVISIONS: 0
APPROVAL: None
INVOLVEMENT WITH FINAL PRINTING:
Printed by Seripop

Despite tales of the inherent difficulty printing with transparent red inks, the real story to this poster is how oddly it suited the actual show. Seripop explain that the show was so action-packed and intense that it created "indoor smog from sweat and cigarette smoke—it was fucking gross."

TITLE: Mile End Invades I'x
CLIENT: Jerusalem in My Heart
SIZE: 18" x 24" (45.72 x 60.96 cm)
PRINTING PROCESS: Screen print
INKS: Latex paint
Are posters what you primarily do for this client? Yes

PROCESS
COMPS PRESENTED: 1
REVISIONS: 0
APPROVAL: None
INVOLVEMENT WITH FINAL PRINTING:
Printed by Seripop

Clearly a lot of thought goes into their work, but for Seripop, "sometimes making posters becomes an exercise in style. This is what we felt like doing here, as all the different parties involved in the actual event were so different. We also often try to do something really different each time we have to do a poster that advertises one of our art shows. So I guess that's why we created this lettering all made with rulers—which we rarely use; we prefer the crooked line. And of course this is our fetish color combo: yellow, orange, red, magenta."

TITLE: Spiders Fake Gigs
CLIENT: Zin Taylor
SIZE: 18" x 24" (45.72 x 60.96 cm)
PRINTING PROCESS: Screen print
INKS: Latex paint
Are posters what you primarily do for this client? Yes

PROCESS
COMPS PRESENTED: 0
REVISIONS: 0
APPROVAL: Zin Taylor
INVOLVEMENT WITH FINAL PRINTING:
Printed by Seripop

Some in the gig poster world have been accused of printing posters for imaginary shows—but imaginary bands? Seripop reveals, "Zin is our bandmate's brother. He commissioned us to create fake gig posters for his fake band, the Spiders. He is an installation artist, and he used them as part of his show at the CAG [Contemporary Art Gallery] in Vancouver."

TITLE: Bop Tart Records Promo
CLIENT: Bop Tart Records
SIZE: 12" x 18" (30.48 x 45.72)
PRINTING PROCESS: Screen print
INKS: Latex paint
Are posters what you primarily do for this client? Yes

PROCESS
COMPS PRESENTED: 1
REVISIONS: 0
APPROVAL: None
INVOLVEMENT WITH FINAL PRINTING:
Printed by Seripop

Seripop created this piece knowing they had a secret weapon: a third color. "We were designing two different posters at the same time for the same client, both budgeted for only two colors." Printing both pieces on the same sheet allowed them to grab an additional color from the other piece, resulting in a heavy black overprint and a complex blue and red pattern they could not have pulled off without the other color to carry the image. All at no extra cost.

TITLE: Coco Rosie Secret Gig Poster
CLIENT: 100-Sided Die
SIZE: 18" x 24" (45.72 x 60.96 cm)
PRINTING PROCESS: Screen print
INKS: Latex paint
Are posters what you primarily do for this client? Yes

PROCESS

COMPS PRESENTED: 1
REVISIONS: 0
APPROVAL: None
INVOLVEMENT WITH FINAL PRINTING:
Printed by Seripop

In creating a poster promoting a show at the warehouse space they share with several artists, Seripop "wanted to keep the show on the down low, as our space only fit 250 people and we knew the headliner would be a big draw." They add, "It's not really legal to have shows in warehouses. So we made the poster cryptic, thinking the effort would dissuade all but the bravest." No luck. After turning away over 600 people, saying hello to the police, and shoveling up broken bottles, they vow "No more shows at our workspace—ever again!"

TITLE: Loosers Tour Poster
CLIENT: Loosers
SIZE: 12" x 18" (30.48 x 45.72 cm)
PRINTING PROCESS: Screen print
INKS: Latex paint
Are posters what you primarily do for this client? Yes

PROCESS

COMPS PRESENTED: 1
REVISIONS: 0
APPROVAL: Loosers
INVOLVEMENT WITH FINAL PRINTING:
Printed by Seripop

As fans of Portugal's improv-noise rock unit Loosers, Seripop felt "that pleasing ourselves visually might hit other people too. Improvisational music calls for a highly organic look. And nothing suggests magic more than Spirograph spirals—at least to us." Getting into the band's mindset, they also felt "diverse elements and really clashing colors seemed appropriate."

TITLE: AIDS Wolf/Creeping Nobodies Gig Poster
CLIENT: AIDS Wolf
SIZE: 12" x 18" (30.48 x 45.72 cm)
PRINTING PROCESS: Screen print
INKS: Latex paint
Are posters what you primarily do for this client? No

PROCESS

COMPS PRESENTED: 1
REVISIONS: 0
APPROVAL: None
INVOLVEMENT WITH FINAL PRINTING:
Printed by Seripop

Paired up with their good friends the Creeping Nobodies, Seripop and their bandmates ventured into a small Canadian town. Determined to "attract all the weirdos in town, this is what we came up with." A beige body "inspired by 1940s commercial art" is surrounded by "lettering shot from the head and the explosion of these weird kinda crafty-looking patterns—probably referring to all those macramé and knitting books we are collecting from the Salvation Army lately."

TITLE: Fantômas/Locust Gig Poster
CLIENT: Fantômas
SIZE: 12" x 18" (30.48 x 45.72 cm)
PRINTING PROCESS: Screen print
INKS: Latex paint
Are posters what you primarily do for this client? Yes

PROCESS

COMPS PRESENTED: 1
REVISIONS: 0
APPROVAL: None
INVOLVEMENT WITH FINAL PRINTING:
Printed by Seripop

Designing one in a series of posters for the Fantômas tour, Seripop responded to "singer Mike Patton's request that each artist do something cute but disturbing." They "collaged a scary kids' book from Italy and some embroidery patterns" along with hand-drawn type and layers of ink to polish off what they call "subtle evil."

TITLE: Daughters/AIDS Wolf Gig Poster
CLIENT: Mandatory Moustache
SIZE: 18" x 24" (45.72 x 60.96 cm)
PRINTING PROCESS: Screen print
INKS: Latex paint
Are posters what you primarily do for this client? Yes

PROCESS

COMPS PRESENTED: 1
REVISIONS: 0
APPROVAL: None
INVOLVEMENT WITH FINAL PRINTING:
Printed by Seripop

Looking to design the perfect poster for the Daughters, described as a "weirdo metal band," Seripop immersed themselves in "classic metal imagery and type such as castles and blackletter" and then proceeded to "make them both kinda off." The intricate detail and medieval feel combined with an absurdist quality to make what they hope is perceived as a "weirdo metal poster."

BIG PUZZLES

What started out as a small studio specializing in the entertainment industry has grown under Drew Hodge's steady hand from Spot Design to SpotCo, a full-service advertising agency filled to the brim with talented creatives that, as *In Theater* magazine says, has created "a quiet revolution in Broadway marketing." Well, they may be quiet by Broadway standards, but they are definitely revolutionary. Breaking through a stagnant time in commercial theater posters, SpotCo has become the champion of the "artistic" poster.

Compared to many of the other firms featured in this book, SpotCo face innumerable hurdles in their creative process and likely deal with the most restrictive set of circumstances, while also having the largest financial responsibility hovering over their work. That they do so with skill and flair made their inclusion in this book a must.

"Big shows mean big puzzles," explains senior art director Gail Anderson. "The sizes and positions of the stars' names in relation to the logo are sometimes contractual givens, and that can be limiting. And sometimes you just really want to make it cool and arty, you know? In your heart, you want to design some cryptic, spare, and fabulous piece or a crazy all-type solution—and then you have to remind yourself that this is the real world and there are real problems that have to be addressed." Principal Drew Hodges adds, "The tougher questions go something like this: What is the emotional promise a poster is making? For us, what will the evening of theater feel like in broad strokes—funny, tension-filled, satirical, big show, small show, modern-day issues, or lifelong classic? Ideally, a poster communicates these emotions so well they are inherent."

This type of work is not all about the struggle against creative restrictions. In reality, it allows for a deep connection to visionaries working in other aspects of the field. "The best part of our work is knowing that it can be part of the success of a show," says Anderson. "People remember it, connect it with the event, and see it in its many incarnations all over town and sometimes across the country, if a show tours. Designing theater posters is interesting because we are really part of the process of getting a show up and running."

KEEP IT SIMPLE

Posters are certainly not all SpotCo does, but they are where SpotCo's heart is. "There is no better feeling than seeing your work featured at an enormous size in the middle of Times Square or in a subway station," says Anderson. "It's fun to see the work become part of the vernacular of its environment. The first time I saw a poster I worked on at the train station, I got off and took a picture of it. I hadn't felt that jazzed about something I'd done in quite some time."

Anderson also gets a charge out of the unique nature of designing a poster, especially considering her past work at *Rolling Stone* magazine. "People stop and chew on magazine pages longer than they do on commercial posters. I had to switch gears from focusing on little details to making big, broad strokes when I started at Spot. Seeing a theater poster in a deli window is pretty humbling. Does it stand out against the clutter? Do you get it pretty quickly? Do you want to steal it?" The answer, more often than not, is—yes!

Anderson is kind enough to draw a parallel in what SpotCo does to the past masters that follows my reasoning for the importance of their work—the commercial component. She notes, "Herbert Leupin, Peter Birkhauser, Niklaus Stoecklin, and Donald Brun are heroes of mine; I am a big fan of the mid-twentieth-century Swiss object posters. I love the fact that they sold toothpaste, luncheon meats, and dress shirts. So lovely, yet completely utilitarian in their final use in stores. I look at the Swiss poster and think, 'Okay, keep it simple, keep it simple.' I look at Paul Rand's work, the WPA posters and the muscular Cassandre posters, and think the same, too. Make your point and move on; people only spare a moment to take posters in when they are getting off the train or passing a theater." As Hodges says, "A successful poster telegraphs a singular emotion, a personality, a visual tune you can sing along with. It should feel like someone made it—it maintains the hand of the individual, whether one or five people contributed to the design."

SELLING TICKETS

"It feels a bit lofty to see what we do as part of a poster movement," says Anderson, "though the idea of that sounds sort of cool, of course. What we do is, admittedly, completely commercial. Our job is to entice you into buying a ticket—or better yet, several tickets." After viewing their work, I am sure we are all tempted. Did you say you like musicals?

"You have to remind yourself that this is the real world and there are real problems that have to be addressed."

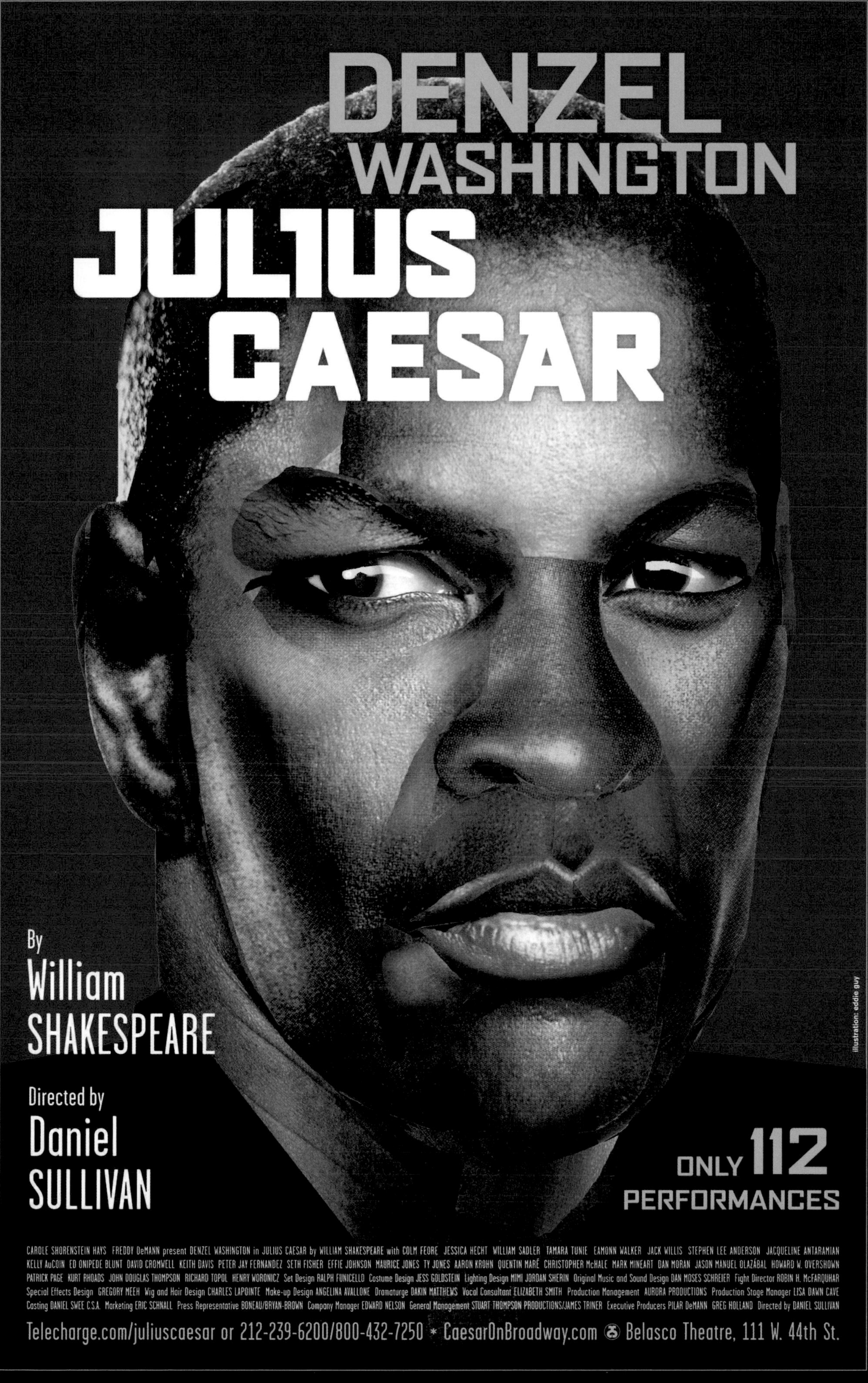

DENZEL
WASHINGTON

JUL1US
CAESAR

By
William
SHAKESPEARE

Directed by
Daniel
SULLIVAN

ONLY **112**
PERFORMANCES

illustration: eddie guy

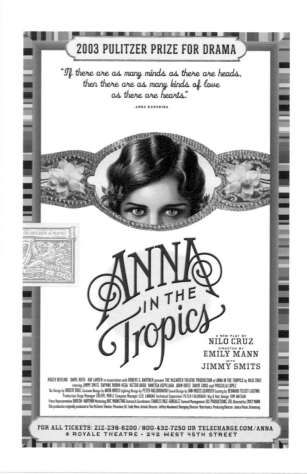

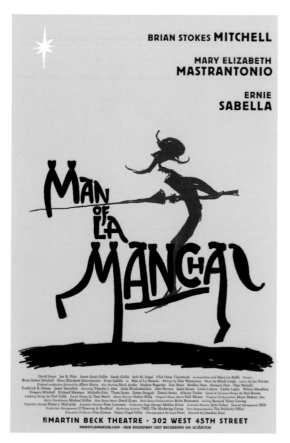

the Ticket you Couldn't get
— UNTIL NOW —

"In this thrilling production, Greek tragedy's most spectacularly vengeful woman has rematerialized as the most ESSENTIAL TICKET of this THEATER SEASON. The show radiates such high theatrical energy—and insight that you can't help grinning through most of it. Ms. SHAW and Ms. WARNER

have created one of the most human MEDEAS EVER. So vivid, so haunting and so damningly easy to identify with. THE ANXIOUS PERFUME that saturates this production is a compound of the PASSION and TERROR that have plagued HUMANS for as long as they have been able to think"

BEN BRANTLEY, THE NEW YORK TIMES 10.4.02

FIONA SHAW

MEDEA

Directed by Deborah WARNER

Direct FROM FIVE 'SOLD OUT' ENGAGEMENTS
→ 84 PERFORMANCES ONLY
Begins December 4
Call Today — TICKETMASTER.COM 212-307-4100/800-755-4000
BROOKS ATKINSON Theatre, 256 West 47th STREET

Design: James Victore Inc.

George C. Wolfe's HARLEM SONG A NEW MUSICAL

LIVE ON STAGE at the WORLD-FAMOUS APOLLO THEATER

WHERE the STREETS ARE PAVED with RHYTHM

TICKETMASTER · 212 307-7171 · APOLLO THEATER · 253 West 125th Street, NYC · HarlemSong.com

Going uptown's as easy as A, B, C, D, 1, 2, 3, 4, 5, 6, & Metro North

I AM MY OWN WIFE

DELPHI PRODUCTIONS IN ASSOCIATION WITH PLAYWRIGHTS HORIZONS PRESENT I AM MY OWN WIFE
BY DOUG WRIGHT STARRING JEFFERSON MAYS SCENIC DESIGN DEREK McLANE LIGHTING DESIGN DAVID LANDER
COSTUME DESIGN JANICE PYTEL SOUND DESIGN ANDRE J. PLUESS PRODUCTION STAGE MANAGER ANDREA "SPOOK" TESTANI
PRODUCTION SUPERVISOR ARTHUR SICCARDI GENERAL MANAGER MIKO COMPANIES, LTD. PRESS REPRESENTATIVE RICHARD KORNBERG AND ASSOCIATES
A WORKSHOP OF I AM MY OWN WIFE WAS PRESENTED BY LA JOLLA PLAYHOUSE, DES McANUFF, ARTISTIC DIRECTOR & TERRENCE DWYER, MANAGING DIRECTOR
DIRECTED BY MOISÉS KAUFMAN

TELECHARGE.COM · 212.239.6200
& LYCEUM THEATRE · 149 W 45TH STREET

TITLE: *Julius Caesar*
CLIENT: Carole Shorenstein Hayes and Freddy DeMann
SIZE: 14" x 22" (35.56 x 55.88 cm)
PRINTING PROCESS: Offset
INKS: 4-color process
Are posters what you primarily do for this client? No

PROCESS

COMPS PRESENTED: 1
REVISIONS: 0
APPROVAL: Show producers
INVOLVEMENT WITH FINAL PRINTING:
Prepared for production

After Hodges and Anderson spoke with the producers, they felt they knew what to deliver. "Denzel Washington starred as Brutus in a modern staging of *Julius Caesar*," says Anderson. "Our task was to position the show as edgy and contemporary, and, of course, the focus was on Denzel making his return to the Broadway stage." The producers loved the intense and brooding Brutus collage artist Eddie Guy created. Surprisingly, only the hairline was actually taken from a picture of the star. "There were no revisions—the best treat in the world for us," says designer Sam Eckersley.

TITLE: *Avenue Q*
CLIENT: The Producing Office
SIZE: 14" x 22" (35.56 x 55.88 cm)
PRINTING PROCESS: Offset
INKS: 4-color process
Are posters what you primarily do for this client? No

PROCESS

COMPS PRESENTED: 3
REVISIONS: 2
APPROVAL: Show producers
INVOLVEMENT WITH FINAL PRINTING:
Prepared for production

"We nailed the basic idea for this one pretty quickly," recalls Anderson, for the controversial play starring puppets in a "real" urban environment. "Once we had the New York subway sign for the logo on fur, it was really a matter of what to do with the puppets. The characters first appeared on a train but were quickly replaced by close-ups once we saw them. They were funny enough on their own—they didn't need props or a set."

TITLE: *La Bohème*
CLIENT: Bazmark
SIZE: 14" x 22" (35.56 x 55.88 cm)
PRINTING PROCESS: Offset
INKS: 4-color process
Are posters what you primarily do for this client? No

PROCESS

COMPS PRESENTED: 3
REVISIONS: 2
APPROVAL: Bazmark
INVOLVEMENT WITH FINAL PRINTING:
Prepared for production

"The only thing more exciting than the challenge of launching one of the world's most beloved operas on Broadway, in Italian, with three sets of leading players, is doing it with legendary director Baz Luhrmann, his graphic and set designer wife Catherine Martin, and his entire team known to the world as Bazmark," says Hodges, who, along with designer Lia Chee, "FedExed concepts to Mr. Luhrmann in Australia while he and his team finished the DVD package of his *Red Curtain Trilogy*." Luhrmann was "a client with high, high standards," who called to say "We actually like them." Hodges explains, "Ms. Martin delivered a logo with popular references to none other than the Coca-Cola logo, befitting the opera's resetting to Paris in the late 1950s. And photographer Douglas Kirkland came through with images of cinematic beauty and sensuality. It all seems perfect for 'the greatest love story ever sung.'"

TITLE: *BKLYN*
CLIENT: Producers Four/Jeff Calhoun, John McDaniel
SIZE: 14" x 22" (35.56 x 55.88 cm)
PRINTING PROCESS: Offset
INKS: 4-color process
Are posters what you primarily do for this client? No

PROCESS

COMPS PRESENTED: 7
REVISIONS: 2
APPROVAL: Show producers
INVOLVEMENT WITH FINAL PRINTING:
Prepared for production

"At the heart of this musical are the street performers and their efforts to lift themselves out of their bleak reality with the music they create," says designer Darren Cox. "We wanted to evoke some of that gritty street feel but at the same time make the art uplifting." After shooting a set in the studio with photographer Geoff Spear, Cox added hand-drawn elements in post-production along with scratches from beat-up old negatives, enhancing the mood.

TITLE: *The Dangerous Lives of Altar Boys*
CLIENT: Think Film
SIZE: 24" x 36" (60.96 x 91.44 cm)
PRINTING PROCESS: Offset
INKS: 4-color process
Are posters what you primarily do for this client? Yes

PROCESS

COMPS PRESENTED: 6
REVISIONS: 6
APPROVAL: Production house
INVOLVEMENT WITH FINAL PRINTING:
Prepared for production

Early sketches for this movie poster—a departure for SpotCo from the closely aligned theater world—focused on the two main characters and the fantasy comic book world that springs from their young minds. Hodges and Cox felt it "might actually be better to immerse the real characters directly in their imagined world." Todd McFarlane illustrated the characters from the animated segments of the film, and SpotCo designed a comic strip for all the elements to coexist in seamlessly.

TITLE: *The Pillowman*
CLIENT: (Boyett Ostar Production) Bill Haber, Robert Fox, Bob Boyett
SIZE: 14" x 22" (35.56 x 55.88 cm)
PRINTING PROCESS: Offset
INKS: 4-color process
Are posters what you primarily do for this client? Yes

PROCESS

COMPS PRESENTED: 12
REVISIONS: 6
APPROVAL: Show producers
INVOLVEMENT WITH FINAL PRINTING:
Prepared for production

This unusual show is set in an unnamed totalitarian dictatorship and centers on the interrogation of a short story writer. "We attempted to evoke some of that bleak and oppressive environment," says Anderson, "but at the same time reveal some of the fantastical elements of the story." They submitted at least a dozen ideas over time—with varying levels of creepiness—before moving forward with this one, designed and illustrated by Cox, with lettering by Mike Rivamonte. "Part of the brief required us to show the two lead actors," says Anderson. "We built a small two-story set out of cardboard that we then digitally doctored the head shots of the actors into. Their bodies are actually those of our coworkers."

Title: *Anna in the Tropics*
CLIENT: Daryl Roth, Roger Berlind
SIZE: 14" x 22" (35.56 x 55.88 cm)
PRINTING PROCESS: Offset
INKS: 4-color process
Are posters what you primarily do for this client? No

PROCESS
COMPS PRESENTED: 6
REVISIONS: 3
APPROVAL: Show producers
INVOLVEMENT WITH FINAL PRINTING:
Prepared for production

Anna in the Tropics is a steamy story of passion and the ability of literature to expand the mind, set in a Florida cigar factory in 1929. "It had just won a Pulitzer and was on everyone's radar when we created the artwork," says Anderson. "Designer Jessica Disbrow and I gave typographer Anthony Bloch a sketch of our title treatment and paired his beautiful lettering with the seductive, well-known cigar label lady. There was no huge epiphany on this one. Our job was to create something beautiful, and the retro design was true to the spirit of the show."

TITLE: *Man of La Mancha*
CLIENT: David Stone, Susan Gallin
SIZE: 14" x 22" (35.56 x 55.88 cm)
PRINTING PROCESS: Offset
INKS: 4-color process
Are posters what you primarily do for this client? No

PROCESS
COMPS PRESENTED: 6
REVISIONS: 5
APPROVAL: Show producers
INVOLVEMENT WITH FINAL PRINTING:
Prepared for production

"We were asked to design an iconic poster for the Broadway revival of *Man of La Mancha*," says Anderson. "The show title was fairly easily transformed into the shape of a horse, as I moved letters around onscreen." Illustrator Ward Schumaker created an ink drawing from Anderson's sketch, and James Victore drew a Don Quixote that served as a tribute to the famous Picasso figure. SpotCo may have even done the job too well, if that is possible. "In the end," says Anderson, "the poster was so old-school that people assumed it was the original show poster when, in fact, the only deliberate similarity was the yellow background."

TITLE: *The Good Body*
CLIENT: The Araca Group, Harriet Newman Leve, East of Doheny
SIZE: 14" x 22" (35.56 x 55.88 cm)
PRINTING PROCESS: Offset
INKS: 4-color process
Are posters what you primarily do for this client? No

PROCESS
COMPS PRESENTED: 6
REVISIONS: 4
APPROVAL: Show producers
INVOLVEMENT WITH FINAL PRINTING:
Prepared for production

"Eve Ensler's latest one-woman show dealt with female body issues," says Anderson, "so we treated the artwork as sort of a follow-up to the poster Spot had created for Ensler's seminal hit *The Vagina Monologues*." The normal-sized, broad-hipped woman has breasts made of scoops of ice cream, playing off a reference Ensler makes to Afghani women hiding in back rooms to secretly eat ice cream. Anderson, Disbrow, and illustrator Isabelle Dervaux faced one last challenge. "We had lots of changes on the ice cream scoops. The boobs were huge at first, and we were asked to take them down a few cup sizes." The best part though, came after the shoot. "There were lots of flavors to choose from for the design—and lots of ice cream to eat when we were done," says Anderson.

TITLE: *Medea*
CLIENT: Roger Berlind, James M. Nederlander, Daryl Roth, Scott Rudin
SIZE: 14" x 22" (35.56 x 55.88 cm)
PRINTING PROCESS: Offset
INKS: 4-color process
Are posters what you primarily do for this client? No

PROCESS
COMPS PRESENTED: 6 or 7
REVISIONS: 3
APPROVAL: Show producers
INVOLVEMENT WITH FINAL PRINTING:
Prepared for production

Hodges and Gail Anderson knew who to turn to for an edgy updating of the Euripides classic *Medea*. Hiring renowned designer and illustrator James Victore to create the typography, they received art that perfectly summed up the performance. "It was a courageous leap of faith on the part of the producers," Anderson recalls. "And the kitchen knife and angry lettering just leapt off the page." SpotCo even emblazoned the front of the theater with Victore's scrawl, to great effect.

TITLE: *Harlem Song*
CLIENT: George C. Wolfe
SIZE: 44.875" x 58.875" (113.98 x 149.54 cm)
PRINTING PROCESS: Offset
INKS: 4-color process
Are posters what you primarily do for this client? No

PROCESS
COMPS PRESENTED: 5
REVISIONS: 2
APPROVAL: Show producers
INVOLVEMENT WITH FINAL PRINTING:
Prepared for production

Harlem Song was a wonderful musical nod to a fascinating part of New York's history. Rather than a Broadway run, it played at Harlem's historic Apollo Theater. "We created a playful marquee with a knocked-back snapshot that a Spot coworker had taken of the Apollo's own marquee," says Anderson. The subway poster appeared in stations all over town, and a huge 60-foot banner hung over the theater. "There was even a McDonald's placemat," says Anderson, "the first time I've ever gotten to eat off my own work."

TITLE: *I Am My Own Wife*
CLIENT: Delphi Productions, David Richenthal, Anthony and Charlene Marshall
SIZE: 14" x 22" (35.56 x 55.88 cm)
PRINTING PROCESS: Offset
INKS: 4-color process
Are posters what you primarily do for this client? No

PROCESS
COMPS PRESENTED: 12
REVISIONS: 8
APPROVAL: Show producers
INVOLVEMENT WITH FINAL PRINTING:
Prepared for production

I Am My Own Wife is the story of a German transvestite who survived the Nazis and, later, the Soviet-dominated communist dictatorship of East Germany. "It was one of the most difficult shows we've ever worked on," says Anderson, "as the subject matter suggests imagery of swastikas and the hammer and sickle. If you look closely at the highlight in the pearls, you'll see them. Subtlety was key here."

★ SPUR (DAVE PLUNKERT) ★

BALTIMORE, MARYLAND, USA

A MAN WHO NEEDS NO INTRODUCTION—AGAIN

Dave Plunkert has set the design world on fire almost too many times to mention. The funny part of it is that he has done so with radically different styles in each instance. We won't mention the high-tech strobe-induced colors and forms he made right after leaving Shepherd College, but we must mention that people to this day are still making a living mimicking this look. The first time the world took notice of him by name was when he engaged in the long love affair with the poster that continues to this day.

Making amazingly sophisticated and challenging posters for a tiny local theater using mostly typographical solutions, Plunkert and his friend Paul Sahre suddenly became hot young guns in the design world, pioneers in the use of modest means for enormous impact that has taken over the silkscreen movement. Sahre admits that these posters are often what he is recognized for.

Far from content to bask in this adulation, Plunkert became one of the most recognizable illustrators in the world with a unique style of collage, drawing, and airbrush that graces top publications and advertisements around the globe. During this period, he still delivered knockout posters, but as a smaller proportion of his portfolio. When Plunkert married a fellow illustrator and started a family, he was able to pursue his love of design as they collectively formed Spur to represent their design and illustration talents. Once the design portion was up and running, his poster work gained weight in the portfolio.

REKINDLED LOVE
Plunkert notes that the boom in poster design "hasn't really affected our bottom line, but doing more posters has increased our profile." Enjoying the "time to experiment with personal and lower-budget projects," he may see a poster movement afoot, but he says, "I'm not getting invitations to the meetings." Plunkert loves the form, as it is "potentially the most artful thing a designer gets to do." Sometimes he is even more determined to do a poster project than those around him. "I typically want to do a poster more than the client wants to do a poster. They can be a tough sell because the idea of hanging a piece of paper up on a city street is not a job most folks want, for some reason." Luckily, he can be very persuasive.

Once the job is in the shop, Plunkert isn't shy about tapping into his influences. "I'll mine just about anyone—Raoul Haussman, George Grosz, Seymour Chwast, Jack Kirby, Picasso. Paul Sahre gave me great advice once: that you can do just about anything on a poster if the client can read the phone number easily." He also shares a deep affinity for the work of "A. M. Cassandre and Paul Rand, for their application of basic principles to creating a beautiful poster, and Art Chantry, for breaking the rules and making something ugly."

When stuck, Plunkert can always fall back on his secret weapon. "Big heads on posters normally work well. If the big head has a hat on, or is smoking, or has something lodged in its eye—even better." You may see a few of those scattered in this review of his work.

Plunkert has come full circle with his work. After plunging back into event posters with assignments for a theater in Madison, he is again earning international acclaim for posters done with minimal resources and budget for a tiny local client, just as he had at the beginning of his career. But this time the client is the Theatre Project. He also continues to reinvent the "big-headed" poster subject and has embraced the current trend for silkscreening and limited editions, somehow making the result look refined yet raw. We can barely wait for what he will dazzle us with next.

"I typically want to do a poster more than the client wants to do a poster."

BITING THE HAND THAT FEEDS YOU
JOYCE HESSELBERTH AND DAVID PLUNKERT
OF
SPUR
AT TOWSON UNIVERSITY
FEB. 20
7:30 pm
CENTER FOR THE ARTS
LECTURE HALL CA241
SPONSORED BY THE ART DEPT.
FREE
www.towson.edu

You have the right to say it.

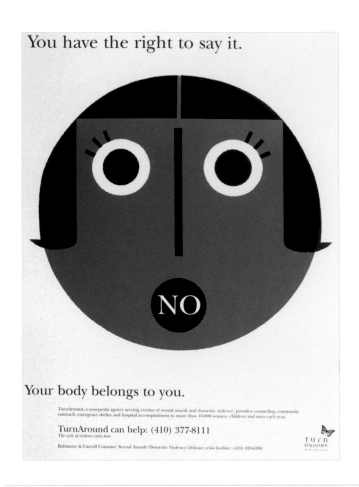

Your body belongs to you.

TurnAround, a non-profit agency serving victims of sexual assault and domestic violence, provides counseling, community outreach, emergency shelter and hospital accompaniment to more than 10,000 women, children and men each year.

TurnAround can help: (410) 377-8111
The cycle of violence ends here.

Baltimore & Carroll Counties' Sexual Assault/Domestic Violence 24-hour crisis hotline: (410) 828-6390

A child is not a toy.

Stop the cycle of sexual abuse.

TurnAround, a non-profit agency serving victims of sexual assault and domestic violence, provides counseling, community outreach, emergency shelter and hospital accompaniment to more than 10,000 women, children and men each year.

TurnAround can help: (410) 377-8111
The cycle of violence ends here.

Baltimore & Carroll Counties' Sexual Assault/Domestic Violence 24-hour crisis hotline: (410) 828-6390

No one should live with fear.

Domestic violence affects the entire family.

TurnAround, a non-profit agency serving victims of sexual assault and domestic violence, provides counseling, community outreach, emergency shelter and hospital accompaniment to more than 10,000 women, children and men each year.

TurnAround can help: (410) 377-8111
The cycle of violence ends here.

Baltimore & Carroll Counties' Sexual Assault/Domestic Violence 24-hour crisis hotline: (410) 828-6390

ROMEO & JULIET
Preston Street 410-752-8558 www.theatreproject.org 45 W. Preston Street 410-752-8
OCT 17-26
2003/04 Season
THEATRE PROJECT

THE MODIFIED
MONOGAMY PROJECT

Preston Street **410-752-8558** www.theatreproject.org 45 W. Preston Street **410-752-85**

BALTIMORE

PROJE

MAR 11-21

2003/04 Season

THEATRE PROJECT

RE

MERICA

CT

Design by SPUR / 410-235-7803 / www.spurdesign.com   Artwork ©2003 David Plunkert

CUL-DE-SAC

Preston Street **410-752-8558** www.theatreproject.org 45 W. Preston Street **410-752-85**

MAY 5-9

THEATRE PROJECT

2003/04 Season

THEAT
BALTIMORE ■
PROJE

Design by SPUR / 410-235-7803 / www.spurdesign.com

TITLE: Biting the Hand That Feeds You
CLIENT: Towson University
SIZE: 16" x 20" (40.64 x 50.80 cm)
PRINTING PROCESS: Screen print
INKS: 2 color
Are posters what you primarily do for this client? n/a

PROCESS
COMPS PRESENTED: 0
REVISIONS: 0
APPROVAL: None
INVOLVEMENT WITH FINAL PRINTING:
Printed by Spur

To promote a talk making fun of Spur's relationship with clients and the design industry, Plunkert wanted a gritty sort of illustration to complement the hand-drawn typography, playful bite mark, and additional fingers. He found a friend in the printing process and pulled the poster himself. He says, "This poster is actually a very poor print job. Uneven color, splotches, hairs—you name it, and it got into the ink. But the poster works better because of that."

TITLE: Turn Around Poster Campaign
"You Have the Right to Say It"
CLIENT: Turn Around
SIZE: 18" x 24" (45.72 x 60.96 cm)
PRINTING PROCESS: 2 color
INKS: Black and match orange
Are posters what you primarily do for this client? No

PROCESS
COMPS PRESENTED: 1
REVISIONS: 0
APPROVAL: Turn Around Committee
INVOLVEMENT WITH FINAL PRINTING:
Inspected the print run

Plunkert, feeling strongly that one poster would not be effective in reaching four very different audiences, had to work hard to sell this poster campaign proposal on domestic abuse to the client. Eventually, Spur did a lot of extra legwork. "We ended up getting the paper donated and designed the posters pro bono to make them fit into their budget."

TITLE: Turn Around Poster Campaign
"A Child Is Not a Toy"
CLIENT: Turn Around
SIZE: 18" x 24" (45.72 x 60.96 cm)
PRINTING PROCESS: 2 color
INKS: Black and match orange
Are posters what you primarily do for this client? No

PROCESS
COMPS PRESENTED: 1
REVISIONS: 0
APPROVAL: Turn Around Committee
INVOLVEMENT WITH FINAL PRINTING:
Inspected the print run

Continuing the campaign on domestic abuse with one focused on children, Plunkert knew that "these posters had to hang in elementary schools, so we opted against photographs of bruised kids for a conceptual approach that was reinforced by repeating simple elements throughout all of the pieces." The simple and bold imagery mixed with a sophisticated sense of placement quickly draws the eye of viewers of all ages. This approach led Plunkert to keep the "toy midsection" to its barest elements.

TITLE: Turn Around Poster Campaign
"No One Should Live with Fear"
CLIENT: Turn Around
SIZE: 18" x 24" (45.72 x 60.96 cm)
PRINTING PROCESS: 2 color
INKS: Black and match orange
Are posters what you primarily do for this client? No

PROCESS
COMPS PRESENTED: 1
REVISIONS: 0
APPROVAL: Turn Around Committee
INVOLVEMENT WITH FINAL PRINTING:
Inspected the print run

During conversations with the client, Plunkert gathered a vital piece of information. "Dogs and cats can be important factors in domestic abuse. Folks will stay in dangerous situations for fear of what might happen to their pet. So including pets is not merely a funny element on the family poster." Rather, it is a direct message and link to viewers who may desperately need the organization's assistance.

TITLE: Theatre Project Series 03–04
Romeo and Juliet
CLIENT: Theatre Project
SIZE: 14" x 23" (35.56 x 58.42 cm)
PRINTING PROCESS: Screen print and offset
INKS: Black offset and then 2 match colors screened
Are posters what you primarily do for this client? Yes

PROCESS
COMPS PRESENTED: 0
REVISIONS: 0
APPROVAL: None
INVOLVEMENT WITH FINAL PRINTING:
Printed by Spur

Developing a "tight type structure that allows the illustrations to be stylistically diverse" was the goal for Plunkert when working on the Theatre Project's 2003–2004 season posters. Printing the posters offset in black for the uniform information and then screening each performance worked out quite well. Plunkert adds, "A key part of the process is no client involvement beyond feeding us dates and titles." This enables him to let his muse run loose.

TITLE: Theatre Project Series 03–04
The Modified Monogamy Project
CLIENT: Theatre Project
SIZE: 14" x 23" (35.56 x 58.42 cm)
PRINTING PROCESS: Screen print and offset
INKS: Black offset and then 2 match colors screened
Are posters what you primarily do for this client? Yes

PROCESS
COMPS PRESENTED: 0
REVISIONS: 0
APPROVAL: None
INVOLVEMENT WITH FINAL PRINTING:
Printed by Spur

Setting a creative time limit for these pieces forces Plunkert to develop imagery that hits quickly and immediately while remaining high concept. "In the case of the Theatre Project posters, I give myself a few hours to come up with the idea and a few hours to do the mechanical," he says. This gives the pieces a sense of energy and simplicity of thought. For this one, he adds, "The poster would hang nicely next to James Victore's famous *Romeo and Juliet.*"

TITLE: Theatre Project Series 04–05 *Seance*
CLIENT: Theatre Project
SIZE: 14" x 23" (35.56 x 58.42 cm)
PRINTING PROCESS: Offset litho
INKS: 2 match colors
Are posters what you primarily do for this client? Yes

PROCESS
COMPS PRESENTED: 0
REVISIONS: 0
APPROVAL: None
INVOLVEMENT WITH FINAL PRINTING:
Printed by Spur

To promote a play where the performers wear rigid masks and do not speak, Plunkert was wise to focus on the ways in which they *do* communicate as well as the late nineteenth-century setting. Through objects and props and an actual séance and actual acts of magic (referenced neatly with a top hat), the story comes to life. Using those same objects and a color palette that matches the actors' masks, the poster prepares the viewer for the unexpected.

TITLE: Oscar Night Poster
CLIENT: AIRS
SIZE: 18" x 24" (45.72 x 60.96 cm)
PRINTING PROCESS: Offset litho
INKS: 3 match colors
Are posters what you primarily do for this client? No

PROCESS
COMPS PRESENTED: 0
REVISIONS: 0
APPROVAL: AIRS Committee
INVOLVEMENT WITH FINAL PRINTING:
Inspected the print run

Creating the invitation first for AIDS Interfaith Residential Services' (AIRS) annual Oscar night fundraiser, Plunkert usually draws a "combination of elements from the invitation" to make up the poster. The event is described as "a sparkling backdrop of city lights across the harbor… provid[ing] the perfect setting as guests arrive and are greeted by a crowd of fans lining the red-carpet runway and continue inside to an unforgettable Hollywood experience." Hence, a little more glitz than Plunkert's usual is called for. He labors hard for this one every year. "I find it a struggle to make the Oscars look cool," he laments.

TITLE: Theatre Project Series 04–05 *Air Dance Bernasconi*
CLIENT: Theatre Project
SIZE: 14" x 23" (35.56 x 58.42 cm)
PRINTING PROCESS: Offset litho
INKS: 2 match colors
Are posters what you primarily do for this client? Yes

PROCESS
COMPS PRESENTED: 0
REVISIONS: 0
APPROVAL: None
INVOLVEMENT WITH FINAL PRINTING:
Printed by Spur

In developing the Theatre Project's 2004–2005 season posters, a funny thing happened to Spur's process. The client remained very hands-off, feeding Plunkert dates and titles only. Plunkert developed a new illustration style for this season that depended on a sense of design. The images were simple or half-toned in order to be screen-printed, but despite the smooth start, this approach was not meant to be. Plunkert reflects, "Originally, these were supposed to be screen-printed by me, but my wife and I had twins, so I couldn't devote the time to print them. To fulfill the contract, I paid the difference for printing these offset on our dime." In this poster, the illustration conveys the amazing intricate aerial acrobatics of the dance troupe and their apparent resistance to gravity.

TITLE: Theatre Project Series 04–05 *A Real "Nigga" Show*
CLIENT: Theatre Project
SIZE: 14" x 23" (35.56 x 58.42 cm)
PRINTING PROCESS: Offset litho
INKS: 2 match colors
Are posters what you primarily do for this client? Yes

PROCESS
COMPS PRESENTED: 0
REVISIONS: 0
APPROVAL: None
INVOLVEMENT WITH FINAL PRINTING:
Printed by Spur

When discussing this play, Plunkert notes how odd it was that the designers had no problem creating powerful imagery or wrapping their heads around the visuals and questions inherent in the bittersweet comedic production. They also saw the power in the title and made it more prominent than most of the work they had done for the Theatre Project. However, "We were fairly uncomfortable throwing around the n-word in production meetings," Plunkert says.

TITLE: Theatre Project Series 03–04 *Cul de Sac*
CLIENT: Theatre Project
SIZE: 14" x 23" (35.56 x 58.42 cm)
PRINTING PROCESS: Screen print and offset
INKS: Black offset and then 2 match colors screened
Are posters what you primarily do for this client? Yes

PROCESS
COMPS PRESENTED: 0
REVISIONS: 0
APPROVAL: None
INVOLVEMENT WITH FINAL PRINTING:
Printed by Spur

Plunkert is unafraid to put a little of the past masters into his work. Here he uses a Saul Bass–like solution to detail the juxtaposition of a man and a cul-de-sac (a set of homes at the end of a street with no outlet). He succeeds, as always, in making it his own. A blaze of orange for the second color accents the tension, as does the rough printing process.

★ SLAVIMIR STOJANOVIC (FUTRO) ★

LJUBLJANA, SLOVENIA

INTO THE FUTRO

The man *Graphis* Magazine hailed as "the undisputed hero of the Serbian design scene" sees his homeland as taking baby steps toward a brave new world. "Slovenia is a small, 2,000,000-person country that became a member of European Union in 2004," Slavimir Stojanovic explains. "Most of the clients got scared of the big new market they found themselves in and pulled the plug on inventive and the groundbreaking creativity that took place in the early 1990s when Slovenia gained its independence."

This led to a year of advertising posters and billboards without much power because they focused solely on selling the product at hand and expressed no creative ideas. "The focus is now coming back down to the basic street poster," he says hopefully. Stojanovic does not plan to wait for that day to arrive, though. Since his days serving some of the country's top agencies, he has always enjoyed creating posters—and now he does so again through his new partnership in Futro. Stojanovic is so proactive that he was preparing to forge an exhibit in Belgrade with twelve giant posters in the downtown square just days after this interview.

Stojanovic is "trying to maintain a healthy balance between Futro's creative and commercial work. In one month we are overwhelmed by product-selling jobs; in the next, along comes a client from paradise who bring us a beautiful project. Because this wonderful other month seems to happen only once a year, we started producing a monthly Futro fanzine," a two-sided folded poster, as a creative outlet. For Stojanovic, the poster "has to be the most entertaining of all the forms of graphic design. It has the power of format. The bigger the better! Posters offer the most artistic freedom. They serves as a visual impulse in everyday life; the stronger the art, the stronger the impulse."

ART AND WORK

"Here in former Yugoslavia, we were strongly influenced by Polish poster masters. But the people who really influenced me as a poster designer are Woody Pirtle and Shigeo Fukuda," says Stojanovic. "My biggest professional influence was Mirko Ilic. I discovered his work in the late 1970s and decided to become a designer. Later I started discovering people like Peter Saville and the music of Massive Attack, Tricky, and Portishead. This, with my early interests in hip-hop and breakdancing, created a mix of seriousness and humor that I try to convey in each project today."

The connection to Ilic makes a great deal of sense when you consider that Stojanovic is committed to an intoxicating mix of creativity, technology, and experimentation. He has even gone as far as splitting Futro into two segments: Futro Art and Futro Work. It is his desire that "art and commercial work feed one another with inspiration," so that "things can be pushed further ahead and inspire other people."

PART OF THE SOLUTION

There is no hiding from the unraveling of the creative environment in Slovenia, but the opportunity to help shape the new environment is also there. "We are a small market where everything changes within a week and we work hard and very, very fast," says Stojanovic. That makes poster work all the more vital. "When I have opportunity to incorporate the most direct logo-design thinking into a poster design, it is the biggest thrill. I love being able to produce something attractive enough on the first glance that people actually take time to decipher the meaning."

Given Stojanovic's giant working scale, viewers will get the message fast. Very, very fast.

"It has the power of format. The bigger the better!"

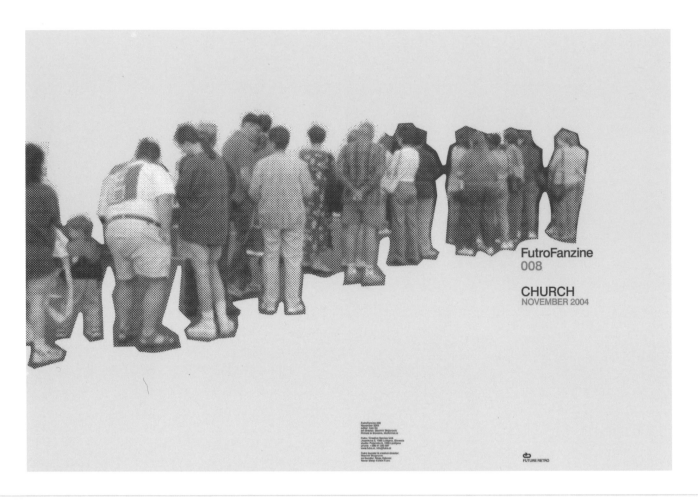

FutroFanzine
008

CHURCH
NOVEMBER 2004

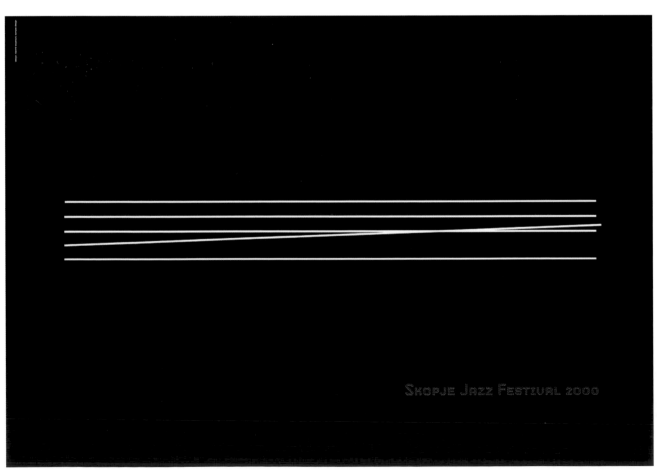

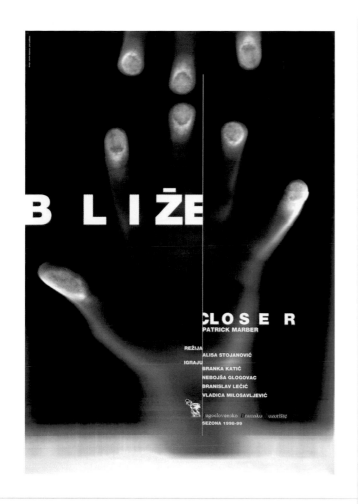

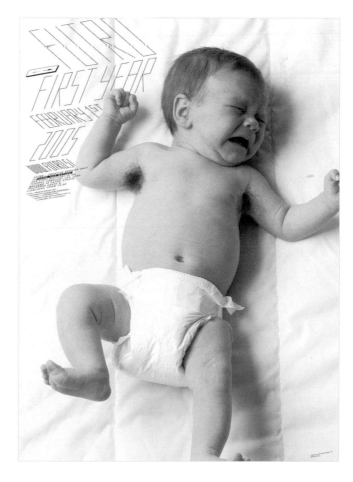

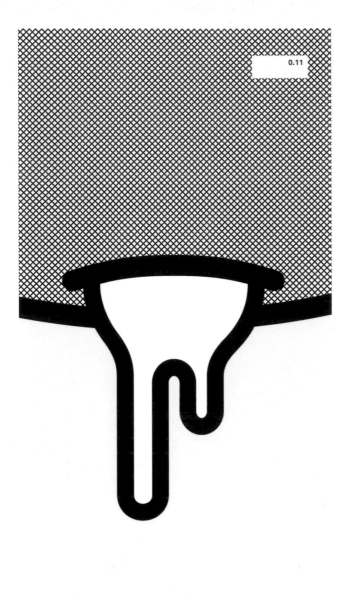

0.11

WELCOME

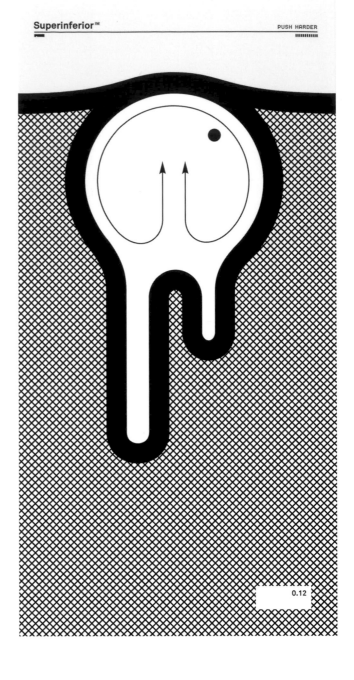

PUSH HARDER

0.12

TITLE: Futro Fanzine 008/Church
CLIENT: Futro
SIZE: 181.10" x 251.97" (460 x 640 cm) for each
PRINTING PROCESS: Offset
INKS: 4-color process
Are posters what you primarily do for this client? Yes

PROCESS
COMPS PRESENTED: 1
REVISIONS: 0
APPROVAL: None
INVOLVEMENT WITH FINAL PRINTING:
Prepared for production and press inspected

Working on the next issue of the Futro fanzine, Stojanovic tied in the design with the evolution of his "Systemerror project, where I take away as much as possible from existing global brand's logos, but they are still recognizable." To complete the picture, he added "sociocultural commentary." When you view both sides of the folded piece, you can appreciate the mix of brand and commentary.

TITLE: Skopje Jazz Festival
CLIENT: Oliver Belopta/SJF
SIZE: 37.01" x 26.77" (94 x 68 cm) each
PRINTING PROCESS: Offset
INKS: 4-color process
Are posters what you primarily do for this client? Yes

PROCESS
COMPS PRESENTED: 1
REVISIONS: 0
APPROVAL: Director of the festival
INVOLVEMENT WITH FINAL PRINTING:
Prepared for production

Stojanovic had the pleasure of designing the poster for this prestigious jazz festival for seven years, and these are some of his best-known early pieces. This particular year saw the most simple execution; the image cleverly plays off a musical notation and the innovative simplicity of the music. It's one of Stojanovic's favorite projects because he had both great freedom in designing it and great affinity for the event. He became so close to the festival that he still considers the director a close friend. This project also afforded him "the opportunity to meet legends like Poy Ayers, Tito Puente, Mahu Dibango, and many more."

TITLE: Closer
CLIENT: Jugoslav Drama Theatre
SIZE: 19.69" x 27.56" (50 x 70 cm) for each
PRINTING PROCESS: Offset
INKS: 4-color process
Are posters what you primarily do for this client? Yes

PROCESS
COMPS PRESENTED: 1
REVISIONS: 0
APPROVAL: Director
INVOLVEMENT WITH FINAL PRINTING:
Prepared for production

Working with his friend Alisa Stojanovic, who directed the play, "ensured we didn't have any problems," he says. The cruel irony of the pressed and reaching fingertips nearly touching but surrounded in darkness combines with the evocative floating typography to create the tension and bleak feeling of the production, which centers on infidelity and the complex web of relationships between two couples.

TITLE: *Waiting for Godot*
CLIENT: Scena kod Vuka
SIZE: 27.56" x 39.37" (70 x 100 cm) for each
PRINTING PROCESS: Offset
INKS: 4-color process
Are posters what you primarily do for this client? Yes

PROCESS
COMPS PRESENTED: 1
REVISIONS: 0
APPROVAL: Director
INVOLVEMENT WITH FINAL PRINTING:
Prepared for production

Invited to design a poster for a production of *Waiting for Godot*, Stojanovic had "just gone through the portfolio of artist Vuk Velickovic. I saw this photograph through incredible coincidence on the same day I received the poster job. I didn't hesitate for a second."

TITLE: Futro Fanzine 007/I Need
CLIENT: Futro
SIZE: 181.10″ × 251.97″ (460 × 640 cm) for each
PRINTING PROCESS: Offset
INKS: 4-color process
Are posters what you primarily do for this client? Yes

PROCESS

COMPS PRESENTED: 1
REVISIONS: 0
APPROVAL: None
INVOLVEMENT WITH FINAL PRINTING:
Prepared for production and press inspected

What Stojanovic calls a "labor of love, right down to having my girlfriend handle the printing," the Futro fanzine is a way "to explore communications further from everyday hard-sell graphic design." Each month the firm sends a folded poster all around the world to disseminate their message and bring a smile to a few faces. For this version, "editor Ivan Ilic was also the photographer. He took a girl on a picnic out of town and came back with these photographs, which immediately triggered my graphic response."

TITLE: Futro First Year
CLIENT: Futro
SIZE: 181.10″ × 251.97″ (460 × 640 cm) for each
PRINTING PROCESS: Offset
INKS: 4-color process
Are posters what you primarily do for this client? Yes

PROCESS

COMPS PRESENTED: 1
REVISIONS: 0
APPROVAL: None
INVOLVEMENT WITH FINAL PRINTING:
Prepared for production and press inspected

To convey that Futro is a "fast-growing small studio," the firm produced this giveaway for clients, colleagues, and friends. "It provoked a lot of diverse reactions," says Stojanovic. He has seen the poster hanging in a number of workspaces, which always makes him feel good.

TITLE: Superinferior 011 and 012
CLIENT: BELEF
SIZE: 48.03″ × 96.06″ (122 × 244 cm) for each
PRINTING PROCESS: Digital
INKS: 4-color process
Are posters what you primarily do for this client? Yes

PROCESS

COMPS PRESENTED: 1
REVISIONS: 0
APPROVAL: Selector of visual programs for BELEF
INVOLVEMENT WITH FINAL PRINTING:
Prepared for production

Produced as part of the Belgrade Summer Festival 2005 (BELEF2005), the Superinferior project comprises "twelve giant posters displayed in a downtown square in Belgrade that are used to tell an autobiographical story of trying to succeed in the Western world," explains Stojanovic. These are the final two of the pieces. You can see his fascination with information design, his bold and simple images, and his mischievous nature.

TITLE: *Bash*
CLIENT: Jugoslav Drama Theatre
SIZE: 27.56″ × 39.37″ (70 × 100 cm) for each
PRINTING PROCESS: Offset
INKS: 4-color process
Are posters what you primarily do for this client? Yes

PROCESS

COMPS PRESENTED: 1
REVISIONS: 0
APPROVAL: Director
INVOLVEMENT WITH FINAL PRINTING:
Prepared for production

Stojanovic produces a few posters each year pro bono for the theater in order to "support culture and our friends as much as we can." In this spirit, he tackled Neil Labut's *Bash*. The vacant smiling facemask relates to the "nothingness" the play is about and "seemed to be right," he says.

STUDIO BOOT

HERTOGENBOSCH, NETHERLANDS

TAKE A LOOK

Edwin Vollebergh paired with Petra Janssen, whom he refers to as "the most beautiful and talented Dutch designer," to form Studio Boot more than ten years ago in their native country, where they are perhaps best known for designing postage stamps. In design circles, however, it is the poster that has built their reputation and brought them acclaim. They have worked with clients as large as Nike on down to the grassroots. In between, they produce now eagerly anticipated Chinese New Year pieces.

The duo also teaches, lectures, and serves on design juries all around the globe.

In their use of the poster as a vehicle for their own communication, they follow in the footsteps of many a proud Dutch designer. Studio Boot even has something in common with the poster movement in the United States in their preference for an organic process and hand-manipulated or created imagery and type. But one look lets you know that they have not yet traded in any of their Dutch flair.

A CLOSER LOOK

Vollebergh knows exactly what to credit for the increase in poster design: "the power of the medium." Harnessing that power in a varied portfolio, Studio Boot has managed to make the poster a creative juggernaut for theaters as well as global makers of athletic gear and equipment. The key is variety in execution. As Vollebergh says, "Don't get stuck on one style. Take the freedom to experiment and make rubbish. Be proud!" It is that pride in the process that allows him to continue to grow and improve a piece—even after it nears a final printing. He admits, "If it doesn't work out as I expected and I'm forced to add an extra layer" of imagery to bring it to the next level, then the studio may be happy, but the poor vendor waiting for the final art may not be.

Vollebergh truly values variety as well as his relationship with his vendors. He allows that the studio "does not like repetition or style domination. A strong influence on our work is the printing method. We like to collaborate with silkscreen printers for the beautiful colors and strong images." That collaboration allows Studio Boot to create a beautiful final piece out of the occasional rough element, such as spray paint or airbrush work.

A LONGER LOOK

Edwin feels that "a poster can be seen as a strong image or message, but with a closer and perhaps longer look, one may find the extra layer with more information and maybe some fun. A poster can grow in appreciation." Mix that strong image with "colors, text, humor, lust, and extras," and you have a recipe for success. He is drawn to the current masters of this mix. "Peret, Alain Le Quernec, Niklaus Troxler—these are all great designers who are still making beautiful work."

Those same qualities inform the special nature of Studio Boot's work. The mix of whimsy and playfulness in the rough edge, spray-painted corner, and hand-drawn typography intertwined with a masterful sense of line and an incredibly sophisticated palette elevates their designs to the realm of the artistic. They also seem to let their joy in the process seep into the fabric of their work. Even pieces made up primarily of black and red manage to have a positive light. Hope radiates from behind the image and type.

"Take the freedom to experiment and make rubbish."

TITLE: Year of the Monkey
CLIENT: Kerlensky Silkscreen Printing
SIZE: 31.50" x 39.37" (80 x 100 cm)
PRINTING PROCESS: Silkscreen
INKS: 2 color
Are posters what you primarily do for this client? Yes

PROCESS
COMPS PRESENTED: 1
REVISIONS: 1
APPROVAL: None
INVOLVEMENT WITH FINAL PRINTING:
Prepared for production and press inspected

Vollebergh had the feeling "it was going to be a good, fun year for the nice ape people. So we made a happy poster with a feel-good image." Using a combination of techniques to achieve a richly detailed image, they layered on incredibly bright primary colors to increase the feel-good vibe.

TITLE: Children's Phone
CLIENT: Oilily and Children's Phone Foundation
SIZE: 32.68" x 46.46" (83 x 118 cm)
PRINTING PROCESS: Offset
INKS: 4-color process
Are posters what you primarily do for this client? No

PROCESS
COMPS PRESENTED: 1
REVISIONS: 1
APPROVAL: Contact at Oilily
INVOLVEMENT WITH FINAL PRINTING: None

Conveying Oilily's connection to modern working women with young children with a seemingly endless list of things to do, Studio Boot still managed to get the colorful aspects of the brand across. The raw elements for the presentation of this poster formed the final elements as well. Vollebergh says, "I made this as a small sketch on a color copier print and finished it on the train on my way to see the client." Working from the original A6 drawing, he then magnified the image and made some minor cleanups and freshened things a touch, but it essentially remains the same.

TITLE: Homage à Toulouse-Lautrec
CLIENT: Anthon Beeke and the City of Toulouse
SIZE: 32.68" x 23.62" (83 x 60 cm)
PRINTING PROCESS: Offset
INKS: 2 color
Are posters what you primarily do for this client? Yes

PROCESS
COMPS PRESENTED: 1
REVISIONS: 1
APPROVAL: Anthon Beeke
INVOLVEMENT WITH FINAL PRINTING: None

Invited by the legendary Dutch designer Anthon Beeke to design a poster trumpeting Toulouse-Lautrec, the studio was honored—and looked forward to the fun ahead. Using a flat rouge and black and a playful hat in reference to the artist's work, Vollebergh admits, "It was difficult to make due to the sophistication of the design audience," and that added a level of pressure. Up to the challenge, Studio Boot produced one of the most memorable pieces in the exhibition.

TITLE: *Kampen*
CLIENT: Theatre of Kampen
SIZE: 32.68" x 46.46" (83 x 118 cm)
PRINTING PROCESS: Silkscreen
INKS: 2 color
Are posters what you primarily do for this client? No

PROCESS
COMPS PRESENTED: 1
REVISIONS: 1
APPROVAL: Two-person committee at the theatre
INVOLVEMENT WITH FINAL PRINTING:
Prepared for production and press inspected

Studio Boot took on a new spin on street-posted artwork. Promoting the upcoming theater season with the concept of "discovery," they hit on a simple idea. Knowing the theater poster would be most visible on street corners, they decided to choose certain colors that would catch the viewer's eyes. "Using these colors, the poster draws attention like a traffic sign!" Vollebergh exclaims. The subsequent brochure based on the poster is a hot commodity, with "people fighting in the streets for it."

TITLE: Leids Cabaret Festival
CLIENT: Arrykies Theatre Productions
SIZE: 32.68" x 46.46" (83 x 118 cm)
PRINTING PROCESS: Silkscreen
INKS: 5 color
Are posters what you primarily do for this client? No

PROCESS
COMPS PRESENTED: 1
REVISIONS: 1
APPROVAL: Two-person committee at the theatre
INVOLVEMENT WITH FINAL PRINTING:
Prepared for production and press inspected

Besides the appeal of having the poster produced in a large format, Studio Boot knew they wanted to get to the essence of the image when the time came to do the final art. Vollebergh gives away some the tips of the trade: "It is a spray image, which we use often, made only with a simple spray can, but without shaking the can too much. That can give a rougher shade than we prefer." In helping keep things "simple and essential," he notes that making a cut-out for this process encourages sticking to basic elements. The result is an evocative come-hither performer peeking out and a hot pink color palette to convey the playful, sexy nature of the cabaret.

TITLE: Nike Butts
CLIENT: Wieden Kennedy
SIZE: up to 118.11" x 216.54" (300 x 550 cm)
PRINTING PROCESS: Offset and silkscreen
INKS: 2 color
Are posters what you primarily do for this client? No

PROCESS
COMPS PRESENTED: 1
REVISIONS: 1
APPROVAL: Contact at Weiden Kennedy
INVOLVEMENT WITH FINAL PRINTING: None

Working with ad agency Weiden Kennedy, Studio Boot took a cheeky approach to a campaign for Nike as they appropriated "French protest posters just as they appear in Paris," but in this case used for the promotion of soccer with Nike as an underground sponsor." Using their spray technique in combination with a simple collage and cut-out, they polished off the message with the simple *X* covering the goal, preventing scoring.

TITLE: Nike Defensif
CLIENT: Wieden Kennedy
SIZE: 118.11" x 216.54" (300 x 550 cm)
PRINTING PROCESS: Offset and silkscreen
INKS: 2 color
Are posters what you primarily do for this client? No

PROCESS
COMPS PRESENTED: 1
REVISIONS: 1
APPROVAL: Contact at Weiden Kennedy
INVOLVEMENT WITH FINAL PRINTING: None

Continuing their Nike series inspired by French protest posters, Studio Boot gave the look a new spin with "a rough cut-out soccer player breaking over the edge of the pattern" and through their bold blocks of typography signifying the other team's defense.

TITLE: Dali Is Born
CLIENT: Patrick and Jolande Van Der Heijden
SIZE: 19.69" x 23.62" (50 x 60 cm)
PRINTING PROCESS: Offset
INKS: 5 color
Are posters what you primarily do for this client? No

PROCESS
COMPS PRESENTED: 1
REVISIONS: 1
APPROVAL: A board of parents
INVOLVEMENT WITH FINAL PRINTING: None

Vollebergh admits the studio "normally only makes birth announcements when they have carte blanche." But for their good friend and working partner, they agreed to do one. They say, "We don't know the kid yet, but she will be just like her wonderful parents." In that vein, they used "an image based on an older sibling and the family's favorite colors" to tie the piece together.

TITLE: The Worst Ice Creams Ever
CLIENT: Rob Van Vijfeiken
SIZE: 32.68" x 46.46" (83 x 118 cm)
PRINTING PROCESS: Offset
INKS: 4-color process
Are posters what you primarily do for this client? No

PROCESS
COMPS PRESENTED: 1
REVISIONS: 1
APPROVAL: Rob Van Vijfeiken
INVOLVEMENT WITH FINAL PRINTING: None

This poster is one of their personal favorites. Vollebergh credits his partner: "Petra made beautiful cut-out type and combined it with this simple, well-known ice cream shape embellished with devil horns." To produce the final art, they sprayed white and red paint directly on a blackboard for the desired effect.

TITLE: *Out Market*
CLIENT: Theatre Kampen
SIZE: 31.50" x 39.37" (42 x 60 cm)
PRINTING PROCESS: Offset
INKS: 4 color
Are posters what you primarily do for this client? No

PROCESS
COMPS PRESENTED: 1
REVISIONS: 1
APPROVAL: Two-person committee at the theatre
INVOLVEMENT WITH FINAL PRINTING:
Prepared for production and press inspected

For the performance of *Out Market* for Theatre Kampen, Studio Boot headed for their usual tools but wanted to make something "classic and underground" at the same time, says Vollebergh. When the time came to finalize the image, they found they had "incredibly complex type for a cut-out image" compared to what they usually risked. Unafraid, they worked on it until they had the desired results, capturing the upright bass player and the musical connection to the show.

TITLE: Year of the Goat
CLIENT: Kerlensky Silkscreen Printing
SIZE: 31.50" x 39.37" (80 x 100 cm)
PRINTING PROCESS: Silkscreen
INKS: 2 color
Are posters what you primarily do for this client? Yes

PROCESS
COMPS PRESENTED: 1
REVISIONS: 1
APPROVAL: None
INVOLVEMENT WITH FINAL PRINTING:
Prepared for production and press inspected

For the Year of the Goat poster, Studio Boot started with sketching. "The actual drawing is very small—6 by 8 cm—with a marker. We always make small sketches, and for this we hardly changed anything." Well, there was *one* little change. "Originally, this was a dog image but we found out at a local Chinese restaurant that it would be the Year of the Goat. Whoops! So we gave the dog milky udders and horns to make it more goatlike."

★ YURI SURKOV ★

MOSCOW, RUSSIA

THEY CALL ME SURIC

The man often known as Suric, Yuri Surkov is one of his country's leading design lights at good time for Russian design. After years of designers working as craftsmen in Russia, this role has waned under the enormous changes the country has undergone. Now, radical creativity is taking hold in all corners of Russia, and designers, especially Surkov, are at the forefront.

Dominating national competitions and representing his country proudly in numerous international collections, he has proven an able ambassador for the renaissance taking place at home. It has been important for the poster to be an integral part of this change, as the medium has a rich history in Russia. Also, for Surkov, "the entire process of creating a poster is magic."

Although he does not see the same energy in Europe, Surkov is excited by the "poster explosion taking place in Asia and the Middle East." At home, he sees the rebound occurring slowly. "I think the number of Russian poster designers is not the same as it used to be; it has decreased. If in the 1990s Russia was represented by hundreds of posters in international exhibitions, now it is represented by no more than ten or twenty," he laments. This does not diminish his enthusiasm. The worldwide poster community is expanding, and designers are able to touch one another's work more easily, thanks to the Internet. Surkov considers himself a big part of the international poster design movement. "This feeling of participation gives me support and inspiration in my work."

NO BOUNDARIES

Surkov "adores the posters made in the 1980s and 1990s." He says his favorite designers make a very long list. "They had a great influence on me as a student, and I still feel this influence on my work," he says. "The biggest inspiration is always the idea for a poster project. If the customer is able to convey the purpose of the project clearly, images start appearing in my head, and at this point anything, especially music, comes into play," as a working inspiration. Surkhov has also famously cited a 1989 visit to Moscow by Massimo Vignelli that enlightened him about the international nature of the design community. All designers share the bond of communicating an idea by creating something even larger than they might have dreamed possible.

It is the idea at which Surkov excels. Even for an intensely stylized poster such as the Golden Bee Biennale solution, Surkov keeps the concept at heart. The poster feels like a bee. Such is the case with all his work. His color choices are inherent to the solution. His designs are often plainly influenced by both nature and technology.

INFLUENCE THE CROWD

Surkov has done the majority of his poster work on social issues. These posters are meant to be "displayed in public places and to influence the crowd." With that in mind, he holds his work to high standards. "If the poster has vivid artistic form and if the artist is honest—if the artist makes his work better than anything he has previously designed, and, of course, if the visual decision is the best representation of the main idea—the poster will be successful." He also has a passion for printing, which is "an integral part of my work," he explains. "I am always involved with it. I love to mix the inks and have the incredible feeling of controlling the process, not to mention the opportunity to touch that first copy right off the press."

That passion for the poster from beginning to end has served Surkov well. He and his likeminded comrades will soon fill Russia with astonishingly challenging design. For the time being, it brings pleasure to our eyes and minds to gauge this progress through the man his countrymen call Suric.

"The entire process of creating a poster is magic."

Let it Bee!

Золотая Пчела 2000 Международная Биеннале Графического Дизайна ▪ Golden Bee 2000 Moscow International Biennale of Graphic Design

NATURA LIST

-posters

Государственный музей
архитектуры им. А.В.Щусева
Флигель «Руина»

МУ
А Р

Yuri Surkov

Академия графического дизайна
Ассоциация «Золотая пчела»
Государственный музей архитектуры им. А.В.Щусева
Международная конфедерация союзов художников
Компания «Экспо-Парк Выставочные проекты»
Центр современного искусства «М АРС»
Галерея Марата Гельмана
Типография «Линия графика»
Фонд поддержки художественных проектов «Арт Москва»
Высшая академическая школа графического дизайна

1.03.04 — 14.03.04

Экологический арт-фестиваль «4-й Блок»

Российская ассоциация графических дизайнеров «4 Блок»   http://www.4block.com
Студия дизайна и рекламы «Про-образ»   http://www.pro-obraz.ru

Государственный музей архитектуры им. В.А.Щусева
Москва, ул. Воздвиженка, 5/25. Экспозиции открыты с 11:00 до 20:00, в субботу и воскресенье с 11:00 до 16:00
Выходной день — понедельник. Тел.: 290—0551. Директор музея — Давид Ашотович Саркисян
www.muar.ru   schusev@muar.ru

Print.LiniaGrafic!

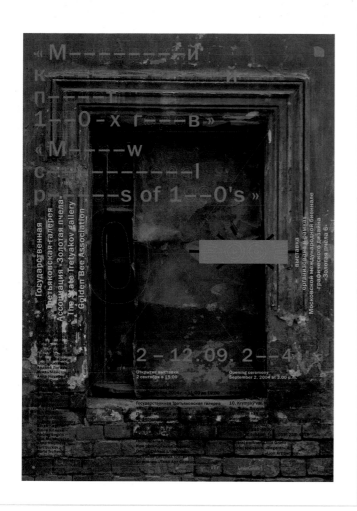

Dream Word

Museum on the Seam—for Understanding, Dialogue & Coexistence

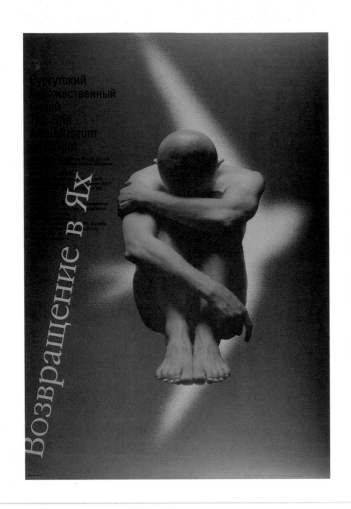

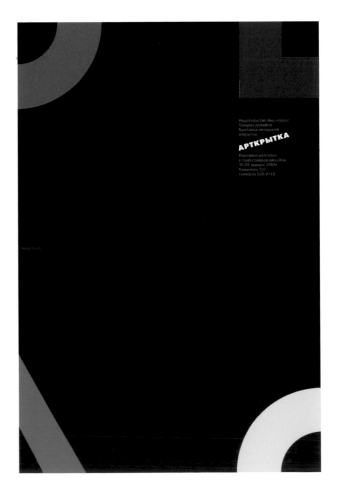

DIE MYTHOLOGIE UND   DIE PRAXIS   DER GEGENWARTSKUNST

The clitoral truth

MOSCOW+   +ПУСТЫНЬ+   +ZURICH

SURIC DESIGN

TITLE: Let it Bee!
CLIENT: "Golden Bee" Moscow International Biennale of Graphic Design
SIZE: 26.9" x 38.6" (69 x 99 cm)
PRINTING PROCESS: Silkscreen
INKS: 2 color
Are posters what you primarily do for this client? Yes

PROCESS
COMPS PRESENTED: 1
REVISIONS: 2
APPROVAL: Curator
INVOLVEMENT WITH FINAL PRINTING:
Prepared for production and press inspected

"I prefer the works in which maximal expressiveness is attained by a minimum of means," explains Surkov. "This poster was chosen because the work surprised me pleasantly. Two circles made up of the lines branching off from the center were superimposed using a little displacement to form a surprising picture. Instead of ordinary lines, the eyes of a bee appear. But this is not the end. Flickering intervals between the lines add motion to the image, and, what is more astonishing, they force the picture to begin to sound! Look at the picture more attentively. Do you hear the vibration of bee wings?"

TITLE: Natura List
CLIENT: Schusev State Museum of Architecture (MUAR)
SIZE: 27" x 38.5" (69.2 x 98.8 cm)
PRINTING PROCESS: Offset
INKS: 4-color process
Are posters what you primarily do for this client? Yes

PROCESS
COMPS PRESENTED: 1
REVISIONS: 2
APPROVAL: Yuri Surkov
INVOLVEMENT WITH FINAL PRINTING:
Prepared for production and press inspected

"A considerable part of my work is devoted to ecological and social themes," says Surkov. "Which is why, when selecting a story for the poster to present my personal exhibition, I decided to use my own image. At first I wanted to name the exhibit 'Soldier of Nature', but then I changed it to 'Natura List'. From my archives, I picked a suitable photograph of me when I was serving in the army. The main solution of the poster is in the central star and, more accurately, in its color," and the inherent associations it has with Russia.

TITLE: Moscow Conceptual Posters of the Nineties
CLIENT: The State Tretyakov Gallery, Moscow
SIZE: 26.9" x 38.6" (69 x 98.9 cm)
PRINTING PROCESS: Offset
INKS: 4-color process and 1 color
Are posters what you primarily do for this client? Yes

PROCESS
COMPS PRESENTED: 1
REVISIONS: 2
APPROVAL: Gallery director
INVOLVEMENT WITH FINAL PRINTING:
Prepared for production and press inspected

For a poster representing the Moscow Conceptual Poster of the 1990s for the State Tretyakov Gallery, Surkov worried about the lack of Russian designers working in the poster medium. Given the state of affairs, "the show could be full of pathos, or have a slight shade of sadness and regret," he says. "This was the first attempt in Russia to present posters as a part of contemporary art. It was rather difficult. The big dash keeps the minor feeling, appropriate to the exhibit. By exposing only first and last letters of the words, I left it for the viewer to guess the rest of the text."

TITLE: Mayakovsky Festival in Moscow
CLIENT: FUTURIZM
SIZE: 26.3" x 37.6" (67.4 x 96.5 cm)
PRINTING PROCESS: Offset
INKS: 4-color process
Are posters what you primarily do for this client? Yes

PROCESS
COMPS PRESENTED: 1
REVISIONS: 2
APPROVAL: FUTURIZM director
INVOLVEMENT WITH FINAL PRINTING:
Prepared for production and press inspected

"The beginning of the twentieth century in Russia was a time of revolutions, struggles for the new future. One of the more active fighters was Mayakovsky," explains Surkov. "He loved revolution, loved struggle. He was a poet with gentle soul who desired to become a fighter and was ready to challenge the entire world, anyone who dared to stand on his path. And what appears on a face of a person who likes to fight?" he asks. "A bruise, of course! But in this case it's not just a bruise—it's text. In this poster, I play a visual game with the viewer. If you look from far away, you can distinguish Mayakovsky's face with a bruise under the eye. If you come closer, the face falls apart into squares—pixels—and instead of the bruise the text is clearly seen. If you come even closer, the program of the entire festival appears in halftones." This poster is special to Surkov, who dedicated it to his painting professor, S. K. Sedelnikov.

TITLE: Coexistence
CLIENT: Museum on the Seam, Jerusalem
SIZE: 26.5" x 38.2" (68 x 98 cm)
PRINTING PROCESS: Offset
INKS: 2 color
Are posters what you primarily do for this client? Yes

PROCESS
COMPS PRESENTED: 1
REVISIONS: 2
APPROVAL: Curator
INVOLVEMENT WITH FINAL PRINTING:
Prepared for production and press inspected

"The goal of this design was to help stop the conflict in the region, force people to make agreements, be more tolerant," explains Surkov. "War is a violation of harmonious equality, because only in equality does harmony exist." He focused on the notion that "we are all different from one another, but compose one whole. 'Coexistence' has three religions peacefully living next to each other symbolically—in one word!" he exclaims.

TITLE: Return to the Yakh
CLIENT: The Fine Arts Museum of Surgut
SIZE: 27.3" x 39" (70 x 100 cm)
PRINTING PROCESS: Offset and silkscreen
INKS: 2 color
Are posters what you primarily do for this client? No

PROCESS

COMPS PRESENTED: 1
REVISIONS: 2
APPROVAL: Curator
INVOLVEMENT WITH FINAL PRINTING:
Prepared for production and press inspected

"I like to work with the Fine Arts Museum of Surgut," says Surkov. "Surgut is a city in Siberia, 3,000 kilometers away from Moscow, its land rich with myths and legends. *The Yakh* in Khant language [Khants are a people of Siberia] has multiple meanings—a river, world, ghost, family. Therefore, the title literally speaks of a return to the inner world. That is why the man on the poster is turned inward, in an embryo-like pose," he says. "The contour of a bird in the background is lifting the man from the ground, indicating his high aspirations." The final touch was printing the piece on Chromalux metallic paper for added impact.

TITLE: Nature Morte
CLIENT: Yuri Surkov
SIZE: 26.1" x 38.6" (67 x 99 cm)
PRINTING PROCESS: Silkscreen
INKS: 2 color
Are posters what you primarily do for this client? Yes

PROCESS

COMPS PRESENTED: 1
REVISIONS: 0
APPROVAL: Yuri Surkov
INVOLVEMENT WITH FINAL PRINTING:
Prepared for production and press inspected

This social poster commemorates the tenth anniversary of the *Chernobyl* nuclear tragedy. Surkov feels "the key to understanding this poster is in the name *Chernobyl*. The depth of this tragedy fits into this word. The name consists of parts: *cherno*, meaning black color, a synonym of mourning, tragedy, death, and *byl*, which is everything that happened in life. Therefore the word symbolizes dead life. Remarkably, *Chernobyl* has the same meaning as *nature morte* in French, *Still Leben* in German, and *still life* in English. Black colored graphics only intensify this gruesome discovery," he adds.

TITLE: Water for Human Kind
CLIENT: Association Pour une Banque d'Images, Paris
SIZE: 27.3" x 39" (70 x 100 cm)
PRINTING PROCESS: Silkscreen
INKS: 2 color
Are posters what you primarily do for this client? Yes

PROCESS

COMPS PRESENTED: 1
REVISIONS: 0
APPROVAL: Association head
INVOLVEMENT WITH FINAL PRINTING:
Prepared for production and press inspected

When you are unsure of your instincts, sometimes you need to trust the instincts of others. "I made this poster very fast," Surkov says. "Since my childhood, I have known that the human body almost entirely consists of water. Life is conceived in water, comes out of water. Water is life, life is water. The concept came to me so easily that I was afraid the poster would be blank. I showed the poster to my colleagues, who assured me that it's very strong. I trusted their opinion, and they were right. This poster became the Laureate of the Triennial of Poster and Eco-Graphic 4th Block in Kharkov, and it won the bronze medal at the International Poster Biennial in Warsaw."

TITLE: ARTCARD Exhibition
CLIENT: IMA Design Gallery, Moscow
SIZE: 27.3" x 39" (70 x 100 cm)
PRINTING PROCESS: Silkscreen
INKS: 5 color
Are posters what you primarily do for this client? Yes

PROCESS

COMPS PRESENTED: 1
REVISIONS: 2
APPROVAL: Curator
INVOLVEMENT WITH FINAL PRINTING:
Prepared for production and press inspected

This piece, which received the Encouraging Prize at the International Exhibition of Graphic Design in Zagreb, was described in what amounted to a perfect summation of Surkov's place in Russian design: "The poster shows a creative continuation of the forcibly interrupted Russian avant-garde." Surkov relates the "elaborate composition based on associations with plastic. The decorative elements in the corners visually remind me of the corners that hold the photographs in place in the photo albums," he says.

TITLE: *SUPREMUS: The Clitorial Truth*
CLIENT: *SUPREMUS*—Intellectual Publishing Project for Visual Art and Popular Culture
SIZE: 27.1" x 38.8" (69.5 x 99.5 cm)
PRINTING PROCESS: Offset
INKS: 4-color process
Are posters what you primarily do for this client? Yes

PROCESS

COMPS PRESENTED: 1
REVISIONS: 2
APPROVAL: SUPREMUS director
INVOLVEMENT WITH FINAL PRINTING:
Prepared for production and press inspected

"*SUPREMUS* is a serious publication about contemporary art produced in Geneva by a publisher," says Surkov. "To shake things up, he always gives a sexual connotation to his publications. So I wasn't surprised when the slogan he offered me for a poster exhibition was 'Supremus. The Clitoral Truth.' As I began to work, I recalled colossal emotions I experienced at the exhibit 'French Lace of the Seventeenth and Eighteenth Centuries.' Everything presented there was handmade by women. It was an astonishing sight!" Surkov related it to the amazing abilities of the modern computer and made a funny association. "I understood that a cross-stitch, an element of old stitching, is similar to a pixel, an element of contemporary computer imaging."

★ SUSSNER DESIGN COMPANY ★

MINNEAPOLIS, MINNESOTA, USA

PURE AND HONEST

Derek Sussner (pronounced *soose-ner*—don't worry, he lets most say it incorrectly for months) set up his eponymous shop along with a crew of creative thinkers in the midwestern design mecca of Minneapolis. It is a city with so much talent that it can be hard to distinguish yourself. However, Sussner has one large advantage: He is not a transplant. He is very Minnesota. And it is his Midwestern qualities that separate him from his pretentious neighbors.

Sussner describes his firm's approach as one that is "aesthetic, informed, and, importantly, intuitive. Our philosophy is best described as a blue-collar work ethic. I believe the best way to connect with anybody is to talk to them as peers—always think of yourself as an equal. Never talk down to anyone, and never be spoken down to, whether it's a wealthy CEO or a hopeful student. I believe that people are smart, and when that is in question, I give them the benefit of the doubt. People will perceive you based on the honest impression you give them."

Honest hard work is a theme that shows up again and again in his poster work, whether a self-promotion piece or a poster for the motorcycle daredevil Evel Knievel. It is the potential the poster has to convey this message that makes it so powerful in his hands. "The poster is such a pure and honest medium," says Sussner. "When we get a poster project, we are like kids in a candy store. There's something special about working in the medium." Sussner Design Company is a full-service firm getting their hands dirty in all manner of design. Yet the poster holds a special place in their hearts—so much so that "if too much time passes without a poster project, we will design one for ourselves."

UNDESIGNED

Asked for his take on past masters of design, Sussner says, "There can't be just one, right?" He finds inspiration in many designers before putting it through the blue-collar filter: "Shepard Fairey and his Obey Giant work, Modern Dog (featured on page 132), Aesthetic Appartatus (featured on page 6), Neville Brody, Carlos Segura (and t26), Ames Design, Templin Brink, Jennifer Sterling, Michael Schwab, Hatch Show, Joe Monnens, and Vaughan

Oliver," just to name a few. But his drive leads him far from design to find solutions. Heavy inspiration can also be found in "Ayn Rand's writings. Music—heavy metal, especially the bands coming from Gothenburg, Sweden. My parents—my upbringing. Personal experiences. Golf—I love it, but it just won't love me back. All things blue-collar. Copy. Copywriters. And, like many, I have a strange fascination for the undesigned," he says.

While the Swedish heavy metal might concern some, I believe it is offset by the mention of his parents. Clients may now return.

SO MUCH WITH SO LITTLE

Sussner credits the rebirth of the poster to "a return to all things tactile and touchable. Even the handwritten note has a renewed fan base. I think the personal touches have become appreciated with all things digital, cyber, emailed, and PDF'd." His appreciation for all things printed runs deep. "I've even kept posters that were sent to me where the design is not great but the printing is beautiful."

When you combine beautiful printing with the ability to capture a great deal with very little, then you have a successful Sussner poster. "What's the outdoor billboard rule—seven words or less?" asks Sussner. "Some of the best posters I've seen were all words. Other great ones are image only. Some are carried only by typography. Some of the best posters, while designed for a specific event or concert, still convey a sense of timelessness."

One timeless thing Sussner Design Company has mastered: hard work.

"I believe that people are smart, and when that is in question,
I give them the benefit of the doubt."

WE JUST SHOWED YOU OUR NOW US MONKEY YOU SHOW YOUR PORT FOLIO

AIGA minnesota's Portfolio One-On-One is a unique event for graphic design students. This two-day program includes studio tours, a vendor exhibit, a panel discussion featuring local senior creatives, how-to portfolio workshops and individual portfolio reviews with professional creatives from the Twin Cities. It's an opportunity for students to get to know other design students and a chance to meet working professionals. The Scholarship for Design Excellence is offered annually at Portfolio One-On-One by the Minnesota Chapter of AIGA. It is awarded to an upper-level graphic design student who demonstrates outstanding aptitude and exceptional creativity. This $1000 award is intended to encourage and further the work of the recipient, and can be used for any purpose. Applicants are required to be enrolled in an accredited college or university in Minnesota, Wisconsin, Iowa, North Dakota or South Dakota that offers a four-year degree in graphic design. This year's event is scheduled to be held Friday, April 7 and Saturday, April 8, 2000 at the Regal Hotel in downtown Minneapolis. Call the AIGA/MN office at 612.339.6904 with questions or to be put on the One-On-One mailing list and sent more detailed event and registration information this March.

THE MINNESOTA CHAPTER OF THE AMERICAN INSTITUTE OF GRAPHIC ARTS IS A NON-PROFIT ORGANIZATION, SERVING THE SPECIFIC NEEDS OF PROFESSIONALS INVOLVED IN GRAPHIC DESIGN AND RELATED FIELDS IN THE MIDWEST REGION. *AIGA*

ALL
VIDEO GAMES
BANNED
EFFECTIVE
IMMEDIATELY
HEY, IT COULD HAPPEN
WITHOUT YOUR INVOLVEMENT IN THE GOVERNMENT YOU ARE POWERLESS TO STOP IT
JOIN THE YOUTH GOVERNMENT COUNCIL AND HAVE A SAY
NO VOICE NO CHOICE

TITLE: AIGA Minnesota Portfolio 1-ON-1 Poster
CLIENT: AIGA (Minnesota chapter)
SIZE: 22" x 31" (55.88 x 78.74 cm)
PRINTING PROCESS: Copier
INKS: Black
Are posters what you primarily do for this client? Yes

PROCESS

COMPS PRESENTED: 1
REVISIONS: 0
APPROVAL: Brainco
INVOLVEMENT WITH FINAL PRINTING:
Prepared the print to be copied

Designing a poster to be displayed at Brainco, the Minneapolis School of Advertising, on AIGA student portfolio day meant getting help from the school's president, Ed Prentiss. Sussner recalled a "mail order ad in the back of a 1950s hunting magazine selling fifteen-dollar squirrel monkeys. I found this a year or so before this poster was designed when I bought a stack of these old magazines on eBay and kept it around for just the right project. I think monkeys are funny, as they make people laugh. Plus, there is a sort of trained-monkey-that-does-tricks-in-the-street-for-spare-change feeling that students can relate to." The final piece was "originally designed at an actual size of 7.5 x 10.5 inches," says Sussner. "Once all the elements were scanned and cleaned up, the final composite was printed on a laser printer at 8.5 x 11 inches and taken to a copy store for large-format copies. The copy machine quality seemed appropriate to both the tone (sarcastic) and to the student audience (limited funds)."

TITLE: The Hunter
CLIENT: Sussner Design Co./
University of Wisconsin, Stout
SIZE: 16.5" x 23.5" (41.91 x 59.69 cm)
PRINTING PROCESS: Digital
INKS: 4-color process
Are posters what you primarily do for this client? Yes

PROCESS

COMPS PRESENTED: 1
REVISIONS: 1
APPROVAL: None
INVOLVEMENT WITH FINAL PRINTING:
Prepared for production and printed

The firm managed to get some extra mileage out of a poster for a speaking engagement that they then modified to use to promote the studio. Sussner explains, "I grew up in rural southwest Minnesota. While I did not grow up on a farm or in the country, we were not far from it. I spent a fair amount of my time hunting critters and birds. When this project came up, it was less a design project and more of a sentimental scrapbook. This image was collaged entirely by hand, with images and ads cut out of old hunting magazines from the 1950s and 1960s. A bit of trial and error, then glued down. Final touches were made on the computer, aged, and then applied to the collage." The copy on the poster says, "I got a stain on my shirt. It might be coffee, it might be blood, and damn it, I don't care."

TITLE: VOBS Fortieth Anniversary Benefit Dinner
CLIENT: Voyageur Outward Bound School
SIZE: 9" x 17" (22.86 x 43.18 cm)
PRINTING PROCESS: Offset
INKS: 2 color
Are posters what you primarily do for this client? No

PROCESS

COMPS PRESENTED: 1
REVISIONS: 5
APPROVAL: Marketing director and event chair
INVOLVEMENT WITH FINAL PRINTING:
Prepared for production and printed

"The poster is an invitation to VOBS's fortieth anniversary benefit dinner and a solicitation of donations to the scholarship program to enable more students to benefit from an Outward Bound experience," explains Sussner. "The art is based on the 1964 logo art for Outward Bound. Historical to VOBS, even a bit sentimental, the poster is a tribute to the past forty years. It is intentionally designed to have a bit of aged feel and to appear as if it was screen-printed." The studio loved being involved with the event. "The most interesting part of it, to me," says Sussner, "was that we were part of an event that was very successful. It's great to have design freedom on a project like this, but as a tool to use in talking to potential new clients, it's nice to be able to show clients work that had actual measurable results—which gives the designer some business credibility." Easy to do when the event doubles its stated funding goal.

TITLE: Flavor CD Release Poster
CLIENT: Flavor
SIZE: 13" x 19.5" (33.02 x 49.53 cm)
PRINTING PROCESS: Digital
INKS: 4-color process
Are posters what you primarily do for this client? Yes

PROCESS

COMPS PRESENTED: 5
REVISIONS: 0
APPROVAL: Lead singer of the band
INVOLVEMENT WITH FINAL PRINTING:
Printed by Sussner Design Co.

Inspired by the band's name (Flavor), the album's name (*Red*), and the title of one of the songs ("PBJ—Strawberry Jelly)," Sussner and crew designed what they felt were truly engaging posters for the group's CD release party. They even overcame severe budget restrictions by running drawing pad paper through their digital printer in two passes to simulate screen-printing. Alas, you cannot please everyone. After the posters were printed, the band decided they were looking for something artistic and alluring, but with a quote or two and a band photo and a photo of the album....

TITLE: Evel Knievel Poster "Leather Saved My Ass"
CLIENT: EK Leather USA
SIZE: 11.5" x 25" (29.21 x 63.50 cm)
PRINTING PROCESS: Offset
INKS: 3 color
Are posters what you primarily do for this client? Yes

PROCESS

COMPS PRESENTED: 8
REVISIONS: 3
APPROVAL: President and Evel Knievel
INVOLVEMENT WITH FINAL PRINTING:
Prepared for production

An overworked former employee could not handle a new project for EK Leather, based around Evel Knievel, the motorcycle daredevil, and Sussner jumped at the chance to fill in. "Some of my favorite toys as a kid were of Evel!" he says with obvious delight. After working up some drawings and reworking them on the computer, "we sent the final layouts via FedEx to the company president and to Evel. The most interesting response that came back from Evel, to whom we never actually spoke directly, was that in the illustration of him, the size of the groin area needed to be enhanced to more accurately reflect the size of his manhood. No kidding."

TITLE: Mille Lacs Band of Ojibwe Youth
Council Poster
CLIENT: Red Circle Agency
SIZE: 15" x 23.5" (38.10 x 59.69 cm)
PRINTING PROCESS: Offset
INKS: 4-color process
Are posters what you primarily do for this client? Yes

PROCESS
COMPS PRESENTED: 1
REVISIONS: 1
APPROVAL: Mille Lacs Band of Ojibwe Chief
INVOLVEMENT WITH FINAL PRINTING:
Prepared for production

Sussner's firm was hired for a unique poster job for a local Indian tribe. "The creative direction we were given was to pose the youth versus the mean old elders in the tribe, to have the posters feel counter-revolutionary. And, of course, there should be a visual reference to the Native American. Interesting note the Native American reference needed to be consistent with the woodland tribe, not southwestern natives. We wanted the posters to look like the wheat-pasted propaganda-style posters you see pasted outdoors on plywood, light poles, and building sides. The idea was to create a poster campaign geared to educate kids on how being on the tribe's Youth Council can directly affect their lives by giving them a voice in their community—or, to be more precise, how *not* being on the council could affect their lives. We needed to show them different ways their rights and freedoms could be infringed upon by others in power. If they have no voice, they have no choice. The posters were placed in schools and youth centers and anywhere else kids hang out."

TITLE: Blue Collar Poster
CLIENT: Sussner Design Co.
SIZE: 17.75" x 25" (45.09 x 63.50 cm)
PRINTING PROCESS: Offset
INKS: 5 color
Are posters what you primarily do for this client? n/a

PROCESS
COMPS PRESENTED: 1
REVISIONS: Numerous
APPROVAL: None
INVOLVEMENT WITH FINAL PRINTING:
Prepared for production and press inspected

Working with the toughest client of all—himself—Sussner brought in reenforcements in the form of photographer Ellie Kingsbury and writer Jeff Mueller. Kingsbury's process proved a turning point in the piece. "She develops the shots directly onto paper with a blue ink," explains Sussner. "She calls them Cyan-O-Types. She tapes off a square area, applies the ink, and exposes a square area. The extra ink that was slopped on the paper also exposes. I loved the whole paper, extra ink and all. So instead of cropping the square photo, we had the whole exposed piece of paper scanned and just set our type on top of it." For the photo, they used their dog as a metaphor for their blue-collar philosophy, going so far as to pose her to look tougher in the shots. One of the "inspirations was the packaging for Cozy Pet Sanitary Panty. When my dog was fixed, the veterinarian told us to have her wear a doggie diaper so she wouldn't stain our house. It is promoted as being very comfortable. On the packaging, there's an illustration of a dog wearing the diaper—and she's smiling."

TITLE: Sussner Six-Year Anniversary Poster
CLIENT: Sussner Design Co.
SIZE: 24" x 32.5" (60.96 x 82.55 cm)
PRINTING PROCESS: Offset
INKS: 3 color
Are posters what you primarily do for this client? n/a

PROCESS
COMPS PRESENTED: 6
REVISIONS: 5
APPROVAL: None
INVOLVEMENT WITH FINAL PRINTING:
Prepared for production and press inspected

For once, taking so long to finish his own promotions really paid off. Sussner explains, "Jeff Mueller and I actually started working on the concept for the poster for our fifth business anniversary. The logo is my hand, and we were going to use it as five fingers for five years in business. Jeff wrote it, and we had sketched it out. But we were busy with paying clients, and the next thing we knew, by the time we started actually designing it a year had gone by. We thought about starting over but instead added a sixth finger to the hand, which we think makes it funnier than with five, added the few new clients to the list, and made it a sixth anniversary poster."

TITLE: The Bremer Magical Mystery Tour
CLIENT: Bremer Bank
SIZE: 11" x 17" (27.94 x 43.18 cm)
PRINTING PROCESS: Offset
INKS: 2 color
Are posters what you primarily do for this client? No

PROCESS
COMPS PRESENTED: 2
REVISIONS: 2
APPROVAL: Marketing communications manager
and senior vice president
INVOLVEMENT WITH FINAL PRINTING:
Prepared for production and press inspected

"We design quite a range of projects for Bremer," says Sussner. "They were one of our first clients. We've worked on everything: ads, website, credit cards, product identities direct mail, newsletters, annual reports, folders, business banking materials, and brochure design. And once in a while we get to go outside of the corporate umbrella with a special event T-shirt, or, in this case, a conference poster." The team created a Beatlesque psychedelic feel with bold colors and then was mildly shocked when they received the go-ahead on the concept. "I still can't believe the bank went for this!" Sussner exclaims.

TITLE: Personal Works Show Invitation
CLIENT: American Society of Media
Photographers (ASMP)
SIZE: 12" x 18.5" (30.48 x 46.99 cm)
PRINTING PROCESS: Offset
INKS: 2 color
Are posters what you primarily do for this client? Yes

PROCESS
COMPS PRESENTED: 3
REVISIONS: 3
APPROVAL: Show chair (and photographer)
INVOLVEMENT WITH FINAL PRINTING:
Prepared for production and press inspected

Working with copywriter Mueller and photographer Ingrid Werthmann on an invitation to an annual photography show by a nonprofit photographers professional organization, Sussner came upon a simple solution. "The pieces in the show are all for sale (profits go to charity), and the work is all photographers' personal work—not work that was commissioned or the outs from a paid commercial photo shoot," he explains. "So we designed the call for entries as a classified ad, and the invite was designed as a light pole sign announcing that pictures were for sale—a rummage sale of photos." Werthmann's image was overprinted with a metallic ink for a simple yet sophisticated effect.

★ THE **HEADS** OF **STATE** ★

PHILADELPHIA, PENNSYLVANIA AND SEATTLE, WASHINGTON, USA

NEWEST OF THE NEW

This dynamic duo is the one that puts the "new" in New Masters. Out of design school only a few years, Jason Kernevich and Dustin Summers have formed one of the hottest design and illustration firms in the United States. In fact, it took only a few months after finishing studies at Tyler School of Art before they realized they needed something more from their day jobs and banded together.

Earning acclaim right out of the gate, they have ridden the swell of enthusiasm for gig posters right to the top of a hotly contested field. Starting out with lesser-known bands, they quickly rose to commissioned work from some of the top touring bands of all time, notably R.E.M. and Wilco.

You can see the influences of others that only just preceded them, including some in this book. (An interesting passing of the torch has occurred from Art Chantry to Patent Pending's Jeff Kleinsmith and now to Kernevich and Summers, all clocking hours in the design department at Sub Pop Records.) They acknowledge being part of a current poster movement but add that the firm "would rather be grouped as a member of a movement of great design—a group of designers using found images, found type, texture, hand-drawn items in reaction to the more glossy computer-driven design that has been prevalent since the first part of this decade." Despite the shared influences, each poster Kernevich and Summers do is very much their own. Using simple hand-executed shapes to make the painstaking separation of hope and reality so clear in their poster for Idlewild, or photographic resources to twist and turn them into the figure-eight record for the Bright Eyes piece, there is one constant: a concept.

CLEAR, SIMPLE, BRILLIANT

Most designers will be pretty lucky to ever have an idea or two, much less a high-falutin' concept. Not the case with the Heads, as each and every piece has one clear and simple, yet brilliant, idea. A signifier of a Heads of State piece is restraint. They take the execution as far as the concept requires—no further. Never overworking or overstylizing a final image, they exit the stage to delirious applause each and every time. When you hold one of their posters, you are amazed at how rough some of the edges are, as the thick silkscreen inks overlap and interact. You can sense their love affair with the medium; you can almost feel the rush of inspiration coming through the paper the poster is printed on. The breathtaking moment is when you step back and view it at a natural distance. The design all comes together, and what seemed spontaneous moments before becomes refined and composed right before your eyes.

This is the type of work that most will take a lifetime to achieve, yet the Heads of State achieved these lofty results right after finishing their studies.

That these guys even exist shows how big a rebirth the poster has experienced. Ten years ago, it would have been unfathomable to start a young design firm around a poster design specialty. Interactive? Sure. Handmade posters? No way. As Kernevich and Summers say, "This section of design has been so stagnant for almost a decade, and now there are many studios, ourselves included, building their whole careers on posters."

GROWING YOUR AWARENESS

When quizzed about what shapes their work, some obvious names pop up: the more free-form work of Paul Rand, Alex Steinwell's album work, and the collage and paintings of Ray Johnson, and of course the sublime work of poster masters such as Milton Glaser, Saul Bass, and Art Chantry. Delving deeper, Kernevich and Summers really give up the goods. "We are here as designers because of mid-1980s metal bands. We drew Metallica and Van Halen logos in our notebooks during fifth-period algebra. We sat on the floor in our Osh-Kosh overalls looking through our parents' collection of vinyl records, just admiring the covers without even knowing why." Now they absorb their surroundings completely. "There's music, there's the weather, and there are lines in books. If you really keep your eyes open, it's hard not to be influenced by everything around you. It's a matter of keeping your senses working during those times when the world decides to tell you a secret."

"It's hard not to be influenced by everything around you. It's a matter of keeping your senses working during those times when the world decides to tell you a secret."

R.E.M.

LANCASHIRE COUNTY CRICKET CLUB
MANCHESTER, UK · JUNE 17, 2005
WITH FEEDER · THE ZUTONS

WITH A.C. NEWMAN AND NEINS · AUGUST 13 · NORTH STAR BAR

BRIGHT EYES JANUARY 28 · THE ACADEMY OF MUSIC

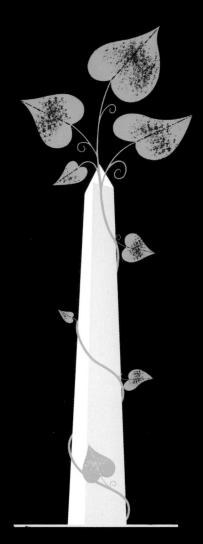

WILCO
JUNE 9TH • 9:30 CLUB
WASHINGTON DC • 2004

TITLE: R.E.M. Manchester
CLIENT: R.E.M. / R.E.M. HQ
SIZE: 18" x 24" (45.72 x 60.96 cm)
PRINTING PROCESS: Silkscreen
INKS: 3-color water based
Are posters what you primarily do for this client? *Yes*

PROCESS

COMPS PRESENTED: 4 each for 4 tour dates
REVISIONS: None
APPROVAL: Michael Stipe and the band's art director, Chris Bilheimer
INVOLVEMENT WITH FINAL PRINTING: None

Sometimes an idea requires a little time to age before it can find the right fit. Summers notes, "I keep a sketchbook, or a few of them, actually. Most of the pages end up being layer upon layer of doodles and ideas, but I also paste in sketches I did on Post-It notes, etc. This image of a stack of books came into my head one day, but at the time I just couldn't make it work." Three years later, when R.E.M. asked Kernevich and Summers to design posters for upcoming concerts around the world, they revisited this idea. As Summers says, "For some reason, it really says R.E.M. to me, sort of playing off the band's long and storied career as a volume of text."

TITLE: Rogue Wave
CLIENT: The North Star Bar
SIZE: 18" x 24" (45.72 x 60.96 cm)
INKS: 3-color water based
Are posters what you primarily do for this client? Yes

PROCESS

COMPS PRESENTED: 1
REVISIONS: None
APPROVAL: Management at The North Star Bar
INVOLVEMENT WITH FINAL PRINTING: None

This poster takes full advantage of the printing process. The spot white was overprinted to make the sheet hanging on the clothesline, allowing a subtle show-through. While the result shows a confidence in the mastering of the art of silkscreening, getting there was a little bumpy. The guys admit they are still learning on the job. "We had the idea for this poster but weren't sure the printing would work out, so we ended up doing something similar but not as complex just to test the overprinting." The extra work paid off, as you can see.

TITLE: Les Savy Fav
CLIENT: TLA
SIZE: 18" x 24" (45.72 x 60.96 cm)
PRINTING PROCESS: Silkscreen
INKS: 3-color water based
Are posters what you primarily do for this client? Yes

PROCESS

COMPS PRESENTED: 1
REVISIONS: 1
APPROVAL: Les Savy Fav and Management at TLA
INVOLVEMENT WITH FINAL PRINTING: None

Part of the appeal of the firm's work is the use of a powerful central image. Finding the right one is a lot harder than one might imagine, and once you have the image in mind, executing it can be equally challenging. Kernevich and Summers explain, "Just as every designer does, we tend to get into slumps. Designing and constructing this poster was a nice departure from the things we had been working on previously. An ungodly amount of time was spent with a copy machine and an X-Acto knife to collage the snakes, but it ended up being a bit of creative therapy." The snake imagery seemed apt for a band that describes its music as "entropy versus evolution, clarity versus confusion, or staying up all night versus sleeping all day."

TITLE: Bright Eyes Philadelphia
CLIENT: R5 Productions
SIZE: 24" x 16" (60.96 x 40.64 cm)
PRINTING PROCESS: Silkscreen
INKS: 2-color water based
Are posters what you primarily do for this client? Yes

PROCESS

COMPS PRESENTED: 1
REVISIONS: None
APPROVAL: Management at R5 Productions
INVOLVEMENT WITH FINAL PRINTING: None

In thinking about a poster for this band, the firm focused on the fact that Bright Eyes had just released two singles making smashing debuts at #1 and #2 on the Billboard single charts, and they were about to simultaneously release two full-length albums. As Summers explains, "The image seems so simple, but it came after a few hours of just staring and sketching and trying to figure how you could make two pieces of vinyl interesting enough to hold a poster."

TITLE: Cat Power
CLIENT: R5 Productions
SIZE: 18" x 24" (46 x 61 cm)
PRINTING PROCESS: Silkscreen
INKS: 2-color water based
Are posters what you primarily do for this client? Yes

PROCESS

COMPS PRESENTED: Each of the Heads designed an option internally and then decided which one to present.
REVISIONS: 3
APPROVAL: Cat Power
INVOLVEMENT WITH FINAL PRINTING: None

This piece captures two of the most distinctive attributes of the firm's work: texture and mildly twisted illustration. Of the origami paper pattern from an over-the-counter craft supply store, Summers notes that it "was used initially on a poster that was to be very stereotypical, domestic, and feminine—an intentionally ironic tone, considering the music." For the illustration, "an old drawing from a children's book inspired me to try something quirky and naïve, but vicious."

TITLE: Idlewild
CLIENT: Capitol Records, EMI/Parlophone
SIZE: 18" x 24" (45.72 x 60.96 cm)
PRINTING PROCESS: Silkscreen
INKS: 3-color oil based
Are posters what you primarily do for this client? No

PROCESS

COMPS PRESENTED: 1
REVISIONS: 1
APPROVAL: Band's Management and the Band
INVOLVEMENT WITH FINAL PRINTING: None

Working in the recording industry often yields inspirational imagery from the band's work. In this case, the piece was inspired by the Idlewild song "A Modern Way of Letting Go." The firm explains, "The image is an exaggerated and metaphorical depiction of severing of a relationship using modern methods." The application of the concept, however, was the key to the true impact of the poster. Kernevich and Summers reveal their secret: "To add to the visual humor and represent how childish even our most adult relationships can become, the image was executed with cut-up pieces of construction paper."

TITLE: Wilco NYC
CLIENT: Wilco, Tony Margherita Mgmt., Chicago
SIZE: 18" x 24" (45.72 x 60.96 cm)
PRINTING PROCESS: Silkscreen
INKS: 3-color water based
Are posters what you primarily do for this client? Yes

PROCESS
COMPS PRESENTED: 2
REVISIONS: 2
APPROVAL: Band's Management
INVOLVEMENT WITH FINAL PRINTING: None

For concert poster design, a really special venue can be as big an influence as the performer himself. For this one, the firm couldn't resist the magic of a storied stage, and that thinking took on a life of its own. The Heads admit, "The fact that this show was held at Radio City Music Hall was the biggest inspiration. Thinking of Art Deco immediately, I knew only the type should convey the charm of Old Gotham. For the main image, I decided to turn to something that has always been in the back of my mind as a truly great visual: Francis Cugat's 1924 painting for the cover of *The Great Gatsby*, published by Scribner. Combining a solemn Jazz Age tone with Art Deco typography was a great jumping-off point and an immediate decision. What took work was making a falling piano look quiet."

TITLE: Built To Spill
CLIENT: Built To Spill
SIZE: 18" x 24" (46 x 61 cm)
PRINTING PROCESS: Silkscreen
INKS: 3-color water based
Are posters what you primarily do for this client? Yes

PROCESS
COMPS PRESENTED: 1
REVISIONS: None
APPROVAL: None
PRINTER: Largemammal Press
INVOLVEMENT WITH FINAL PRINTING: None

Less is often more for the Heads of State. Summers notes that the final execution here is "a super-simple poster. There was so much more to this, but we just took away and took away until it ended up being just the building and type. We tend to do that a lot, start off with too much going on and then whittle it down to only its more necessary parts. This started out as a very busy piece with the upside-down city—but in the sky there were clouds, people falling, airplanes, hot air balloons, basically just a ton of garbage that made the poster much too busy." When discussing the city image and its orientation, they say, "It's basically just a stripped-down interpretation of the band name. When we approach a poster, we explore many ways to portray that band or its music. Sometimes we work off lyrics; sometimes we work off the sound of the music or the feeling we get from the music. Sometimes we try to interpret the band name in an unexpected way, but we try not to be too gimmicky." What they do accomplish is strength by subtraction.

TITLE: Wilco Washington D.C.
CLIENT: Wilco
SIZE: 18" x 24" (45.72 x 60.96 cm)
PRINTING PROCESS: Silkscreen
INKS: 3-color oil based
Are posters what you primarily do for this client? Yes

PROCESS
COMPS PRESENTED: 18
REVISIONS: 1
APPROVAL: Band's Management Company TMM Chi
INVOLVEMENT WITH FINAL PRINTING: None

This project was "probably one of the fastest posters we've ever designed," say the Heads of State. Summers explains, "After going through a few rounds of ideas, designing around eighteen different posters for this show and being totally worn out at midnight or so, Jason presents this image of the leaves that he had found but wasn't quite sure what to do with it. I immediately saw the vine wrapping around the Washington Monument, and about forty-five minutes later the poster was done." He continues, "That's one of the most exciting things about working with another person, the Ping-Pong effect, where one person finds something but isn't sure exactly how to make it work, so the other steps in with a fresh perspective."

TITLE: Califone
CLIENT: North Star Bar
SIZE: 18" x 24" (45.72 x 60.96 cm)
PRINTING PROCESS: Silkscreen
INKS: 3-color water based
Are posters what you primarily do for this client? Yes

PROCESS
COMPS PRESENTED: 1
REVISIONS: None
APPROVAL: Promoter
INVOLVEMENT WITH FINAL PRINTING: None

The Heads try to get off easy describing this piece as "completely based off a Califone song called 'Don't Let Me Die Nervous'." While the inspiration holds true, the execution reveals a love affair with the golden age of animation and comics. The subtle shifts in the halftone create shading and radiant light, showcasing a thorough mastery of the silkscreening process that belies the small number of years they have been at this.

TITLE: Hot Hot Heat
CLIENT: R5 Productions
SIZE: 18" x 24" (45.72 x 60.96 cm)
PRINTING PROCESS: Silkscreen
INKS: 3-color water based
Are posters what you primarily do for this client? Yes

PROCESS
COMPS PRESENTED: 1
REVISIONS: None
APPROVAL: Promoter
INVOLVEMENT WITH FINAL PRINTING: None

The Hot Hot Heat poster proved a turning point for the firm. They relate, "This was one of our earlier posters. It was done at a point when we relied a little too heavily on clip art and found imagery and hadn't really explored drawing things ourselves. Where we would have tried to find a piece of art or imagery of a fire hydrant, we instead went down the street and took a picture. This was a crossing point into a more hand-done, rough-hewn style."

TITLE: Magnetic Fields
CLIENT: Red Ryder Booking
SIZE: 18" x 24" (45.72 x 60.96 cm)
PRINTING PROCESS: Silkscreen
INKS: 3-color water based
Are posters what you primarily do for this client? Yes

PROCESS
COMPS PRESENTED: 4
REVISIONS: 2
APPROVAL: Band and Tour Manager
INVOLVEMENT WITH FINAL PRINTING: None

Sometimes the work of others seeps in and provides profound inspiration. Kernevich and Summers note, "This poster plays off of the Magnetic Fields library of love songs, maybe their darker side. We had been looking at a lot of wood cuts, block-printing, but we also drew inspiration from the work of Seripop (see page 154) and Yo Rodeo and their use of twisting and interlocking bizarre forms. Keeping one's eyes up and drinking in one's surroundings are essential parts of growing as a designer.

★ THINKMULE ★

PEORIA, ILLINOIS, USA

INTRODUCING MR. MULE

It is hard to believe that Jeremy Pruitt is located in the heartland of the United States. For one thing, under the persona he assumes for his art and design ventures—Mr. Mule, or, more often, Thinkmule—he can be found all over the Internet as a contributor to numerous fringe design and art sites and collections. His daily correspondence is with like minds from all over the globe. Some of these connections even end up in collaborations, including magazines, installations, and anything else people can get their hands on. Thinkmule is so well known in these circles that he could be anywhere and seems to be everywhere.

A passion for art and a seemingly unquenchable thirst for work have led to an extensive body of work for a young upstart. His unique drawing style, honed every day in his sketchbook, separates his work from that of his peers. His sense of design and typography cannot be denied, and on occasion, those skills alone can carry a piece. But the posters all seem to have his hands on them, and the more evident that is, the more engaging the result. He uses doodles, primitive drawings, and ripped and pasted images, and then scribbles over the top of them. There is a sense of dirty work involved in his design, yet the final product is true and complete.

The best possible medium for the work of Thinkmule has always been the poster, a canvas he is unable to resist. Pruitt is shy, however, about hearing his name connected to a "movement." He says, "I am just doing what I like, and it happens to be popular at the moment, but I am by no means on the front edge of any 'new movement'." Whether he likes it or not, he will find his name in those conversations with increasing frequency.

PRIMITIVE AND HONEST
Thinkmule's appreciation for art history and the art of primitive cultures gives his drawings a particular focus. He also has a deep regard for patterns and their intricacies. The viewer can see that attention to detail combined with his intuitive line work. Pruitt adds, "Outsider art has had a big impact on my work the last few years. It seems very pure and honest to me." He combines this with his love of many other art movements. An appreciation of Jean-Michel Basquiat and Cy Twombley mixes with folk art and the art of the insane. The influence of his design heroes, Lester Beall, Stenberg Brothers, Lucian Bernhard, Alexander Rodchenko, El Lissitzky, Saul Bass, Herbert Matter, and H. R. Erdt, seeps into his work.

Pruitt brings along all of this visual baggage, plus a keen observation of his environment, when working on a poster. Noting his love for the freedom of such assignments, he still feels a sense of responsibility to promote the band, event, or cause and make an "honest representation" of the message or music. Pruitt knows the jobs arrive on his desktop not so he can do a "random visual exercise for my own benefit" but rather so he can build excitement and fill venues.

Sometimes Pruitt is too successful. His Iron and Wine poster had a very difficult time staying posted around town promoting the show; the prints were stolen by appreciative onlookers almost immediately after they were hung.

CONNECTED
Thinkmule's posters are about "making a connection," says Pruitt, whether between a music fan and Thinkmule's interpretation of the band's music or the greater connection with the poster community at large. He loves the online communities (such as gigposters.com) that have sprung up where "poster lovers have a place to see what was or is going on at the moment, talk about posters, and have a resource on making posters." He knows it is not just the single poster artist that is carrying this torch. "The design shops have helped by doing award-winning work, and as more and more people have seen it, the interest has grown." A growing community of creatives, from the world's largest agencies down to the lone designer and his stunning work and clever moniker—all are connected by their love of one thing: the poster.

"Outsider art has had a big impact on my work the last few years. It seems very pure and honest to me."

THURSDAY, JULY 29TH
★ O'LEAVERS ★
9:30PM 21+ $5

The Minders

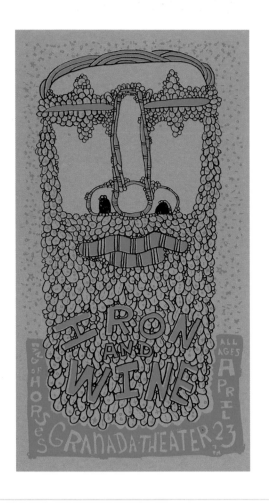

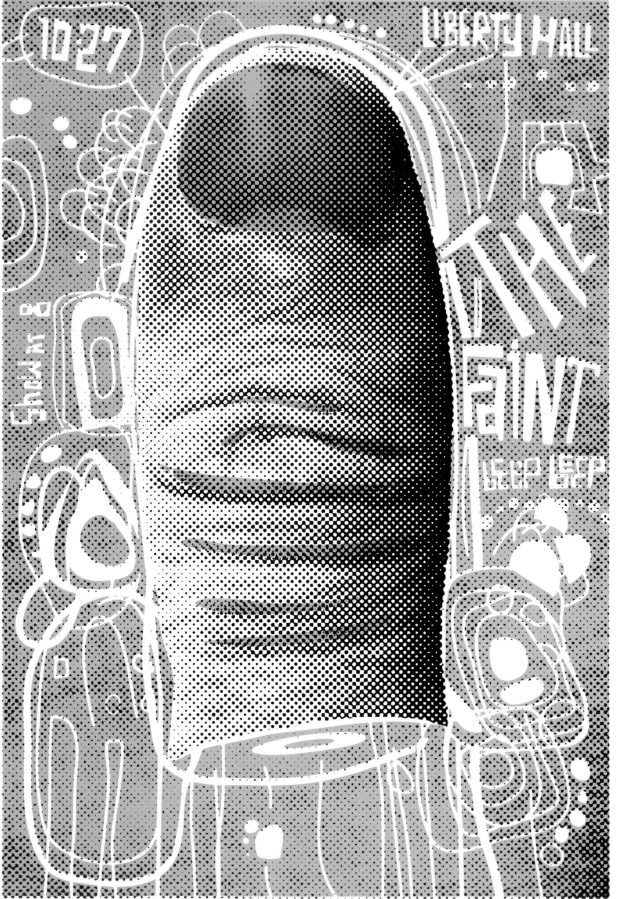

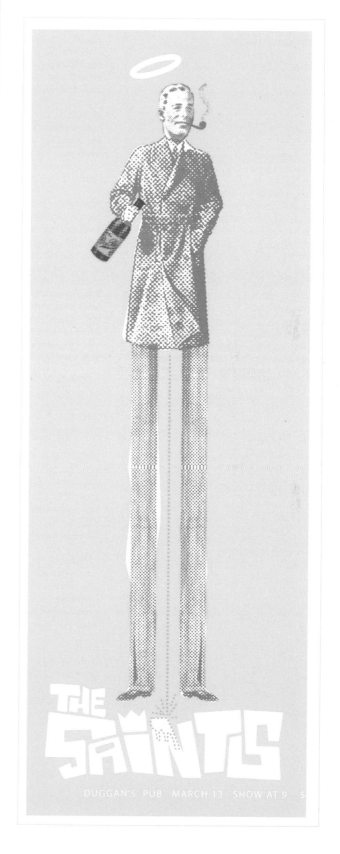

TITLE: Minders
CLIENT: One Percent Productions
SIZE: 8.5" x 14" (27.94 x 35.56 cm)
PRINTING PROCESS: Digital
INKS: 4 color
Are posters what you primarily do for this client? Yes

PROCESS
COMPS PRESENTED: 1
REVISIONS: 0
APPROVAL: Promoter
INVOLVEMENT WITH FINAL PRINTING: None

It's funny, the little details you can pick up on when researching your subject matter. Pruitt was "watching TV and sketching. I really liked the name of this band, and in the photos I saw, I noticed a pair of these groovy glasses on one of the dudes. I loved the look and simply had to use it." After some initial drawings, he found himself at an impasse and went to the grocery store to clear his head. "Watermelon was on sale, so I decided to pick one up, and as I was thumping on it to make my selection it hit me—put the glasses on the melon. On the way home, I thought of the type running through the vine. Rushed in to take a digital photo of the melon and an old pair of horn-rimmed glasses I had." A short time spent drawing the type, and this masterpiece was complete.

TITLE: Iron and Wine
CLIENT: Jacki Becker
SIZE: 12.5" x 19" (31.75 x 48.26 cm)
PRINTING PROCESS: Silkscreen
INKS: 2 color
Are posters what you primarily do for this client? Yes

PROCESS
COMPS PRESENTED: 1
REVISIONS: 0
APPROVAL: Promoter
INVOLVEMENT WITH FINAL PRINTING:
Printed by Thinkmule

When you're excited about a project, your first idea can ring true immediately. Pruitt says, "I love this band, and this was actually the first rough sketch I did for the project. I just worked it and refined it further. I did the rough half-size and then tightened it up. I did the entire drawing in one sitting." When he decided to add the second color, he "started doing that by putting the first drawing on the light box and just adding elements here and there." Tight on time, the project "came together really fast, but I think that was a good thing in this case." This piece is also part of his evolving process and is "all by hand, which is my favorite style now."

TITLE: Ween
CLIENT: One Percent Productions
SIZE: 12.5" x 19" (31.75 x 48.26 cm)
PRINTING PROCESS: Silkscreen
INKS: 3 color
Are posters what you primarily do for this client? Yes

PROCESS
COMPS PRESENTED: 1
REVISIONS: 0
APPROVAL: Promoter
INVOLVEMENT WITH FINAL PRINTING:
Printed by Thinkmule

For the unconventional band Ween, Pruitt wanted to do something a little fun and wacky. However, he didn't want to duplicate the efforts of others. "I was going to do a boobs poster, and then I remembered Aesthetic Apparatus had done one for another band. But I didn't give up on boobs. I just switched to dog boobs. I don't have a thing for dog boobs, mind you—it just seemed to fit with this idea of 'weening'. But the dog is not a normal dog, and she runs around shooting milk all over the place. I originally had the dog have a long neck and the nipples went up the neck, but I thought the dog on the go with nipple spray was funnier."

TITLE: Tortoise
CLIENT: Jacki Becker
SIZE: 8.5" x 11" (21.59 x 27.94 cm)
PRINTING PROCESS: Digital
INKS: 4 color
Are posters what you primarily do for this client? Yes

PROCESS
COMPS PRESENTED: 1
REVISIONS: 0
APPROVAL: Promoter
INVOLVEMENT WITH FINAL PRINTING: None

"Right around the time I did this poster, I had just bought some matchbox art—the little labels you stick on matchboxes from Europe. They were really cool and very old-school and mechanical in their printing," reveals Pruitt. "I wanted to do something like it, very simple and bold, with straightforward color. I had done a sketch randomly some time before that of a saw cutting a cloud in half, and I thought it would be a great image for the poster. The type was inspired by some I had seen in an old Art Deco book I have. I love the feel of it—and so I made my own."

TITLE: Rent Money Big
CLIENT: Rent Money Big
SIZE: 11" x 17" (27.94 x 43.18 cm)
PRINTING PROCESS: Digital
INKS: 4 color
Are posters what you primarily do for this client? Yes

PROCESS
COMPS PRESENTED: 1
REVISIONS: 0
APPROVAL: Band
INVOLVEMENT WITH FINAL PRINTING: None

Pruitt was familiar with the local band Rent Money Big and their "fun and energetic shows," which he wanted to capture on the poster for an upcoming performance. He worked fast based on his knowledge of the client, making an energetic red swirl "with a pencil, blowing it up enormously on a copy machine," and combining with other elements he had on hand to make a striking figure.

TITLE: These Arms Are Snakes
CLIENT: Jacki Becker
SIZE: 8.5" x 11" (21.59 x 27.94 cm)
PRINTING PROCESS: Xerox
INKS: 1 color
Are posters what you primarily do for this client? Yes

PROCESS

COMPS PRESENTED: 1
REVISIONS: 0
APPROVAL: Promoter
INVOLVEMENT WITH FINAL PRINTING: None

Something so raw and spontaneous can take a lot of planning, says Pruitt. "I really wanted the piece to capture the band's vibe. I knew I had some of this art already, and I wanted this piece to be a combination of different elements, texture and grit. I first just worked with my idea and did a thumbnail drawing and got a picture of what I wanted it to be in my head. I remember cutting some of it out with scissors and arranging it. I scribbled and tweaked. Scanned. I would say this one was a move for me in that I liked the more hands-on approach and it started me moving in the direction of doing all my posters by hand. I originally was going for the background to be orange, but I thought the gray fit better and was more heavy-duty. Orange was too happy, and I don't like happy."

TITLE: The Faint
CLIENT: Jacki Becker
SIZE: 12.5" x 19" (31.75 x 48.26 cm)
PRINTING PROCESS: Silkscreen
INKS: 2 color
Are posters what you primarily do for this client? Yes

PROCESS

COMPS PRESENTED: 1
REVISIONS: 0
APPROVAL: Promoter
INVOLVEMENT WITH FINAL PRINTING:
Printed by Thinkmule

Pruitt admits some projects need a little more thought. "This was the second concept I came up with," he says. "I was going to do a poster of a goat. I had read about these goats that faint and fall over. I thought that would be a funny poster. I don't know if anyone would have gotten it, but what the hell. I then did some other sketches and thought of some stuff that makes you faint. Like cutting off your thumb! I started to think about how that would make you feel—like woozy and shit." A quick photograph of his thumb later, and concept number two is a winner.

TITLE: The Makers
CLIENT: One Percent Productions
SIZE: 12" x 18" (30.48 x 45.72 cm)
PRINTING PROCESS: Digital
INKS: 4 color
Are posters what you primarily do for this client? Yes

PROCESS

COMPS PRESENTED: 1
REVISIONS: 0
APPROVAL: Promoter
INVOLVEMENT WITH FINAL PRINTING: None

Pruitt is a collector of sorts, which can come in handy. "I was looking through some old car magazine —I have a ton of old magazines. I like the art and feel of them. I was looking specifically at an old car ad. A lot of old car ads used to show the engines, and that inspired me. Wouldn't it be a great idea to do an engine skull?" he thought. Following a few variations, Pruitt had the engine skull of his dreams.

TITLE: The Saints
CLIENT: The Saints
SIZE: 8" x 19" (20.32 x 48.26 cm)
PRINTING PROCESS: Digital
INKS: 4 color
Are posters what you primarily do for this client? Yes

PROCESS

COMPS PRESENTED: 1
REVISIONS: 0
APPROVAL: Band
INVOLVEMENT WITH FINAL PRINTING:
Printed by Thinkmule

For the local band the Saints (not the world-famous ones from Australia), Pruitt thought a lot about their stage show. "They cuss a lot and flip off the crowd and spit on the crowd. Real nice guys, though." With that in mind, he "came up with the idea of an angel peeing on a cloud." After further thought, he "thought it might be cooler to have a "1950s-style figure in heaven because the 1950s were such a life-was-so-good time and I am sure they were just as messed up as us." After the figure was set up to be drinking and urinating on the band's name, it looks like he surely doesn't belong in heaven and may even have a secret agenda. "He's no saint," says Pruitt, "Pee boy!"

TITLE: Arcade Fire
CLIENT: Jacki Becker
SIZE: 12.5" x 19" (31.75 x 48.26 cm)
PRINTING PROCESS: Screen print
INKS: 2 color
Are posters what you primarily do for this client? Yes

PROCESS

COMPS PRESENTED: 1
REVISIONS: 0
APPROVAL: Promoter
INVOLVEMENT WITH FINAL PRINTING:
Printed by Thinkmule

When he works in his hand-drawn style, Pruitt seems to find himself building designs differently. Listening to Arcade Fire, Pruitt "started to add pieces to each portion of the poster inspired by different songs." Tightening the composition to where he wanted it, Pruitt "redrew the eyes several times and ended up combining several pieces of the drawing digitally afterwards." Sweating the details paid off, as this piece has been a major success.

★ THIRST (RICK VALICENTI) ★

CHICAGO, ILLINOIS, USA

SETTLE DOWN FOR A MINUTE

There may be an uproar about the inclusion of Rick Valicenti as a "New Master," as he has hardly been hiding his talents all these years. However, one is hard pressed to think of a designer whose work seems fresher and more modern and cutting-edge in execution than Rick. His ability to be years ahead of the curve is astonishing, and when the time came he simply could not be left out. It is important to note his focus on the poster as a medium, as it has been a constant in his portfolio. It is also the arena in which his ever-evolving personal design seems to be expressed at the highest pinnacles in his life.

For Valicenti, the poster has always been a barometer of what makes his journey so special—the choices he makes as well as the ones he does not. "The best part of designing a poster is the hardest part of designing a poster—deciding what to actually print. Unlike when designing a catalog or book, the designer has but one page to express the program, the event, or the system, not 32 or 332 pages! I thoroughly enjoy the challenge," he says. As a caution, he adds, "All design processes are a mine filled with compromise. The designer, or I should say the best designers, are the ones who can consistently conceal compromise in their final output. The poster has but one surface to serve design's many masters seated at the conference table. The best posters make everyone happy—including the designer."

A TRIP TO THE MOVIES
One might expect to find Valicenti's finger on the pulse of the design underground, that he is seeing our world in a way that many of us cannot possibly imagine. Not true at all. As far as the poster is concerned, he is aware of what is transpiring in music and political poster design, but he sees it the same way millions of others do—at the movies. "The Hollywood poster harkens back in some weird way to the classic advertising posters of the early twentieth century," says Valicenti. "While some of them were not great, the same can be said of today's Hollywood product. However, every once in a while a minor classic bubbles to the surface and in some cases transcends the lifespan of the movie itself. The gold *Austin Powers II* poster, the recent *Star Wars 3*, and the retro *Catch Me If You Can* quickly come to my mind." He views his role as a designer for the Lyric Opera in Chicago as having the same demands of those promoting films.

His projects "share the same sense of spectacle and production value, and with that need to communicate on many of the same formal levels." He is unapologetic about the influence of the work displayed at your local theater as he draws this parallel. "Know this for certain: The hallways in our modern cineplexes are today's equivalent to the European kiosk-lined streets of the past."

Besides taking inspiration from his Friday- and Saturday-night visits to the movies, Valicenti harkens to designers past. "Cassandre is my model," he says, "but no designer practicing today can escape the influence of modern masters like Bass, Matter, Beale, Tanaka, Hoffman, Brockman, Weingart, and Greiman." For something a little looser, he is also a "sucker for the 1960s posters of Mosoco [Mouse.]"

CONCEPTUAL PRECISION
The poster can be the most challenging medium, and the most rewarding as well. It is both of these aspects that keep someone of Valicenti's caliber engaged in its pursuit. "The poster, at the end of the day, is Composition 101, which should not be confused with Layout 101 or Typography 101," he says. "The best posters are done with conceptual precision and visual economy. Success is getting it all right at the same time."

Ladies and gentlemen, "success."

"The poster has but one surface to serve design's many masters seated at the conference table."

'That was then...this is whenever **Rick Valicenti** *7 feb 05 Vancouver* GDC/BC

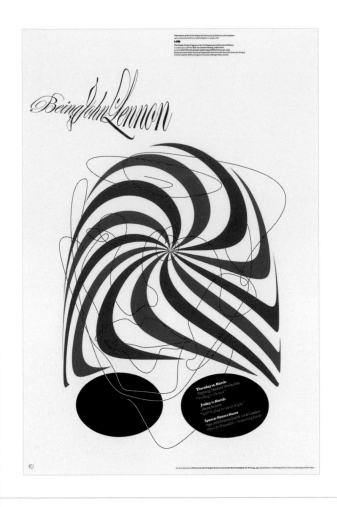

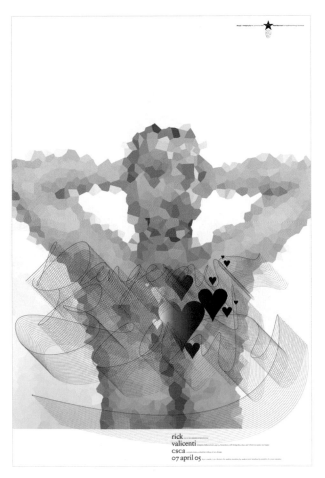

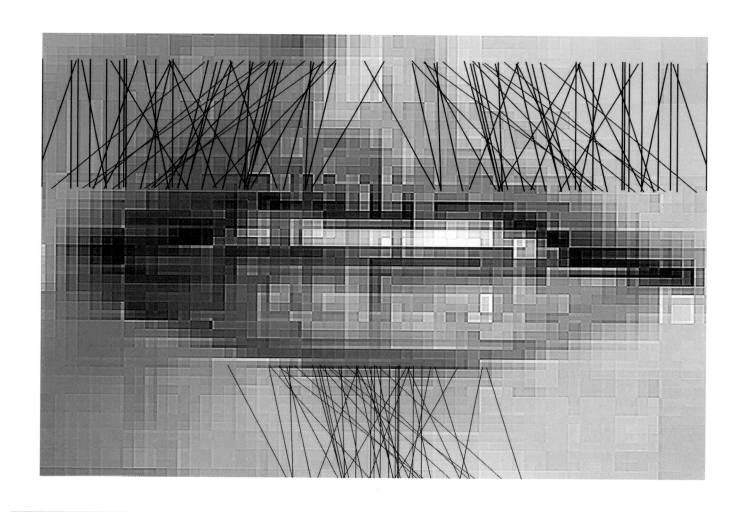

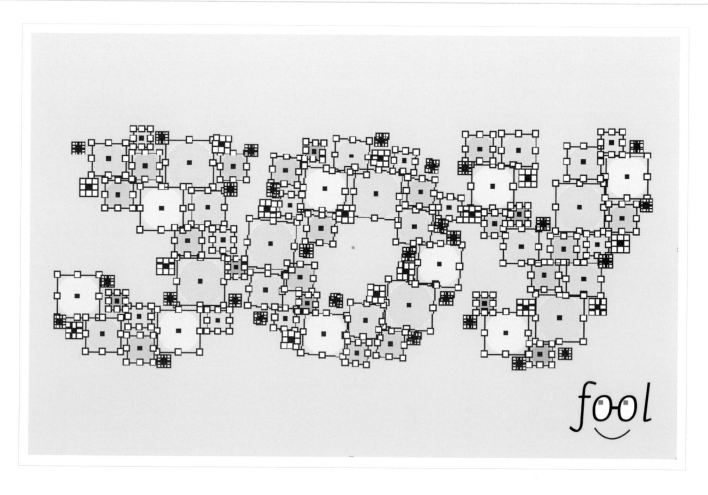

WAGNER **THE RING**

LYRIC OPERA OF CHICAGO 2005

2003 **LYRIC OPERA OF CHICAGO 2004**

TITLE: Vancouver
CLIENT: Vancouver, BC, Society of Graphic Designers
SIZE: 24" x 36" (60.96 x 81.44 cm)
PRINTING PROCESS: Offset
INKS: 4-color process
Are posters what you primarily do for this client? Yes

PROCESS
COMPS PRESENTED: 0
REVISIONS: 0
APPROVAL: Thirst
INVOLVEMENT WITH FINAL PRINTING:
Provided paper and print specifications

After thirty years of marriage, Valicenti and his wife separated. This poster is the first of many dealing with that struggle. "A personal transformation like this never comes easy, and graphic design is hardly the cure. Graphic design, however, can serve as both a mirror and a reflection of the feelings I have been experiencing. While I am the creator of this work, the making process is in no way perceived as a substitute for a proper introspection, which has been happening concurrently. Overwhelmed with a dark sadness, this image shows a deflated professional me seated under the tree of happiness and love. My jester's cap complete with glowing promotional signage seems torn and tattered. I created an image of myself that seems to be molting as I transform into a new future."

TITLE: Alabama One
CLIENT: University of Alabama, Birmingham
SIZE: 24" x 36" (60.96 x 81.44 cm)
PRINTING PROCESS: Offset
INKS: 4-color process
Are posters what you primarily do for this client? Yes

PROCESS
COMPS PRESENTED: 0
REVISIONS: 0
APPROVAL: Thirst
INVOLVEMENT WITH FINAL PRINTING:
Provided paper and print specifications

Working through this difficult period, Valicenti admits, "I found myself so disturbed by both the process of making the Vancouver portrait and reflecting on it that I forced myself to get repositioned in a happier place. As Valentine's Day approached, I recited the old adage 'She loves me, she loves me not'. The Illinois cardinals accented the cold snowy outside, as I kept focused on being happy." This is side A of a poster promoting his lecture and workshop at University of Alabama Birmingham.

TITLE: Alabama Two
CLIENT: University of Alabama, Birmingham
SIZE: 24" x 36" (60.96 x 81.44 cm)
PRINTING PROCESS: Offset
INKS: 4-color process
Are posters what you primarily do for this client? Yes

PROCESS
COMPS PRESENTED: 0
REVISIONS: 0
APPROVAL: Thirst
INVOLVEMENT WITH FINAL PRINTING:
Provided paper and print specifications

A few days later, while working on side B of the Alabama poster, Valicenti felt "the forced positive outlook of the 'be happy' graphic still did not ring true. It almost seemed like I had run away and was hiding from myself. I recalled that John Lennon had run away once to Los Angeles for what has infamously become known as the 'lost two weeks'. Just that recollection took me to my own archive of a graphic created in February 2004 while on a vacation in Belize. While experimenting with a few of the effects in a recent version of Illustrator, I designed a book jacket for an unwritten novel, *Being John Lennon*. Feeling like this mythical persona of John Lennon, I decided to use it as the darker of the two sides of me at that point in time. To refashion this graphic, I pulled a contour line drawing of myself, also created in a happier 2004. Together these two expressions of myself made the accurate impression of me in 2005."

TITLE: me ego
CLIENT: Columbus Society of Communication Arts
SIZE: 24" x 36" (60.96 x 81.44 cm)
PRINTING PROCESS: Offset
INKS: 4-color process
Are posters what you primarily do for this client? Yes

PROCESS
COMPS PRESENTED: 0
REVISIONS: 0
APPROVAL: Thirst
INVOLVEMENT WITH FINAL PRINTING:
Provided paper and print specifications

The final piece of Valicenti's separation exploration, "this image is deceivingly simple but seems to complete this trilogy of self-expression. What might appear as a happier, bolder self is probably just one man testing the waters of stepping out of his own skin. Again, without even a kernel of an idea, I found myself meandering the Internet for imagery. I stumbled upon an image of what appeared to be a balding middle-aged man with a piece of paper covering his face. I borrowed this very low-resolution image and enlarged it only to find it very soft as a result. The crystal filter was applied, but still there was a white field and a balding head. With a bit of cutting and pasting I had configured a new face and hair in my own image."

TITLE: *View from the Bridge*
CLIENT: Lyric Opera of Chicago
SIZE: 24" x 36" (60.96 x 81.44 cm)
PRINTING PROCESS: Offset
INKS: 4-color process
Are posters what you primarily do for this client? No

PROCESS
COMPS PRESENTED: 3
REVISIONS: 3
APPROVAL: General director and PR/marketing director
INVOLVEMENT WITH FINAL PRINTING: Provided paper and print specifications and press inspected

Valicenti has enjoyed a long and happy relationship with the Lyric Opera of Chicago. Designing the world premiere poster for Arthur Miller's *View from the Bridge*, his brother and he "created a simple photo shoot consisting of two lights for the portrait session with the opera's lead, Kim Josephson." He dug into his files and found "the water image, a photograph from my own archive, which when printed red became both the blood and the red of the Italian flag. The bridge suspension pattern was created by accident as I suffered through without a well-designed layout. A few Photoshop filter sequences on top of a very low-resolution screen grab of a bridge detail and I had the beginnings of this tangled web representing emotional turmoil. Barry Deck's Euniverse font design was given its first commercial application beyond Barry's use of it in *Raygun* magazine. It was converted to path and modified so it appeared to float in the waters below. An acid green plane completed the flag motif and at the same time created a tumultuous sky."

TITLE: South Carolina
CLIENT: In Series 2
SIZE: 24" x 36" (60.96 x 81.44 cm)
PRINTING PROCESS: Offset
INKS: 4-color process
Are posters what you primarily do for this client? Yes

PROCESS
COMPS PRESENTED: 0
REVISIONS: 0
APPROVAL: Thirst
INVOLVEMENT WITH FINAL PRINTING:
Provided paper and print specifications

Valicenti's self examination did not completely end, but it did take a light-hearted turn. "Didn't everyone want to be like Britney Spears—popular, beautiful, loved by the masses worldwide, rich, rich, rich, and moderately talented?" asks Valicenti. "Just thinking about the possibilities of being like Britney made me want to smile. And with that, a light bulb went off over my head—Britney's charm is her girl-next-door smile. Given that I have had facial hair for the better part of my adult existence, I wondered what I would look like if I could smile like Britney. On close examination, this image provides a detail."

TITLE: Joy (Fool)
CLIENT: Kent State University
SIZE: 24" x 36" (60.96 x 81.44 cm)
PRINTING PROCESS: Offset
INKS: 4-color process
Are posters what you primarily do for this client? Yes

PROCESS
COMPS PRESENTED: 0
REVISIONS: 0
APPROVAL: Thirst
INVOLVEMENT WITH FINAL PRINTING:
Provided paper and print specifications

Thirst treats the computer much in the way that the silkscreen crowd cherishes a copy machine. Valicenti confesses, "Sometimes doing design is just something playful. Sometimes being a play fool is sitting down with the laptop and having no idea what one is going to make when a new document is initiated. In this case I was making dots, and the dots clustered to become a letter. Hardly a revolutionary idea, but after the *O*, I added a *Y* and then the *J*. I thought I was done, but the dots were too big to fit on the tabloid field, so I selected all and set the reduction to what I thought was 50 percent. It had actually been set to 5 percent. The dots had remained selected and actually looked cooler than the circles themselves. I did a screen grab, opened it in Photoshop, increased the image size some 300 percent, set the enlargement to nearest neighbor, added a handful of sharpen passes, and it was a moment of joy when I pushed save."

TITLE: *The Ring*
CLIENT: Lyric Opera of Chicago
SIZE: 24" x 36" (60.96 x 81.44 cm)
PRINTING PROCESS: Offset
INKS: 4-color process and touchplate of blue
Are posters what you primarily do for this client? No

PROCESS
COMPS PRESENTED: 2
REVISIONS: 3
APPROVAL: General director and PR/marketing director
INVOLVEMENT WITH FINAL PRINTING: Provided paper and print specifications and press inspected

Thirst could not help but be inspired by the performance, as "Lyric's Ring Cycle opens with a breathtaking surreal underwater experience. Acrobats are suspended with bungee cords swimming the depths of the three-story proscenium." Valicenti says, "Capturing this experience seemed like the most appropriate iconic image for Wagner's *Ring*. Dan Rest's horizontal series of 35mm documents were scanned and lovingly recomposed, enhanced, and turned into a dreamlike digital tableau. Our custom font for the Lyric was set in a straightforward, almost Hollywood-product fashion and printed in silver."

TITLE: *Faust*
CLIENT: Lyric Opera of Chicago
SIZE: 24" x 36" (60.96 x 81.44 cm)
PRINTING PROCESS: Offset
INKS: 4-color process
Are posters what you primarily do for this client? No

PROCESS
COMPS PRESENTED: 5
REVISIONS: 2
APPROVAL: General director and PR/marketing director
INVOLVEMENT WITH FINAL PRINTING: Provided paper and print specifications and press inspected

Valicenti notes, "The seasonal commemorative Lyric Opera of Chicago posters have a life of their own in that there are any number of influences surrounding the various productions. Sometimes it is the thematic content, other times it may be the set, or in this case it was the costume designs. Robert Perdziola presented his ideas for both sets and costumes as beautiful gouache sketches. Robert, Susan Mathieson-Mayer, the Lyric's marketing wonder, and I thought it best to characterize this production with a sketch of Samuel Ramey as a colorful Mephistopheles. Robert created the painting full of Old-World gesture and gusto. Our composition was reminiscent of Bavarian advertising posters once Thirst's Robb Irrgang combined Bodoni poster with Jonathan Barnbrook's Bastard's initial *F*. The actual poster printed was on Gilbert Paper's Realm Natural to give it an aged patina."

TITLE: All About the Money
CLIENT: ESPN/Thirst
SIZE: 24" x 36" (60.96 x 81.44 cm)
PRINTING PROCESS: Offset
INKS: 4-color process
Are posters what you primarily do for this client? No

PROCESS
COMPS PRESENTED: 3
REVISIONS: 3
APPROVAL: Art director
INVOLVEMENT WITH FINAL PRINTING: Provided paper and print specifications and press inspected

Asked by *ESPN* magazine to illustrate an article featuring athletes making exorbitant amounts of money, Valicenti set out to create some diamond-encrusted digital bling. "My friend Matt Daly, the digital effects guru at Digital Kitchen, wrote a script in Maya giving the settings on steroids an unpredictable expression all their own. Many hours later, the scene was rendered at a high enough resolution for a billboard. *ESPN* actually used only a small area including six diamonds for the entire spread. I felt like I had been sent to the locker room after delivering a great performance before the game was over. In my own version of overtime, I encouraged Chicago's Graphic Arts Studio to print an edition of 1,000 for their use and my reward."

TITLE: Fall 2000
CLIENT: Illinois Institute of Technology/
College of Architecture
SIZE: 24" x 36" (60.96 x 81.44 cm)
PRINTING PROCESS: Offset
INKS: 4-color process
Are posters what you primarily do for this client? Yes

PROCESS
COMPS PRESENTED: 1
REVISIONS: 2
APPROVAL: Dean of Architecture
INVOLVEMENT WITH FINAL PRINTING: Provided paper and print specifications and press inspected

Valicenti's innate creative ability allows a level of exploration that is not recommended for beginners. He confesses, "It is always a pleasure to make something from virtually nothing. In the spirit of pulling a thread, I enjoy just pulling and tugging at what I have and see where it leads—no ideas, no thumbnails, just trust that with time and focus something right will be revealed. I had a fairly simple assignment to make a poster for the IIT/College of Architecture Lecture Series and include the names, one photo, and the school's name. The first thing I did was misspell ARCHIITECTURE, as only IIT could do. The next area of my attention was the photograph taken in Italy of one of the student compositions. To understand it, I indulged in tracing the forms. One thing led to another before I felt I had arrived somewhere that I always wanted to go."

TITLE: I Gave at the Office
CLIENT: Thirst
SIZE: 24" x 36" (60.96 x 81.44 cm)
PRINTING PROCESS: Offset
INKS: 4-color process
Are posters what you primarily do for this client? n/a

PROCESS
COMPS PRESENTED: 0
REVISIONS: 0
APPROVAL: Thirst
INVOLVEMENT WITH FINAL PRINTING: Provided paper and print specifications and press inspected

Thirst's work is constantly evolving. Says Valicenti, "Most of my days are spent on the phone. Needless to say, I often find myself lost in the unconscious act of doodling. A few years ago, Chad Johnston, then a recent graduate of Iowa State University, contacted me about a collaboration. I responded by asking Chad if he would like to convert a handful of my doodles into vector art. For about a year or so, Chad would forward his Illustrator files and I would form objective images and return them to him. He then would have his way and send them back. Never once did we imagine anything specific, but we amassed a fusion of our imaginations. This led to a book with Rob Wittig, who took our titles as his launching point in writing allegorical tales that are universal in theme and weird in meter. All of this activity is essential in the research that defines the years of Thirst work. It is from these activities that I pull solutions for much of my commercial work."

★ MARTIN WOODTLI ★

ZÜRICH, SWITZERLAND

NEW SWISS

A lot has been written about Martin Woodtli and the new vanguard of Swiss designers, who seek challenging clients but often shy away from large accounts with corporate backing, choosing instead to live project to project on work for clubs, theaters, and galleries. The most obvious assessment of this new wave of designers is their lack of affinity for the famed Swiss International Style. Some would say the pursuit of the poster is contrary to popular Swiss design today.

The experimentation inherent in some of this work, particularly with typography, might warm hearts in Berlin more than in Woodtli's home city, Zürich, but it is more important to see the one striking similarity with his Swiss forefathers Woodtli shares: The man is meticulous—a craftsman's craftsman.

That he works for cultural clients with small budgets seems to fly in the face of economic reasoning. Yet Woodtli simply cannot help himself, forming intricate silkscreen patterns and knockouts—some that the man he famously interned for, Stefan Sagmeister, declared would be impossible to print in America. It appears Woodtli is persuasive with printers as well as clients.

He has a powerful desire to see these designs through, as well as the energy to make them happen. "There is always something to discover, to organize, to develop," he says. "One is confronted with what lies on the inside of a problem and what can be left aside. This can be frustrating until you break through to the final reward." He adds, "This, for me, makes the poster always an engaging exercise—and never boring."

AN EXTRAORDINARY THING

Woodtli believes firmly that collaboration with the customer is a big part of achieving a successful final product. "You notice quickly who you can work with. If there is a power struggle, it can become problematic very quickly." Building a sense of trust, however, means "you can release the limits on what can be created." It is this trust that he finds inspirational. The process interests him more than past designers or his surroundings. However, he says, "I do appreciate the work that has come before me in this medium, and it always gives me hope that I am alone on this earth, fighting this daily struggle. Creating a poster can be an extraordinary thing, and I hope others explore its possibilities." He leaves it to history to sort out the details.

Volumes are already being written about him; his work is found in international collections and museums. Woodtli himself has been kind enough to leave a brilliant monograph behind. It is staggering in its accomplished portfolio of work, given his young age. The Swiss have even nominated him for a federal design prize.

OBSESSIVE ENERGY

Woodtli returns to his theme of energy when talking about poster design. "The poster requires intelligence, communication abilities, artistic sensibilities and talent, and sure and steady hands to guide it. It also requires endurance. I do not think that genius occurs accidentally or suddenly emerges. Design requires a great deal of energy from me. Obsession on its objectives is needed, as well as a sense of responsibility to conveying the message."

He applies this obsessive energy to his role in the collaboration, "listening, considering, stimulating, verbalizing, and then visually communicating" the solution to the problem at hand. He also offers a unique service: tender, unadulterated love of design channeled through the hands of a master. The youngest member of the AGI upon his induction, he applies these talents to a client base that most certainly would not be able to afford them had he chosen a different approach for his business. Hearing him talk, it is obvious he could not have it any other way. Luckily, we can all visually reap the spoils.

"I do not think that genius occurs accidentally or suddenly emerges. Design requires a great deal of energy from me."

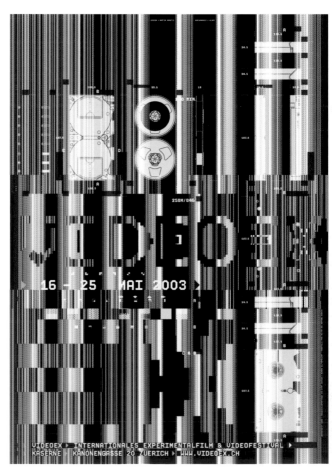

Design: Martin Woodtli , Serigraphie: Uldry

14.

SCHAFFHAUSER

KAMMGARN

16. MAI . 17. MAI

JAZZFESTIVAL 2003

Museum
für Gestaltung
Zürich

9. Februar bis
5. Juni 2005

• Ausstellungsstrasse 60, 8005 Zürich

TITLE: Sportdesign
CLIENT: Museum für Gestaltung Zürich
SIZE: 35.3" x 49.9" (90.5 x 128 cm)
PRINTING PROCESS: Silkscreen
INKS: 5 color
Are posters what you primarily do for this client? Yes

PROCESS
COMPS PRESENTED: 1
REVISIONS: 0
APPROVAL: Museum Director
INVOLVEMENT WITH FINAL PRINTING: Yes

It is perhaps with the Museum where Woodtli most firmly realizes his quest to deliver "authored graphics" showcasing his singular vision and style. The Museum für Gestaltung demands that the posters promoting its exhibitons be works of art in and of themselves. In doing so, they have hired a who's who of Swiss designers. In this select group, it is Woodtli who is called upon most often to deliver. His design for an exhibit on "Sport Design" and the "social, cultural, and even technical phenomenon associated with the strive for all things athletic," as the program states, shows the reason why. What at first seems a simple typographic *S* styled after those worn as jersey numbers turns into so much more upon closer inspection. Soon you are faced with an arena, a racetrack, fields seemingly destined for soccer, handball, volleyball, and everything in between, among other references. Not to mention the stunningly intricate printing and use of color. A simple *S* never held so much meaning.

TITLE: Lichtecht
CLIENT: Museum für Gestaltung Zürich
SIZE: 35.3" x 49.9" (90.5 x 128 cm)
PRINTING PROCESS: Silkscreen
INKS: 4 color
Are posters what you primarily do for this client? Yes

PROCESS
COMPS PRESENTED: 1
REVISIONS: 0
APPROVAL: Museum Director
INVOLVEMENT WITH FINAL PRINTING: Yes

"What fascinates us with light in everyday life?" the Lichtecht exhibit program asks. Showcasing art that confronts this question, designer Martin Woodtli pondered the intellectual question himself. Playing on the use of brightness, reflection, darkness, and shadow, he created a piece that perfectly encapsulates the exhibit. Applying type via light in any way conceivable, he creates odd juxtapositions from multiple sources and angles to further the intellectual study for the viewer. Most would have settled on one successful application of this concept but not Woodtli; he uses a different application for each individual block of information to create a masterpiece.

TITLE: Trickraum
CLIENT: Museum für Gestaltung Zürich
SIZE: 35.3" x 49.9" (90.5 x 128 cm)
PRINTING PROCESS: Silkscreen
INKS: 4 color
Are posters what you primarily do for this client? Yes

PROCESS
COMPS PRESENTED: 1
REVISIONS: 0
APPROVAL: Museum Director
INVOLVEMENT WITH FINAL PRINTING: Yes

To sum up all the possibilities for an animated film festival that focuses on the manipulation of narrative and architectural forms to create "dreamlike impressions," Woodtli knew he could not focus on any one film. Instead he used typography to create a play on our perceptions of his own. The twisting forms and bizarre dimensionality cause the viewer to question what he knows about a seemingly simple image. This strikes at the very heart of the festival's intent, as a two-dimensional application becomes alive and challenges our eyes!

TITLE: Door2Door 2003
CLIENT: Marcel Henry and Beate Engel, Stadtgalerie Bern
SIZE: 35.3" x 49.9" (90.5 x 128 cm)
Printing Process: Silkscreen
INKS: 4 color
Are posters what you primarily do for this client? Yes

PROCESS
COMPS PRESENTED: 1
REVISIONS: 0
APPROVAL: Marcel Henry and Beate Engel
INVOLVEMENT WITH FINAL PRINTING: Yes

For the owners of an art gallery in Bern, Woodtli wanted to express the variety of an event that would feature more than 90 works of art, from painting, sculpture, and music to computer-generated experiments and performance art. He also knew he wanted to capture the feel of the "Door2Door" title in the promotional poster. Creating intersecting shapes of bold color and his trademark eye for detail, Woodtli manages to have the type and composition play tricks on the eye, giving the effect of "doors" that are open and closed, dimensional and flat. All with silkscreening, the flattest printing process possible.

TITLE: VideoEx 2003
CLIENT: Patrick Huber, Kunstraum Walcheturm
SIZE: 35.3" x 49.9" (90.5 x 128 cm)
PRINTING PROCESS: Silkscreen
INKS: 5 color
Are posters what you primarily do for this client? Yes

PROCESS

COMPS PRESENTED: 1
REVISIONS: 0
APPROVAL: Festival Director
INVOLVEMENT WITH FINAL PRINTING: Yes

The Videoex festival celebrates experimental film and video annually in Woodtli's hometown of Zürich. Combined with experimental live music and other acts, the event is focused squarely on the future of this art form. Woodtli, in turn, celebrates the video in all its glory in his design promoting the event. Using video test patterns, his diagrams and informational illustrations, and a dramatic use of color and detail, he captures the "feel" of both video and the future like few before him. He certainly is not finished, though: the staggering detail in the layout of colored bars creates subliminal letterforms and shapes.

TITLE: Einfach Komplex—Bildbäume und Baumbilder in der Wissenschaft
CLIENT: Museum für Gestaltung Zürich
SIZE: 35.3" x 49.9" (90.5 x 128 cm)
PRINTING PROCESS: Silkscreen
INKS: 4 color
Are posters what you primarily do for this client? Yes

PROCESS

COMPS PRESENTED: 1
REVISIONS: 0
APPROVAL: Museum Director
INVOLVEMENT WITH FINAL PRINTING: Yes

"Einfach Komplex" is a contrast in terms—"simply complex." The exhibition is built around trees "with their simple trunk and complex branches," as the program states. The exhibit would flesh out into computer simulations and cartography, among other scientific applications. It is here that Woodtli took his inspiration. His intricate and somehow humanistic form of technical diagramming has never been applied better than it has here. Using a simplified color palette makes the attention to detail all the more obvious. He perfectly connects the scientific analysis of an organic object so vital to the exhibit.

TITLE: Schaffhauser Jazz Festival 2003
CLIENT: Urs Rollin, Hausi Naef
SIZE: 35.3" x 49.9" (90.5 x 128 cm)
PRINTING PROCESS: Silkscreen
INKS: 3 color
Are posters what you primarily do for this client? Yes

PROCESS

COMPS PRESENTED: 1
REVISIONS: 0
APPROVAL: Festival Director
INVOLVEMENT WITH FINAL PRINTING: Yes

"Because music does not emerge from the air in an empty room," the Scahaffauser Jazz Festival has taken it upon itself to showcase and bring together the most exciting jazz and improvisational artists they can to Switzerland. The festival strives for a social impact as well as an aesthetic one. Woodtli reflects this feeling accurately in his poster, with intricately intersecting colors and forms merging a painterly artistic feel with a very modern and techy application. The layered feel of the piece, for a silkscreen, is staggering. Once again, he astonishes us in his mastery of the process. Upon closer inspection, the forms take the shape of the festival's trademark flowers for an added effect.

TITLE: Play
CLIENT: Museum für Gestaltung Zürich
SIZE: 35.3" x 49.9" (90.5 x 128 cm)
PRINTING PROCESS: Silkscreen
INKS: 4 color
Are posters what you primarily do for this client? Yes

PROCESS

COMPS PRESENTED: 1
REVISIONS: 0
APPROVAL: Museum Director
INVOLVEMENT WITH FINAL PRINTING: Yes

For an exhibition that "looks at the individual, social and design aspects of play, showing the phenomenon as a human need, cultural asset, and emotional life focus," Woodtli took his lead from the "fun" aspect. Blocky type is sent astray from a pop art explosion, all washed in a glow of bright, dynamic color. Little dingbats and a steady hand with halftones again belie the skill and craftsmanship in Woodtli's designs. Somehow he manages to pull off a wildly artistic execution while not losing his connection to some of the most simple shapes and memories we carry with us: those of our toys.

★ THE **NEXT WAVE** ★

THE NEXT GENERATION OF POSTER MASTERS IS NOT FAR BEHIND

As this project developed, it quickly became obvious that not everyone whose work warranted display could be included. In fact, hundreds of talented people would have to be left out. However, some designers stand out as obvious bearers of the future of poster design, and a survey of their talents was irresistible. When the next volume of this book is undertaken, years from now, we will not have far to look to find those to profile. Here are a select few to keep your eye on.

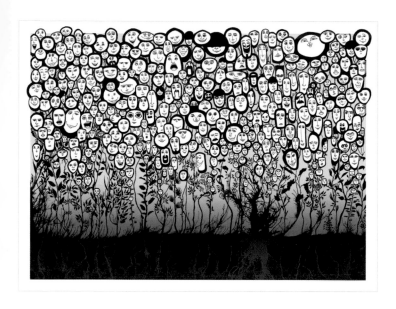

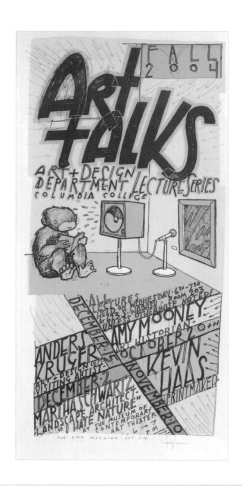

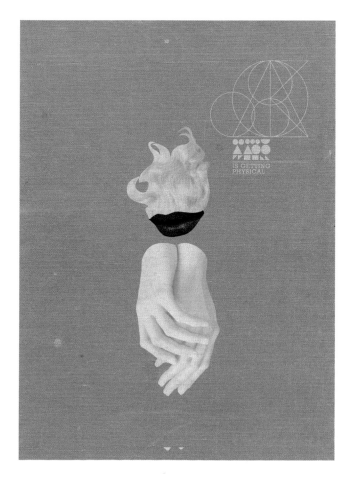

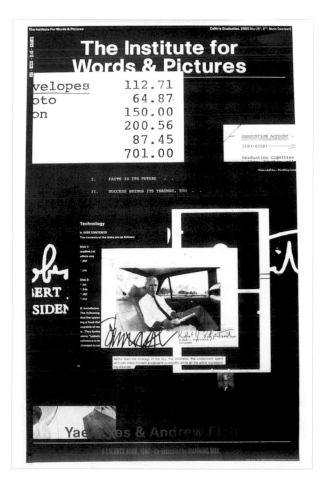

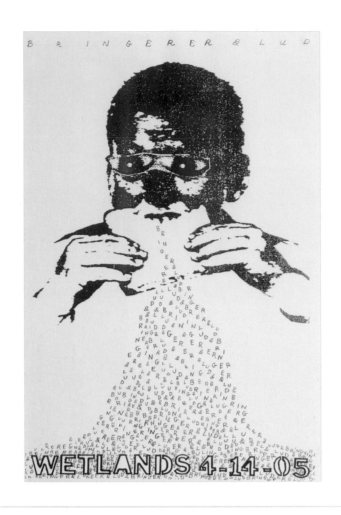

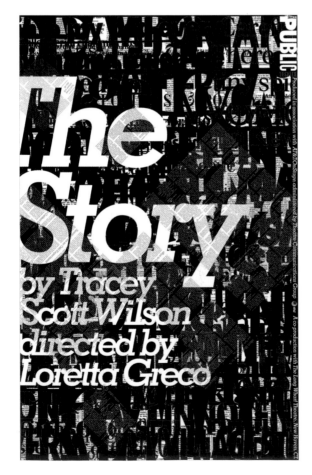

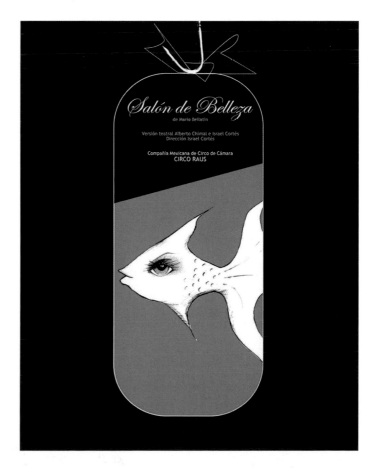

344 DESIGN (USA)

TITLE: 344 Flowers
CLIENT: 344 Design LLC
SIZE: 24" x 18" (60.96 x 45.72 cm)
PRINTING PROCESS: Offset
INKS: 2 color and clear varnish
Are posters what you primarily do for this client? No

PROCESS

COMPS PRESENTED: 1
REVISIONS: 0
APPROVAL: 344 Design
INVOLVEMENT WITH FINAL PRINTING:
Prepared for production and press inspected

Stefan Bucher at 344 has been producing self-promotional posters for the past few years, "sometimes thoughtful, sometimes funny, always personal." What they had been was clean and graphic. Bucher finally buckled under the modernism in his other work and decided to "let a nice, big drawing stand on its own without explanation." Announcing the arrival of spring, "the poster features 344 faces that I drew and scanned individually over a period of three weeks—roughly 20 faces a day—so I could figure out the best composition on the computer. I then spent another few weeks drawing stalks, then leaves. All were done separately. Once those were scanned and assembled, I thought—hmm, it's not quite enough. So I added a root system in clear varnish. How can you have flowers without roots?" Bucher asks. "A lot of people have asked me whether the faces are portraits of friends. I'm shocked and flattered that anybody could think that I'd have 344 friends. If I had that many friends, I wouldn't be drawing obsessive things like this. I do have some very good friends, though, and I was glad that I could give them this poster as a gift."

THE BIRD MACHINE (USA)

TITLE: Art Talks Lecture Series
CLIENT: Columbia College of Art and Design
SIZE: 12" x 24" (30.48 x 60.96 cm)
PRINTING PROCESS: Silkscreen
INKS: 4 color
Are posters what you primarily do for this client? Yes

PROCESS

COMPS PRESENTED: 1
REVISIONS: 0
APPROVAL: Department head
INVOLVEMENT WITH FINAL PRINTING:
Printed by The Bird Machine

Chicago's The Bird Machine has at its disposal the talents of Jay Ryan, Mat Daly, and Diana Sudyka. For this piece, Ryan made a humorous observation using one of his trademark animals and his brilliant hand-drawn typography to have the "actual art talk." As is usually the case with his work, once a concept was settled on from an initial sketch, he "scanned in the pencil line work and then photocopied it onto transparencies. Then he hand-cut rubylith to make the separations and burn the screens." Next, Daly lent his masterful hand to the printing. Soon after, the client had an amazing final product embellished with Ryan's unique style and The Bird Machine's gorgeous printing.

BOSS CONSTRUCTION (USA)

TITLE: Annual Marvin Gaye Tribute Concert
CLIENT: Tha Movement Production Company
Size: 10" x 23" (25.4 x 58.42 cm)
PRINTING PROCESS: screen print
INKS: 3 color
Are posters what you primarily do for this client? Yes

PROCESS

COMPS PRESENTED: 2
REVISIONS: 2
APPROVAL: Vice president and production manager for Tha Movement
INVOLVEMENT WITH FINAL PRINTING:
Printed by BOSS Construction

Andrew Vastagh, the main man behind BOSS Construction, likes to immerse himself in his subject matter whenever possible—in this case, promoting a concert poster for a performance based on Marvin Gaye's *Here My Dear* album. He repeatedly listened to the album, knowing the tale of divorce and financial strife that helped form this concept album about Gaye's marriage to Berry Gordy's daughter. "I began thinking of themes and imagery to convey what I had listened to. Themes of 1970s modern décor and colors began making their way into my treatment of this poster. Browns, rich maroons, and flashy golds came to mind, and abstract shapes overlapping one another were a given. I then started taking literal images from the lyrics of the record; wedding rings and pretty sparrows flying away were a couple of repeating motifs," says Vastagh. "I then went to my old trusty turntable and pulled out my *Soul Classics of the Seventies* record. I thought I'd give it a listen and get into the groove. That's when it hit me: records! Records are a perfect shape and index relaying the period I wanted the piece to live in. I then proceeded to abstract their geometric shapes with the light reflecting off them and the dot pattern reminiscent of old comic books and designs of that era," and pulled all of the pieces together.

DIRK FOWLER/F2 (USA)

TITLE: Loretta Lynn
CLIENT: Canyon Amphitheater
SIZE: 13" x 20" (33.02 x 50.80 cm)
PRINTING PROCESS: Letterpress
INKS: 2 color
Are posters what you primarily do for this client? Yes

PROCESS

COMPS PRESENTED: 1
REVISIONS: 0
APPROVAL: Promoter
INVOLVEMENT WITH FINAL PRINTING: Printed by F2

Dirk Fowler, the man behind F2 Design, enjoys the close proximity of his family to his creative process on occasion. "Being a lifelong fan of Loretta and her music made this design an exciting opportunity. I really wanted it to be special," says Fowler. "All of my posters are hand-cut and hand-printed on a Vandercook proof press, so I try and keep the design as simple as possible. The image is usually secondary to the idea or concept for me. I'd been sketching and working on the idea for a while. I had the image laid out on the computer just as the finished piece appears, except for the tuning pegs. I thought I was pretty much where I wanted to be with the design when my wife, also a designer, who hadn't seen any of my drawings, walked by and glanced at the image on my monitor. Literally, from across the room, she said, 'Cool, her head looks like a guitar.' I was so angry that I hadn't seen that, but she was right. I added the tuning pegs immediately. It definitely made the image. That's how a concept is born."

MARYAM ENAYATI (IRAN)

TITLE: 100th Birthday of Sadegh Hedayat
CLIENT: Seyhoon Gallery, 5th Color
SIZE: 27.56" x 39.37" (70 x 100 cm)
PRINTING PROCESS: Digital
INKS: 4-color process
Are posters what you primarily do for this client? Yes

PROCESS

COMPS PRESENTED: 1
REVISIONS: 0
APPROVAL: Maryam Enayayti
INVOLVEMENT WITH FINAL PRINTING:
Prepared for production

Maryam Enayati is part of the new poster movement of Iran and, importantly, a woman within that movement. She was asked to participate in an exhibition celebrating an important figure in Iranian culture, Sadegh Hedayat, by the 5th Color, a band of Iranian designers dedicated to elevating design in their country. "Sadegh Hedayat is the most famous writer in Iran," says Enanyati. "He is well known for his distinctive hat as well, so using that as a starting point, I put the 100 celebrating his birthday so that the zeros acted as his eyes."

DECODER RING DESIGN CONCERN (USA)

TITLE: Modest Mouse/Hand That Feeds You
CLIENT: Modest Mouse
SIZE: 18.5" x 24.5" (46.99 x 62.23 cm)
PRINTING PROCESS: Screen print
INKS: 2 color
Are posters what you primarily do for this client? Yes

PROCESS

COMPS PRESENTED: 1
REVISIONS: 0
APPROVAL: Band and manager
INVOLVEMENT WITH FINAL PRINTING:
Prepared for final production

The three partners of the Decoder Ring Design Concern, Paul Fucik, Christian Helms, and Geoff Peveto, were entrusted by the band Modest Mouse and their management to design posters for each of their shows on their 2005 tour. "We sat down at a dive bar here in Austin and came up with the idea of a poster series, with each poster based on an individual lyric or song," explains Helms. "When we got down to discussing approval, we suggested a number of scenarios. In response, Isaac [the lead singer] said something that few designers ever hear and we were absolutely floored by: he told us that he loved what we do and trusted our vision and our understanding of his band. He didn't want to direct us in any way or even see the posters before the show. He wanted to be surprised when he showed up at each city." This one of the series, designed by Helms, is a reflection on the band's obligation to appear at radio and television appearances. "Often they end up sabotaging those events, directly or indirectly, out of spite and turning off some potential fans. Hence the bite-the-hand-that-feeds-you cliché. When I heard the lyric "Well I'm gonna act up but not in your fucking play," it seemed like the perfect subtext to reinforce the visual message," he says.

QIAN QIAN (CHINA)

TITLE: Control
CLIENT: Qian Qian
SIZE: 39.37" x 27.56" (100 x 70 cm)
PRINTING PROCESS: Digital
INKS: 4-color process
Are posters what you primarily do for this client? Yes

PROCESS

COMPS PRESENTED: 1
REVISIONS: 0
APPROVAL: Qian Qian
INVOLVEMENT WITH FINAL PRINTING:
Printed by Qian Qian

Since departing from his position at Ogilvy in Beijing, designer Qian Qian has been exploring social issues through teaching design and through the poster. "This piece is my comment on today's media-saturated society. People, as an audience, are fooled and controlled. I seldom watch TV. I hope people may give a thought to what they're watching on TV when they see this poster." He is aware this may be wishful thinking, but he is prepared to wish.

FUSZION COLLABORATIVE (USA)

TITLE: Shake Your Booty Fashion Show
CLIENT: Shake Your Booty
Size: 12" x 18" (30.48 x 45.72 cm)
PRINTING PROCESS: Screen print
INKS: 1 color
Are posters what you primarily do for this client? Yes

PROCESS

COMPS PRESENTED: 2
REVISIONS: 2
APPROVAL: Shoe store owner
INVOLVEMENT WITH FINAL PRINTING:
Prepared for production

FUSZION Collaborative designer John Foster and the owner of Shake Your Booty Shoes and Accessories have a long working relationship that has positioned the store as the funkiest boutique in Washington, D.C. When the store agreed to hold a fashion show, they knew they did not have much of a budget to promote it. Foster recommended "plastering an economical poster, printed with the store's signature hot pink, in all of the trendy clubs, shops, and restaurants to build a buzz in town." For the poster, he wanted to make a model that was sexy but not too distinct and to have her adorned with noticeable shoes. "I have a soft spot for boots," he admits. "I also wanted to be sure that the clothing felt modern and edgy without being defined as a certain outfit." After a few failed experiments piecing together Xeroxed images, Foster nearly abandoned the concept. Undeterred, he drew the model he needed, along with his favored boots. "I kept some of the texture from the Xeroxes and ended up using those to make the dress have the feel I was hoping for."

DAN GRZECA (USA)

TITLE: 2005 Empty Bottle Festival of Jazz
and Improvised Music
CLIENT: Empty Bottle
SIZE: 19" x 26" (48.26 x 66.04 cm)
PRINTING PROCESS: Screen print
INKS: 4 color
Are posters what you primarily do for this client? Yes

PROCESS

COMPS PRESENTED: 1
REVISIONS: 0
APPROVAL: Festival directors
INVOLVEMENT WITH FINAL PRINTING:
Prepared for production

Artist and designer Dan Grzeca's work must be seen in person to be properly appreciated. I have never seen screen-printing so close to painting in feel but will attempt to do it justice. Having worked with Chicago's free jazz music scene and festival directors Ken Vandermark and John Corbett for ten years, Grzeca is given free reign. "The main concern I have

is to be sure to spell the European names correctly. The Scandinavians throw me for a loop," he admits. He likes to add a sense of improvisation to the process, to mimic the music in some way. "The image and text were all hand-drawn spontaneously using a reverse drawing process on clayboard. I then worked into the drawing a positive sense with a bit of ink and brush. The title lettering was just sketched out so as to be open to improvisation in the final drawing," he says. Once Grzeca is happy with his "improvised" artwork, the process remains creative as he works closely with his printer to decide on color, registration (sometimes intentionally off a little), transparency and opacity for each layer of ink.

WYETH HANSEN (USA)

TITLE: Secrets
CLIENT: The Free Library
SIZE: 18" x 24" (45.72 x 60.96 cm)
PRINTING PROCESS: Silkscreen
INKS: 5 color
Are posters what you primarily do for this client? Yes

PROCESS

COMPS PRESENTED: 1
REVISIONS: 0
APPROVAL: Curator
INVOLVEMENT WITH FINAL PRINTING:
Printed by Wyeth Hansen

For a group show at The Free Library in New York curated by Mark Owens, artist and designer Wyeth Hansen was hoping for better luck than the year before. "Our studio cat had tracked ink across all the finished posters the morning of the exhibition last year. That was awesome," he laughs. With months to ponder his piece for the show, he still found himself printing the night before. Owens had "asked for something large and simple and colorful. I designed this poster with the thought in mind that it could be cut down into 16 equal-sized flashcards from which young children could learn the hidden secrets of the universe—hence the title. In this case, the secrets of the universe are bad puns on questionable pseudoscience buzzwords." The printing did not go as smoothly as the design, but with a little ink to spare and a set of helping hands, he was able to keep it away from the cat.

EIKE KÖNIG (GERMANY)

TITLE: BookaShade
CLIENT: BookaShade/Get Physical Music
SIZE: 23.4" x 33.1" (59.4 x 84.1 cm) A1
PRINTING PROCESS: Offset
INKS: 4-color process
Are posters what you primarily do for this client? No

PROCESS

COMPS PRESENTED: 4
REVISIONS: 1
APPROVAL: Band members
INVOLVEMENT WITH FINAL PRINTING:
Prepared for production

Promoting a new release for the group BookaShade, designer Eike König and his firm, Hort, developed a system of interlocking individual elements "in order to make the act of remixing visually apparent." The band makes "wonderful, minimalist house music akin to film scores," explains König. He combined elements he felt shared that sentiment—used papers, old canvases, and the legendary Rockwell font—to pull the elements together. The final product is a study in thick simplicity.

ZAK KYES (UK)

TITLE: The Institute for Words and Pictures
CLIENT: California Institute of the Arts
SIZE: 26" x 42" (66.04 x 106.68 cm)
PRINTING PROCESS: Diazo
INKS: 1 color
Are posters what you primarily do for this client? No

PROCESS

COMPS PRESENTED: 2
REVISIONS: 0
APPROVAL: Committee of CalArts faculty, students, staff, and the Office of Student Affairs
INVOLVEMENT WITH FINAL PRINTING:
Prepared for production

Locating one of the few remaining Diazo printing companies in Los Angeles (Diazo is a process, favored for blueprints, involving a chemical process using ammonium hydroxide and diazonium salt), designer Zak Kyes created a series of posters to accompany a book he put together with another designer. "This poster series conceals shreds of information from a larger, deconstructed fantasy called The Institute for Words and Pictures (www.instituteforwordsandpictures.com). The IFW&P is a fictional pocket novel documenting an imagined and reconstructed CalArts program during the 1980s." Kyes set about staging the rumor that the project had been canceled at press and the book was just recovered, or invented, depending on your perspective. Confusing yet engaging. Revered director for the design program at CalArts Louise Sandhaus declared, "The IFW&P serves as an irreverent tribute to a new standard of standards. Good, bad, or ugly isn't the point. Trying everything is."

RON LIBERTI (USA)

TITLE: Bringerer and Lud
CLIENT: Bringerer
SIZE: 11" x 17" (27.94 x 43.18 cm)
PRINTING PROCESS: Photocopy
INKS: 1 color
Are posters what you primarily do for this client? Yes

PROCESS

COMPS PRESENTED: 1
REVISIONS: 0
APPROVAL: Bringerer
INVOLVEMENT WITH FINAL PRINTING:
Printed by Ron Liberti

Ron Liberti's skills are as diverse as his imagery is wild. Although his trusted hands have created design in music, radio, movies, commercials, and videos, his poster work has intrigued the world. Ron's printmaking skills are applied in the best possible way for each piece, which may result in a screen print, photocopy, painting, or some bizarre combination of all of the above. What he doesn't do is design on the computer. Manipulation is the aspect that pulls them all together. For Bringerer, he took the "original image of this tiny detail of a Norman Rockwell painting. I blew it up, shrunk it down, tweaked it, pasted, etc. Stenciled *Wetlands* on the bottom with my trusty Sharpie." Looking it over and not fully satisfied, Liberti "wanted some action, so I decided on bread crumbs falling to make the letters of the bands. They turned into ants crawling up, which I liked even more," he admits. "I really dig the movement, and I like thinking about this big-eyed, ant-eating kid. He's become a bit of a mascot for us."

LURE DESIGN (USA)

TITLE: *Cyrano de Bergerac*
CLIENT: Orlando UCF Shakespeare Festival
SIZE: 12" x 20" (30.48 x 50.8 cm)
PRINTING PROCESS: Screen print
INKS: 2 color
Are posters what you primarily do for this client? Yes

PROCESS

COMPS PRESENTED: 1
REVISIONS: 0
APPROVAL: Marketing director
INVOLVEMENT WITH FINAL PRINTING:
Printed by Lure

Working closely together with the festival's marketing director over the years, Lure Design's team of Paul Mastriani and Jeff Matz built up a high level of trust. Each poster has its hurdles, as designer Mastriani explains. "*Cyrano de Bergerac*, by Edmond Rostand, was challenging because everyone pretty much knows the story of the man with the large nose, and although we thought that that image was very important, we didn't want to present it in the traditional way. Within the script, there was a reference to a white feather and its representation of Cyrano's soul. So it seemed natural to have the feather be the main graphic and Cyrano's silhouette knocking out of it. The type, a mix of altered fonts and handlettering, was used to reflect writing with a quill pen—imperfections, ink splatters, and flowery gestures." While they were happy with the results, "*the Cyrano* poster is bittersweet for us," admits Mastriani. "It is one of our favorite posters and one of the first we screenprinted ourselves. Unfortunately, it was one of the last posters we created for the Orlando UCF Shakespeare Festival. The marketing director we had worked so closely with moved on to another position."

JOE MARIANEK (USA)

TITLE: *The Story*
CLIENT: The Public Theater
SIZE: 30" x 48" (76.2 x 121.92 cm)
PRINTING PROCESS: Screen print
INKS: 3 color
Are posters what you primarily do for this client? Yes

PROCESS

COMPS PRESENTED: 1
REVISIONS: 1
APPROVAL: Marketing director and producer
INVOLVEMENT WITH FINAL PRINTING:
Printed by GrafX

Working with creative director Paula Scher at Pentagram's New York office, designer Joe Marianek had the opportunity to work on the barometer of the return of poster design, as mentioned in this book's introduction: the season of performances at New York's famed Public Theater. *The Story*, Marianek notes, "is about a newspaper reporter who reveals a labyrinth of race, social politics, ambition, and truth while investigating a murder." Using clipped newspapers to create an unending texture, the feeling of the complexity of the reporter's situation becomes evident.

OCTAVIO MARTINO (ARGENTINA)
TITLE: *Zoo*
CLIENT: España Cordoba, Centre for the Arts
SIZE: 27.56" x 37.40" (70 x 95 cm)
PRINTING PROCESS: Offset
INKS: 4-color process
Are posters what you primarily do for this client? No

PROCESS
COMPS PRESENTED: 2
REVISIONS: 1
APPROVAL: Centre committee, including director, curator, and others
INVOLVEMENT WITH FINAL PRINTING:
Prepared for production

The Centre for the Arts puts out a monthly poster to promote upcoming activities. This particular poster was to hold two months' worth of information. "It was chaos to me," says designer Octavio Martino. "The activities arranged for these two months were so diverse, so heterogeneous, and so tight in the calendar, like animals in a yard! And I said, why not?" Sticking to his pop-culture feel for the Centre's materials, he began to sketch. The couple "was originally a black and white photograph from the 1950s, which I had to add color to, and put a top on the lady," he laughs. "I thought it would be appropriate to choose domestic animals because of their relationship with human beings, as a cultural state, but I was not sure about which animals to pick and how many, and I got kinda stuck. I had a CD full of these animals, and I thought, if I use them all, then I don't need to choose!" Zoo indeed.

NOTHING SOMETHING (USA)
TITLE: Black Angus, *Ladies of Leisure*
CLIENT: Black Angus
SIZE: 25" x 37.5" (63.5 x 95.3 cm)
PRINTING PROCESS: Offset
INKS: 4-color process
Are posters what you primarily do for this client? No

PROCESS
COMPS PRESENTED: 1
REVISIONS: 2
APPROVAL: Black Angus owners
INVOLVEMENT WITH FINAL PRINTING:
Prepared for production and press inspected

Nothing Something's Kevin Landwehr loves working with the fashion industry in New York City. "Fashion designers can be such characters!" he exclaims. "Eccentric, intelligent, fun, funny, and intensely warm if they like you; take caution if they don't. Only in the fashion world do your clients show up to a meeting in matching pink jumpsuits with bottles of champagne in hand." With the help of consultant Devin Becker, Landwehr designed a poster for an event for the Black Angus brand. The look relies heavily on their current mode of thinking. "For work that advertises events, we tend to use typography, controlled chaos, and a sense of history as our primary tools. Modern and postmodern poster design so often relies on the image or the idea for emotional impact. I wouldn't presume to criticize the approach

of modernity, but I can tell you this: Right now we're into regression. Computer, television, and cell phones; we're all staring at screens for 75 percent of our days, so we love it and clients love it when we channel the past into something beautiful and emotionally compelling," he says. It would be awfully hard to argue against this piece on the subject of compelling beauty.

THE SMALL STAKES (USA)
TITLE: Built to Spill
CLIENT: Slim's
SIZE: 18" x 24.5" (45.72 x 62.23 cm)
PRINTING PROCESS: Silkscreen
INKS: 4 color
Are posters what you primarily do for this client? Yes

PROCESS
COMPS PRESENTED: 1
REVISIONS: 1
APPROVAL: The Small Stakes
INVOLVEMENT WITH FINAL PRINTING:
Printed by The Small Stakes

Jason Munn, the man behind the Small Stakes moniker, is a master of the simple, direct, and often artful performance poster. Few in the gig poster game are as conceptual as he is. Working on a poster for Built to Spill, a band he really enjoys, Munn felt "a little added pressure. When you are making a poster for a band you really respect, you don't want to let them down." This basic concept had been with Munn for a long time, and when he was hired for the Built to Spill job he knew it was a perfect fit. Working digitally and with painted brushstrokes, he had one final change. "The poster was originally going to print on white paper with a dark gray paint can. I made the switch to dark gray paper stock right at the last minute and switched the can to metallic silver. I love the way color shifts and gets muted on dark paper."

RYAN WALLER (USA)
TITLE: The Heart Is a Lonely Hunter
CLIENT: Re:UP/Selective Hearing Gallery
SIZE: 20" x 20" (50.80 x 50.80 cm)
PRINTING PROCESS: Silkscreen
INKS: 3 color
Are posters what you primarily do for this client? No

PROCESS
COMPS PRESENTED: 1
REVISIONS: 0
APPROVAL: Curator
INVOLVEMENT WITH FINAL PRINTING:
Printed by Ryan Waller

As part of "The Unbearable Brightness of Neon" collection for San Diego's Re:UP/Selective Hearing Gallery, New York artist and designer Ryan Waller created a kitschy set of 1980s-influenced tiny ghosts swallowed by a graphic heart shape. Little idiosyncrasies in each print in the small run made them all "unique and special," he says. His playful ghost images, paired with a color palette that plays tricks with your eyes due to its similar tonality allow a quick consumption of the image. Upon closer inspection, the viewer is rewarded with the abundance of tiny details.

LOURDES ZOLEZZI (MEXICO)
TITLE: *Beauty Parlor*
CLIENT: Experimental Theatre Company
SIZE: 27.17" x 37.01" (69 x 94 cm)
PRINTING PROCESS: Silkscreen
INKS: 3 color
Are posters what you primarily do for this client? Yes

PROCESS
COMPS PRESENTED: 2
REVISIONS: 2
APPROVAL: Director
INVOLVEMENT WITH FINAL PRINTING:
Prepared for final production and press inspected

At the beginning of each project for director Israel Cortes, designer Lourdes Zolezzi meets with him to have a "roundtable discussion to go over everything about the aesthetic and concept surrounding the performance. Certain scenes and the entire process are covered in these talks." These discussions can last for hours or even days, but when they are complete "an image is born," exclaims Zolezzi. This particular play revolves around "the relationship between beauty and death and a moment of humanity in our brief existence," she explains. Zolezzi loves to manipulate the process during the printing, even adding silver ink to parts of the fish illustration during this run.

★ AFTERWORD ★

YOUR FIRST KISS

"The poster is my favorite medium because it has touched me since I was a little child in the fifties and sixties," says Niklaus Troxler. "I had encounters with the posters of Herbert Leupin, Donald Brun, and Josef Müller-Brockmann in the streets. They inspired me to study graphic design, and I chose to carry on the tradition of the poster designer."

"I discovered posters back in the 1960s when I saw a psychedelic poster [one of Mouse's skull-and-roses posters] in a used bookstore," recalls Art Chantry. "I bought it and stared at it. Over the next few months I began to find other wonderful local similar posters on walls and telephone poles in my city. It was posters and later comic books and record covers that led me into graphic design. I imagine that is actually true for the lion's share of graphic designers in America. I don't think I'm alone in that history."

"Since I began creating posters more than thirty years ago, the medium has been rumored to be near death. That's proven to be wrong," says noted designer and educator Lanny Sommese. "Posters continue to find their way into the living spaces of the world. However, they are more than decoration, nowadays, or collectibles or advertising ephemera—they are emblems of the values, aspirations, and dreams of the persons whose walls they adorn."

AN OCEAN CAN'T DIVIDE US

"In many cases, poster design offers a respite from the designer's day-to-day client-related stuff, and they never have to hear the word 'branding,'" says Sommese. "The advantage of the poster over other media is that a poster is more visceral and because of its size it is immediate and confrontational. It is more expressive. It is fun!"

"If a poster isn't beautiful in the traditional sense, it can get by being startling and impactful," says Paula Scher. "What matters most is the graphic impact." Sommese laughs that "feeling that the primary function of a poster was to demand attention on the street, one of my teachers many years ago jokingly told me how to create an effective poster image. 'When in doubt, make it big or red,' he said. "Or, better still, make it big and red—and mix in a little sex."

Sommese notes a "new attitude among many designers, especially Americans, about the use of their skills in areas outside of commercial practice—to use their talents to make things better and serve society, humanity, nature, etc." This same drive can be seen in our international cast, but it particularly manifests itself in another way for the American designers—a return to hand work and organic design and a movement away from the computer and even the photograph. The European designers have continued a loving relationship with technology and industrial assistance. Yuri Surkov's design relates heavily to his love of nature, as does Slavimir Stojanovic's—yet their application of that imagery is heavily influenced by its production on the computer. Even the work of Jianping He and Fang Chen relies heavily on photography and its technical capabilities.

The Berlin contingent represented here uses technology and its inspired style of illustration to advance their concepts and to increase the graphic impact available. Pedram Harby showcases how the computer has made sophisticated manipulation of type and images possible, allowing practitioners in seemingly remote areas of the design world to speak to a worldwide audience. Those in the Next Wave section show that this is becoming more and more prevalent.

The designer included here that best bridges this philosophical gap should not come as a surprise. He is a skateboard- and soccer-obsessed idealistic young designer located in the land of poster masters of the past and home to some of the most collectible posters of the past century: Poland's Jakub Stepien, who designs under the Hakobo moniker. Seeing his sophisticated take on the notion of designing for rock bands, you know the gap between his thinking and execution and those of Patent Pending or the other leading lights of the American underground is very small.

IT'S PERSONAL

What all of the designers showcased here share is a unique take on the medium. "The concoction of my idealistic poster requires a dash—sometimes more—of the designer's idiosyncratic way of looking at things," says Sommese. "This idiosyncratic approach is shared by all exceptional poster designers and is a commonality among the individuals in this collection."

"I feel a poster must have a personal style and convey an artistic message; personal interpretation is very important," says Niklaus Troxler. "Moreover, the design of the poster must be true to the medium—that is to say, it is essential that I create a poster. The solution is simplicity: The message has priority over form, creativity over aesthetics, and expression over perfect design. If it succeeds, it is because beauty must follow. If the result appears new and simple, one is left wondering why something so elementary was not realized before. It recalls the invention of the wheel and subsequent amazement that it worked."

A SMALL PIECE OF CAKE

Rene Wanner has done more than anyone else to bring the international poster community together through his webpage (www.posterpage.ch) and his blog. He knows that he is able to capture only a small portion of what is being produced, especially as few enter prominent contests, admitting "the Biennale [and other contests and exhibitions] and Graphis are only a small piece of the cake." International superstars still seem to find their way toward these collections, but they usually arrive a few years past their true innovative periods. "Thousands of poster artists are out there practicing who have no idea what they are doing and are doing everything exactly wrong. Yet it works great," says Chantry. "The natural restrictions of poster art have been ignored, and a whole new sort of design object has emerged. The result is a lot of bad and ignorant posters. But best of all, hundreds of amazing new talents are emerging as well. "Exposure through the Internet has allowed "completely invisible voices to explode out of the gate, redefining modern posters."

The reality is that despite waning interest in some quarters, there are more poster designers than ever, as Chantry mentioned. The poster, more than any other medium, leaves the mark of the designer. I point you in the direction of www.posterpage.ch and www.gigposters.com and ask that you scour the Internet and annuals and competition and soak in the energy inherent in the power of the poster. I hope this book inspires some to apply their own talents to what should be considered the most important historical application of graphic design. "Design history is often documented by the means of posters," notes Troxler. "On a single level, the poster clearly lays out both the contents and the translation of an idea" like no other medium.

I hope you, the reader, will give a little of yourself and design a poster. I look forward to you joining one of the most exciting times in design history.

–John Foster

★ DIRECTORY OF DESIGNERS ★

AESTHETIC APPARATUS
Minneapolis, MN USA
www.aestheticapparatus.com

FRANÇOIS CASPAR
Paris, France
www.francoiscaspar.com

FANG CHEN
Shantou, China
fchen02@yahoo.com

CYAN
Berlin, Germany
www.cyan.de

ODED EZER
Givatayim, Israel
www.ezerdesign.com

HAKOBO (JAKUB STEPIEN)
Lodz, Poland
www.hakobo.art.pl

HAMMERPRESS
Kansas City, MO USA
www.hammerpress.com

PEDRAM HARBY
Tehran, Iran
www.setavand-group.com

JIANPING HE
Berlin, Germany
Wuxi, China
pingposter@t-online.de

HENDERSONBROMSTEADARTCO
Winston-Salem, NC USA
www.hendersonbromsteadart.com

FONS HICKMANN (M23)
Berlin, Germany
www.fonshickmann.com

JEWBOY CORPORATION
Tel Aviv, Israel
www.jewboy.co.il

ANDREW LEWIS DESIGN
Vancouver Island, BC Canada
www.alewisdesign.com

LITTLE FRIENDS OF PRINTMAKING
Madison, WI USA
www.thelittlefriendsofprintmaking.com

LUBA LUKOVA
New York, NY USA
www.lukova.net

METHANE STUDIOS
Atlanta, GA USA
www.methanetudios.com

MODERN DOG
Seattle, WA USA
www.moderndog.com

PATENT PENDING DESIGN
Seattle, WA USA
www.patentpendingindustries.com

SANDSTROM DESIGN
Portland, OR USA
www.sandstormdesign.com

SERIPOP
Montreal, QB Canada
info@seriopop.com

SPOTCO
New York, NY USA
ganderson@spotnyc.com

SPUR DESIGN (DAVE PLUNKERT)
Baltimore, MD USA
www.spurdesign.com

SLAVIMIR STOJANOVIC (FUTRO)
Ljubljana, Slovenia
www.futro.si

STUDIO BOOT
Hertogenbosch, Netherlands
edwin@studioboot.nl

YURI SURKOV
Moscow, Russia
suric@tushino.com

SUSSNER DESIGN COMPANY
Minneapolis, MN USA
www.sussner.com

THE HEADS OF STATE
Philadelphia, PA USA
Seattle, WA USA
www.theheadsofstate.com

THINKMULE
Peoria, IL USA
www.thinkmule.com

THIRST (RICK VALICENTI)
Chicago, IL USA
www.3st.com

MARTIN WOODTLI
Zürich, Switzerland
martin@woodt.li

NEXT WAVE

344 DESIGN
344design.com

BIRD MACHINE
Chicago, IL USA
www.thebirdmachine.com

BOSS CONSTRUCTION
Nashville, TN USA
avastagh@excite.com

DECODER RING DESIGN CONCERN
Austin, TX USA
www.thedecoderring.com

DIRK FOWLER (F2 DESIGN)
Lubbock, TX USA
www.f2-design.com

MARYAM ENAYATI
Tehran, Iran
m_enayati@hotmail.com

FUSZION COLLABORATIVE
Alexandria, VA USA
www.fuszion.com

DAN GRZECA
Chicago, IL USA
grzeca@earthlink.net

WYETH HANSEN
Brooklyn, NY USA
www.wyethhansen.com

EIKE KÖNIG
Frankfurt, Germany
www.hort.org.uk

ZAK KYES
London, UK
www.zak.to

RON LIBERTI
Carrboro, NC USA
ronliberti@hotmail.com

LURE DESIGN
Orlando, FL USA
www.luredesigninc.com

JOE MARIANEK
Brooklyn, NY USA
joe@joemarianek.com

OCTAVIO MARTINO
Cordoba, CBA Argentina
octaviomartino@arnet.com.ar

NOTHING SOMETHING
Brooklyn, NY USA
www.nothingsomething.com

QIAN QIAN
Springfield, MO USA
q2design@gmail.com

THE SMALL STAKES
Oakland, CA USA
www.thesmallstakes.com

RYAN WALLER
Brooklyn, NY USA
www.victoryleague.com

LOURDES ZOLEZZI
Mexico City, Mexico
www.zolezzistudio.com

DEDICATION

This book is dedicated to my father, who survived cancer during its writing—by having a misdiagnosis and subsequent surgery he may not have needed. That scenario is perfect for his personality. I will always treasure the talks we had when we both thought he was dying.

This book is also dedicated to Cornel Windlin, one of the first designers I approached for inclusion. He was unable to participate this time; I cannot wait to lead off my next book with his incredible work.

ACKNOWLEDGMENTS

I owe a huge debt of gratitude to the amazing people who gave so much of themselves to this book—the designers. I cannot thank you enough. But I will try the next time I see you in person. Prepare for a big Foster bear hug. You can now rest easy and know you do not have to dread my late-night emails or badgering phone calls. I hope that I have done your awe-inspiring work the justice it deserves.

An enormous thank you to Kristin Ellison at Rockport for believing in this project when it seemed like no one would. You have been a rock and a great friend throughout.

This book couldn't have been completed without the help of everyone here at FUSZION. Special thanks always to the boss, Rick Heffner. Amazingly, my beautiful wife and daughter allowed me to write another one of these. I kiss them both as often as I can to penalize them further.

To the numerous people I am unable to list and, most important, the enormous talents showcased here, a big fat kiss is coming your way when we see each other next.

—John Foster

ABOUT THE AUTHOR

John Foster's posters have been seen in numerous collections and publications including *Communication Arts*, *HOW*, *Print*, the Smithsonian's Museum of Design in Atlanta, and too many others to mention. He is also the author of *Maximum Page Design* (HOW Design Books.)

FUSZION staff pictured are: Phil Foss, John Foster, Christian Baldo, Rick Heffner, Kristen Argenio, Khoi Tran, and Sue Smith

ABOUT FUSZION

Based in Alexandria, Virginia, FUSZION Collaborative is a full-service design studio that specializes in unique, creative solutions for print and interactive applications. FUSZION's diverse client base spans from entertainment to advocacy. Visit them at www.fuszion.com